D1474259

Martin Heidegger on Being Human

Studies in Philosophy

CONSULTING EDITOR :
V. C. Chappell, *The University of Chicago*

A Random House Study in the History of Philosophy

Richard Schmitt
Brown University

martin heidegger

on being human

an introduction to
SEIN UND ZEIT

GLOUCESTER, MASS.

PETER SMITH

1976

acknowledgments

I am indebted to the Council of the Humanities of Princeton University for appointing me Alfred Hodder Fellow for 1963–1964, to the Guggenheim Foundation for a grant during 1965–1966 and to Brown University for summer stipends in 1965 and 1966.

I am very grateful to the Princeton Philosophy Department for their hospitality during my year there. Many portions of this book have profited considerably from my conversations with Professor Victor Gourevich.

Professor Heidegger has kindly given permission to quote from his so far unpublished lectures "Grundprobleme der Phänomenologie," which he gave in Marburg, Germany, during the summer of 1927. Professor Koichi Tsujimura of the Kyoto National University of Kyoto, Japan, first drew my attention to these lectures and allowed me to microfilm his copy.

The Max Niemeyer Verlag of Tübingen, Germany has granted permission for translation of passages from *Sein und Zeit*.

Portions of Chapters 1 and 5 appeared in *Inquiry*, X (1967) in a paper entitled "Can Heidegger be understood?" The editor of *Inquiry* has kindly given his permission to incorporate sections of that paper in the present book.

contents

Martin Heidegger on Being Human

1

ontology

In this book I shall explain
those portions of Martin Heidegger's *Sein und Zeit*[1] which
one needs to understand if one is at all going to gain access
to it. These sections throw light on the problems that Heidegger attempts to solve and the sorts of solutions that he proposes for them.

We usually give explanations, in whatever area it may be,
only in response to questions. An explanation is not readily
intelligible unless one knows the question to which it is a
response. Thus also in the present case. Explanations of
Heidegger's text are helpful only if we have some idea of
what needs explaining. It is clear to everybody who reads
S & Z that some explanations are needed because the book
is very difficult to understand. But it is not equally clear
what it is that needs to be explained, what it is that makes
the book so difficult.

An examination of the opening passages will reveal difficulties that recur throughout.

The task is, then, to raise once again *the question about the meaning of being*. Are we nowadays even perplexed at being unable to understand the expression "being"? Not at all. The first task is, therefore, to awaken once again an understanding for the meaning of this question. The goal of the following treatise is to work out concretely the question about the meaning of "being" [1]. . . . The above-mentioned question has nowadays fallen into oblivion . . . [2].

In this passage it is not clear what the central question is. Sometimes it is formulated as "What is the meaning of the expression 'being'?" [see also 11], sometimes as "What is the meaning of being?" Those two questions are quite different. The first concerns the meaning of an English word. The second concerns the state or condition of being. The first is a question about a word in a particular language and thus can only be answered by someone who knows that language. The second question is not about anything linguistic at all and answering it does not require that one know a particular language. The difference between those two questions illustrates the difference between what philosophers call "using an expression" and "mentioning an expression." Heidegger seems to have overlooked that distinction.

The passage does not make clear, moreover, why the question concerning the meaning of being, whatever its precise formulation should be, needs to be raised again. It seems false, certainly, that we do not understand the question "what does the expression 'being' mean?" or that we have forgotten how to ask it. It is by no means obvious that we do not know what being means or do not know how to ask questions about it. What is true, of course, is that philosophers have lately tended to neglect both questions not out of sheer forgetfulness but because they have persuaded themselves that the questions are philosophically unproductive. Philosophy, they are inclined to say, has come a long way since Plato and Aristotle first raised questions of this sort; on some points we are not as confused as they were. Today, they say, we know that no important philosophical insight emerges from such an inquiry.

In the first section of *S & Z*, Heidegger explains that philosophers have come to regard questions about being as idle questions. He suggests that their reasons for avoiding all such traditional questions are mere "prejudices." [2] It would seem therefore that he himself recognizes that questions about "being" have been put aside for philosophical reasons and that they have not simply been forgotten. But if that is what he believes, why does he begin solemnly by accusing us of having forgotten how to ask the traditional questions about being (or "being")? He seems to offer two incompatible explanations for the present lack of interest in ontology. On the one hand, philosophers are said to refuse to ask what being or "being" means; on the other hand, they are said to have forgotten how to ask that question. But I can refuse to do only what I could do if I wanted to. Something that I have forgotten how to do, I could not do even if I wanted to. I can therefore also not refuse to do it.

The first difficulty was that Heidegger seemed to be asking two distinct questions—the questions about the meaning of being and the meaning of the expression "being"—as if they were one and the same. Now we find him apparently asserting two distinct views, which are incompatible, as if they were one and the same. A closely related difficulty is exemplified by his discussion of the prejudices that prevent philosophers from talking about "being." His arguments appear incoherent: they do not prove what they seem intended to prove or they use premises that Heidegger seems committed to reject.

The first prejudice is said to be the view that "being" is the most general concept. Heidegger points out that philosophers have generally agreed that being is not a genus. It must therefore belong to entities analogically. But no one has succeeded in giving a clear account of the nature of the relevant concept of analogy.

If one says, therefore, that "being" is the most general concept, one cannot be saying that it is the most clear concept, which does not stand in need of any further discussion. On the contrary, the concept of "being" is rather the most obscure [3].

It is difficult to see the connection between premises and conclusion in this argument. Let us suppose that Heidegger argues in this way: "If you regard being as the most general concept, you must treat its relationship to entities as analogical because being is not a genus. But the concept of analogy has never been adequately clarified; it seems false, therefore, that being belongs to entities analogically. Hence being is not the most general concept." This argument shows that to view "being" as the most general concept is a prejudice, because being demonstrably is not the most general concept. But the argument does not show that being must again be made the object of philosophical inquiry. In fact, it would seem quixotic to argue that the failure of many generations of good philosophers to clarify and establish a doctrine of being demonstrates the need for taking up the question once more. We might just as well argue that the study of astrology and phrenology should be resumed with renewed vigor. If past failures justify relinquishing those subjects, surely past failures should also justify our reluctance to do ontology in the traditional style.

But perhaps we have misconstrued Heidegger's reasoning. Perhaps we must read his paragraph in this way: "Being is the most general concept; it is therefore analogical. But philosophers have thus far failed to make clear what the analogy of being consists in. The analogy of being can, however, be made clear. [This statement, we must assume, is an unstated premise in this argument.] Therefore we must resume the traditional project and ask 'What does the expression "being" mean?'" If this is his argument, he certainly does provide some grounds for resuming the questions about

"being" but only at the cost of using as a premise a statement that he wants to reject as a "prejudice"; namely that
being is the most general concept. The conclusion depends on
that premise although Heidegger does not want to accept it.

If, therefore, the initial statement in Heidegger's paragraph
is false, the paragraph does not show what Heidegger wants
it to show. If the initial statement is true, he has no grounds
for regarding it as a prejudice. Similar incoherences prevent
us from understanding the discussion of the other two alleged
prejudices: that "being" is indefinable and that everyone
has an intuitive understanding of "being." The indefinability
of "being" is said to require us to take up once more the
question about the meaning of "being." Its intuitive trans-
parence is said to demonstrate its obscurity [4].

Briefly, the second argument could be read as follows: "Because being is indefinable, the failure of past ontologies to find
a definition is no reason for rejecting all inquiries into being
that do not seek to define 'being.' " Here the "prejudice"
that being is indefinable would be used as a premise. Alternatively, Heidegger may be arguing that it is false that being is
indefinable, hence we must try to find a definition. But if
this is the task, we cannot also claim that we do not understand what the question concerning the meaning of "being"
means. The discussion of the third prejudice contains no
argument but seems only to yield a willful paradox.

A further difficulty arises in Heidegger's justification for
concentrating, in *S & Z*, on the question of what it means to
be a human being. His reasoning seems to produce a false
conclusion because it uses a transparent falsehood as a premise.

Heidegger has several arguments to justify beginning the
renewed inquiry into the meaning of "being" by investigat-
ing the meaning of being human. One argument concludes
that the discussion of human beings is the proper starting
point for this new venture in ontology because the questions
about being are asked by human beings:

Therefore, elaborating the question about being means rendering transparent the being that asks the question with respect to its being [7].

Commentators have repeatedly cited this argument as if it supported the desired conclusion.[3] But it clearly does not do so. If we accepted Heidegger's argument, we would be forced to conclude that the answer to any question must be prefaced by a discussion of what it means to be human, for, after all, all questions are asked by human beings. But we certainly do not expect a treatise on physical chemistry to begin with a discussion of human nature, although human beings do raise the questions to which physical chemistry provides the answers. Heidegger's argument is a bad one whether it applies to ontology or physical chemistry because the implicit premise—that one must always begin to answer a question by talking about the one who asks it—is false. But what if it is true only in ontology that inquiry must begin with questions about the questioner? In that case Heidegger's argument uses as one of its premises the conclusion that is to be established.

Sometimes Heidegger's statements are incoherent; sometimes they are obviously false; sometimes they are unclear because important distinctions are not observed. These are some of the difficulties one encounters in reading *S & Z*. These difficulties call for explanations. Specifically, we need an answer to this question: Why is it that what seems clearly incoherent, patently false or obviously unclear to us seems plausible and important to Heidegger? This question indicates the direction that our explanations must take. The first section of *S & Z* provides some hints as to the outline of the explanations required.

The view that "being" is indefinable does not imply that there is no problem about being but rather that

a way of characterizing entities that is justified within certain limits . . . is not applicable to being [4].

We are "justified," says Heidegger, to speak about definitions when we talk about entities (I translate *"Sein"* as "being" and *"Seiendes"* as "entity"). It is appropriate (whether
true or false) to say of entities that they can or cannot be
defined. But this sort of talk does not apply to being. That
being is indefinable is not said, by Heidegger, to be a prejudice because it is false but because it is utterly inappropriate
and misleading to talk about being in this way. Similarly, it
is inappropriate to say of being that it is the most general
concept. Being is presumably a pervasive feature of the world.
But calling it "the most general concept" is not the most
felicitous formulation for this pervasiveness. The continued
failures of philosophy have shown that it is impossible to
clarify the notion of analogy as used in this context. We must
not conclude, however, that there is nothing to which a term
like "being" is applicable or that it is not legitimate to inquire into the matter. All that we are entitled to conclude
from the failures of traditional ontology is that it chose to
phrase its questions in a vocabulary that led to philosophical
dead ends. Heidegger takes the stubborn obscurity of the notion of analogy as a sure sign that the formulations that first
led philosophers to talk about analogy in their discussions of
being are the source of the philosophical failures.

But for the very reason that these formulations led to failure, we should feel encouraged to resume the question—but
not as it has been put in the past. Rather, we should try to
find a new way of formulating it. Similarly, if the traditional
notions of definition are not applicable to being, the question
whether being is or is not definable is not philosophically
fruitful. Instead we must try to develop a new vocabulary in
which that feature of being that the tradition captured in the
unfortunate phrase "Being is indefinable" can be stated so
as to do it justice and to avoid insoluble philosophical puzzles. The fact that being is indefinable, that is, that the notion
of definition is not a useful one when we talk about being,
therefore does require us to reopen the entire question in or-

der to find notions that are more apt and more illuminating. Hence Heidegger concludes the first section of *S & Z* :

> Consideration of the prejudices reveals not only that there is no *answer* to the question about being but also that the question is obscure and without direction. Salvaging the question about being requires, therefore, that we first elaborate the *question* adequately [4].

Elaborating the question, we understand now, means finding the vocabulary that is more appropriate to it than vocabularies used in the past. Once we understand this point, we are in a better position to resolve the difficulties we discussed earlier.

What seemed so incredible at first, that Heidegger accuses us of being unable to ask what "being" means, now seems intelligible. For we are not told that we are unable to ask for the meaning of a perfectly familiar (if not very clear) word in English (or German). Instead we are told that we do not know how to put the question that philosophers have misleadingly put as "What does 'being' mean?" This question in English (or in any language) does not adequately express what is at issue. The task is to understand what sort of vocabulary is needed so that the question can be formulated. The task undertaken by Heidegger in *S & Z* is to provide the outlines of such a new philosophical vocabulary.

Heidegger's apparent vacillations between different formulations of the question that is to be revived in *S & Z* is not evidence of his neglect of the distinction between use and mention. (In fact, I shall argue in Chapter 3 that a crucial feature of the sort of language that Heidegger recommends to us and uses in *S & Z* is that failure to differentiate use from mention does not generate puzzles.) When he asks, "What does the expression 'being' mean?" he is not, as we just saw, asking a lexicographical question about a word in an existing natural language. The question is rather one for which no adequate formulation has been found thus far, one to which the words in use in natural languages are not adequate. In the first paragraphs "being" appears in quotes repeatedly not in order to suggest that the inscription " 'being' " functions as the name of a word in English, but in order to remind us that we are using a word that is not the most appropriate for what we are referring to; instead it is the word that has been used in the past to refer to something for which, thus far, no better word is available. Indeed, to "learn to ask the question about the meaning of 'being' " is to find the proper word to refer to what thus far has improperly been called "being." (The same applies of course to the word "meaning.")

If this is Heidegger's project, it is not inconsistent to assert both that we have forgotten to ask what "being" means and that we are refraining from asking the question because we are misled by prejudices. There is, Heidegger thinks, a philosophical issue that is now formulated, quite misleadingly, as "What is the meaning of 'being'?" This poor choice of terminology has frustrated the entire inquiry. Most philosophers, having forgotten the original issue, have written off the entire enterprise because they found the question, as now formulated, unproductive. They mistook the question in its present form for the philosophical issue itself instead of considering the question merely as one possible formulation of the issue. Thus their refusal to continue ontological reflection, not only is not incompatible with but is, on the contrary, a symptom of their having forgotten the original issue concerning what we now call "being."

A new vocabulary is needed to revive that issue. It may seem, at first, that we need only replace the term "being" in order to formulate our question more happily. But if it is misleading to express the pervasiveness of being as "Being is the most general concept," we also need new concepts in order to make this point less awkwardly. We need replacements for terms like "concept" and "general." Similarly, the inappropriateness of speaking of definitions of being leaves us without terms in which to talk about what we are doing when we think about being. Besides a replacement for the concept of being we need a refurbished vocabulary to apply to our thinking about it. We also need to reexamine and renovate our vocabulary for talking about language. Uses of language are misleading in familiar senses of that term if words are used in ways in which they are not ordinarily used and no explanations of the unusual uses are given, or if words are used in several different senses at the same time, or if the meanings of words shift from one use to the next without notifying the reader of that shift. If traditional discussions of being had been misleading in any of these familiar senses, no new vocabulary would have been needed, but only a more careful use of the old one. When we use the term "misleading" here, however, it is used in an unfamiliar way, which needs to be explicated. We need new ways for differentiating clear from misleading uses of language. We also need a new account of the relationship of words to things, if, as we saw earlier, the use-mention distinction is not important in Heidegger's language. But reconsidering what it means to think and talk goes a long way toward reconsidering, more generally, what it means to be a human being. In ways that will soon become more explicit, the search for a new vocabulary for ontology does require that we reexamine traditional concepts used to describe human beings:

> If the question about being is to be posed explicitly and to be asked so as to be completely transparent. . . . the elaboration of the question requires . . . that we explore the way in which one looks toward being, in which one understands and formulates its meaning conceptually [7].

Heidegger's choice of starting points follows from his diagnosis of past failures. Ontology must begin with a discussion of human beings (as it is they who ask what "being" means) because their misconceptions about themselves, about what it means to think and what it means to talk, frustrated all ef-

forts to make clear what being means. Heidegger's justification for beginning a discussion of ontology with man presupposes his explanation for the failure of the tradition: An
inadequate philosophical vocabulary for talking and thinking
about human beings prevented philosophers from asking what
being means. Because we do not know what the question about
the meaning of being is, we are in no position to assess this
diagnosis. But we know now that Heidegger is looking for a
new philosophical vocabulary. "Being is not accessible in the
same manner as entities, instead it must be brought into view
in a free design (*Entwurf*) as we shall still have to show. This
designing we call . . . 'phenomenological construction.' "[4]

Vague talk about "a new philosophical vocabulary," however, does not throw very much light on Heidegger's enterprise in *S & Z*. A discussion of what he means by "ontology"
will provide a more specific account of this enterprise.

II

Ontology deals with being. Ontological statements are
therefore statements about being. If past ontological statements were inadequate for lack of an adequate vocabulary,
we must begin by finding a new one. But what assurance do
we have that such a vocabulary is available? Perhaps we can
find no better vocabulary than the one used thus far. If Heidegger's inquiry is even worth beginning, he must assume
that better vocabularies are within our reach. He must also
assume that we are in a position to recognize that vocabulary
should we find it. He must assume, in other words, that we
are sufficiently familiar with being, in general, and with human being, in particular, to be able to speak of each as it
needs to be spoken of:

The meaning of being must therefore already be available to us somehow. We suggested that we are never

without some understanding of being. From it springs
our explicit question about the meaning of being as well
as our inclination to grasp it conceptually in certain
ways. We do not *know* what "being" means. But as soon
as we ask "What *is* 'being'?" we make use of some understanding of "is" without however being able to formulate the meaning of "is" conceptually. . . . *This average and vague understanding of being is a fact* [5].

The question about the meaning of being has led us to assume that we already understand being. It has not led us to
assume, however, that we are able to talk about it. On the
contrary, our inability to talk about being at all adequately
provides the impetus for this inquiry. The understanding of
being that Heidegger assumes we have is therefore inarticulate. Heidegger calls this inarticulate understanding "preconceptual understanding." [5] The term "understanding" is used
in such a way that it is perfectly consistent to claim that one
understands something although one is unable to formulate
one's understanding. In this way, Heidegger assumes that we
understand "being" although we do not have the concepts in
which to phrase our understanding:

"Being" is, of course, presupposed in all ontologies, but
not as an available *concept* and that is what we seek [8].

What is this nonconceptual understanding on which the entire enterprise rests? As the answer is not immediately clear,
a good portion of *S & Z* consists of an attempt to make it
clear.

Does everyone have this preconceptual understanding of
being or do only some favored philosophers?

Whenever we utter a sentence, for instance, "To-day is
a holiday" we understand the "is" and with that something like being. . . . The shout "fire!" means "fire
broke out, help is needed, let whoever is able save himself—bring his own being to safety." [6]

The point of this homely example is clear: If anyone has an understanding of being, everyone who uses language does. The understanding of being is a universal human trait. A further question forces itself upon us at this point: Is it a contingent or a necessary fact about human beings that they possess this preconceptual understanding of being? Heidegger opts for the latter. It is of the very essence of human being, which he calls "dasein," that it has a preconceptual understanding of being. (I shall follow the now established convention and treat "dasein" as the English translation of "*Dasein*." "Dasein" denotes human beings but is not synonymous with "human being" in the sense of a "person.") Heidegger wants to differentiate the sense in which dasein is, from the sense in which things, events, states, properties are said to be. The sense of "to be" in which dasein is, therefore will be called "existence." Possessing an understanding of being, including an understanding of human being, now called "dasein," is an essential feature of dasein. Existence we are told "is possible only where there is understanding of being." [7]

The preceding paragraph provides a fuller statement of the reasons for beginning to clarify the question about "being" with a discussion of dasein, of what it means to be a human being. The question about "being" cannot be clarified unless we have a better grasp of the preconceptual understanding, which we must assume to exist if the project is to be at all promising. But this preconceptual understanding is, in turn, a necessary condition for being a human being:

> When we inquire after the possibility of understanding anything like being, we do not invent this being or forcibly mold it into a problem, perhaps even in order to take up once again a question in the philosophical tradition. . . . The question about being as question about the possibility of having a concept of being . . . stems from a preconceptual understanding of being. Thus the question about the possibility of having a concept of being is

pushed back a step to the question about the nature of the
understanding of being, in general. The . . . task of laying the ground for metaphysics thus transforms itself
into the attempt to throw light on the inner possibility of
understanding being.[8]

Heidegger calls this inquiry into human being with an eye to
the preconceptual understanding of being "fundamental ontology" [13]. The only portions of *S & Z* that are published
are those dealing with fundamental ontology. *S & Z* as we
have it is an essay on fundamental ontology. This formidable
term must now be explicated.

Fundamental ontology is the ontology of human beings. The
term that needs to be explicated, therefore, is simply the more
general term "ontology." Because it is a familiar term,
commentators have treated it with contempt. Although Heidegger's opening declarations that *S & Z* represents a new
departure in philosophy should have discouraged the assumption that he uses words that are familiar to us with equally
familiar meanings, writers about Heidegger have put little
effort into explicating "ontology." Usually they content
themselves with the observation that the distinction between
ontological and (what Heidegger calls) "ontic" discourse parallels the distinction between being and entities.[9] This observation is, of course, perfectly correct; ontology is discourse
about being. But the task of Heidegger's new ontology is to
enable us, for the first time, to ask what "being" means. It
is of no use to us to explicate the term "ontology" by reference to another term that is said to be so unfamiliar that we
are unable even to ask what it means.

Heidegger himself has drawn this distinction between ontological and ontic discourse with greater precision than his
commentators. We find a series of explicit suggestions in
S & Z.

We are told that normative statements in which men state
how they would wish to live their lives, or what their obliga-
tions are, exemplify ontic statements [312]. So do statements

expressing one's *"Weltanschauung,"* complaints about the
corruption of human nature or general expressions of one's
pessimism [179]. Also ontic is all talk about how one incurs
moral guilt as well as some discussions of the meaning of the
concept of "moral guilt." We are making ontic statements
when we ascribe guilt or reject ascriptions of guilt; in some
cases even talk about what "guilt" means is ontic [280].
What are ordinarily called "factual" statements and questions are another class of ontic statements. Statements and
questions in science are ontic [11], and that, one suspects,
does not only apply to the empirical sciences but also to mathematics [see 9]. But ontic also are the sorts of factual statements we make in everyday life. Ontological questions and
statements, on the other hand, are most obviously exemplified
by the discussions about fundamental concepts in the sciences.
The controversies between intuitionism and formalism in mathematics, the controversies about the concepts of space and
time in physics, the argument about teleology and mechanism
in biology—all are examples of ontological disagreements [9–
11]. Ontology provides a "system of categories" [*ibid.*]. In
a later work, Heidegger states flatly that "the accepted name
for the discussion of the being of entities is 'doctrine of categories.'" [10] Ontological statements are statements about
categories. (Heidegger distinguishes between categoreal concepts applicable only to dasein and categoreal concepts applicable to all other entities: The former he calls "existentials," reserving the term "categories" for the latter. I
ignore this distinction in the present discussion and use "category" to refer to any kind of categoreal concept.) The distinction between ontic and ontological talk closely parallels
the familiar distinction that is often referred to by contrasting factual statements with statements about categories.

By identifying the ontic-ontological distinction as the distinction between understanding of and talk about facts and
understanding of and talk about categories, I have rendered
Heidegger's assumptions more familiar, but I have not clari-

fied the distinction he draws. For the distinction between talk about facts and talk about categories is no clearer than the distinction between ontic and ontological talk. Nor can we find a criterion for ontological statements in Heidegger. He does, however, provide some rather firm suggestions for an explication of the terms "ontic" and "ontological."

"Ontology" is the name for "the explicit theoretical inquiry into the meaning of the [being of] entities" [12]. Ontology states what "being" means. Such explicit ontological knowledge and understanding are to be differentiated from the sort of understanding that we all have but have not yet been able to put into words. Heidegger calls the latter understanding "preontological." This preontological understanding is "preconceptual." The precise task of ontology is to find the concepts in which this understanding is to be expressed. Heidegger's ontology will provide "the proper set of concepts" [6] demanded by the preontological understanding of being. But what sort of understanding is this? Here are some examples of this understanding: No one in his right mind would shake a doorknob and twist the hand stretched out to greet him. If, to take a rest, I were to sit down on a person, I would either apologize profusely or ostentatiously neglect to do so. I would not dream of apologizing to a stone. We understand preontologically what tools are insofar as we reach for them only under very specific conditions and in specific ways, and insofar as we know how to use them [69]. We understand persons preontologically as the owners of these tools [117–118]. We might ask the fisherman whether we may borrow his boat, but we do not ask the boat whether we may borrow the fisherman. All these are examples of our preconceptual, preontological understanding of different categories or of different senses of "to be." We understand these different senses of "to be" and therefore conduct ourselves appropriately in relation to entities that belong to different categories. The task of ontology is to provide the vocabulary for formulating this understanding.

It would be a mistake to conclude from these examples that possessing preontological understanding is a disposition, for instance, to make or to assent to statements about fishermen and their boats and the categoreal differences between them. Possessing preontological understanding is a necessary feature of being human. It is not a necessary feature of human beings to be able to make or assent to true statements about the categoreal features of things. To make such statements is a "theoretical" [12] and, more specifically, philosophical enterprise, and it is not necessary to be a philosopher in order to be human. Preontological understanding is not dispositional knowledge that certain statements are true. I demonstrate preontological understanding not by talking but by acting (although sometimes, of course, the acts are linguistic ones). This concept of understanding will be discussed in detail in Chapter 5.

Because Heidegger is notorious for his neologisms, one might think that recommending a new philosophical vocabulary consisted in introducing them. But this is not true. At times, Heidegger does, of course, introduce neologisms. He coins the expression "ready to hand (*zuhanden*)," for instance, to designate objects of use, like tools and materials; but sometimes he simply alters, more or less radically, the established meaning of a word. The expression "ready to hand" has been mentioned; its companion expression is "present on hand (*vorhanden*)," which applies to all things that are not ready to hand.[11] The familiar German word *"vorhanden"* ordinarily means "present," or "available" but is now restricted by Heidegger to apply only to a limited range of things present or available, and its meaning is changed correspondingly. Of course, we could have used established words to make this distinction. Ordinary language by no means prevents us from drawing the distinction that Heidegger wants to stress. We could have contrasted objects of use, for instance, with things to which the question "What is it for?" does not apply. But using the expression "ready to hand"

and "present on hand" is easier. Both neologisms and new uses of terms are mostly introduced for the sake of convenience. In other cases ordinary language allows us to make distinctions without alterations in customary usage or without using new coinages. Thus, when Heidegger insists that persons are different from things, he uses both "persons" and "things" in perfectly ordinary ways. Here nothing would be gained by novel language and therefore Heidegger uses ordinary locutions.

Introducing a new philosophical vocabulary does not consist in coining new words or using familiar words in new ways. The properly philosophical task consists in explaining the differences, say, between persons and things or between what is ready to hand and what is present on hand. These differences are not altogether novel. They are recognized in ordinary conduct and often also in ordinary speech. They are differences of which we have preontological understanding. New only are Heidegger's explanations of these differences. The new vocabulary is needed in order to give these explanations. Using a particular philosophical vocabulary commits one to explaining distinctions in specific ways. The traditional vocabulary committed us to treating "being" either as a generic or as an analogical term. The vocabulary is such that these are the only alternatives. Similarly, as we shall see in the next chapter, the traditional vocabulary does not allow us to explicate the difference between objects of use and other things—a distinction that we understand preontologically, of course—in the way that seems appropriate to Heidegger. Hence the need for a new philosophical vocabulary that consists of distinctions drawn and explicated in philosophically unfamiliar ways.

S & Z is an essay in ontology. Not all philosophical explications of terms or of distinctions are properly ontological. Not all philosophically interesting distinctions bear on different senses of "to be." The difference between philosophical explications, in general, and the more narrowly ontological explications will emerge at the end of this discussion of the passages in which Heidegger explains what he means by "ontology."

One clarifies ontological distinctions by explaining, for instance, the different sense in which some terms are to be used when talking about persons or when talking about things. Persons, Heidegger claims, are not *in* the world in the same sense of "in" as water is *in* a glass or clothes are *in* the closet [54]. That they are in the world in this special sense is a necessary feature of persons. It is, moreover, a feature that we do not know from our observations of ourselves and other persons. Features of entities that belong to them necessarily and that are not known to us through observation are often called the "criterion" for being, or being called, an entity of a certain type. Saying that persons are in the world in a special sense of "in" therefore provides a partial criterion for being a person. The clarification and explication of terms or concepts that one undertakes in ontology provides partial or complete criteria for the concepts and the correct application of the corresponding terms. Providing a new vocabulary means finding new criteria.

In this way, Heidegger singles out persons by recommending this special sense of "in" as part of the criterion for being a person. This was not a criterion used by traditional philosophers. On the other hand, he rejects parts of the criteria used in the tradition. Philosophers have sometimes affirmed and at other times denied that each person has a self. Heidegger wants to argue instead that it is precisely a characteristic of persons that some of them have a self and others do not. This argument is one element of his novel explication of "person," which differs from that to which philosophy textbooks have accustomed us. Similarly, "world" is explicated in novel ways; first Heidegger distinguishes senses of "world" that have not traditionally been distinguished by philosophers and then he provides partial criteria for the new senses introduced. Thus, one new sense of "world" is char-

acterized by the applicability of the question "Whose world
is it?"—a question to be answered by naming or describing
a person. In like manner, Heidegger wants to set forth and
distinguish between two senses of "thing" where the philosophical tradition recognized only one; he claims that objects
of use are essentially different from objects to which the
question "What is it for?" does not apply. The new philosophical vocabulary is introduced by drawing philosophical
distinctions where none were drawn before, providing novel
criteria for terms and concepts that, in some cases, replace
traditional criteria.

Ontology not only draws distinctions and explains them;
it also gives reasons for accepting criteria offered in explanation of the different senses of words. These reasons fall into
two classes. The first is the familiar "assembling of reminders," the reference to ordinary modes of behavior or ways of
talking. Thus, in introducing the distinction between objects
of use and things that are not objects of use, Heidegger points
out that one's familiarity with objects of use, unlike one's
familiarity with other things, requires not only that one look
at them but also that one actually use them; he also points
out that often we use them most effectively when we pay no
particular attention to them [69]. But what shall we make of
these observations? We are trying to draw distinctions with
some precision and to explain the distinctions. The observations cited—as is usually true of references to familiar conduct or patterns of speech—suggest that there is some sort of
distinction here. But the same observations are often compatible with alternative sets of terms and explanations of them.
In order to defend any particular set, we therefore resort to
the second class of reasons, which Heidegger uses much more
frequently and which is much more like various forms of re-
ductio argument (I shall discuss the special sense of "argument" applicable here in the last chapter): If we explicate
ontological features and distinctions in a certain way, by
providing criteria, partial or complete, we shall commit our-

selves to denying statements that we know to be true and to
assert others that we know to be false. Typical of these arguments are Heidegger's criticisms of Cartesian and post-Cartesian philosophy: If we take "world" in the sense in which
philosophers have usually taken that term, as the totality of
objects of theoretical knowledge, it follows that "I know that
there is a world" implies that "I know that there is a world
by inference from the evidence available to me." But, Heidegger says, there is no such inference [202 ff.].

We can now sharpen the distinction between ontic and ontological statements. Factual judgments rest on observations;
the explanations of criteria for the use of ontological terms
obviously do not rest on observations. But observation statements or generalizations from observation are not the only
kinds of ontic statements. Statements in science are ontic, and
thus theories in science are also examples of ontic statements.
It would seem that scientific theories are very closely analogous to ontologies because they are supported by the same
pattern of reasoning. One rejects a theoretical statement for
the same reasons one rejects an ontological one—because one
would commit oneself to making false factual statements if
one accepted the theoretical or the ontological statement. At
this point the difference between ontic (scientific) and ontological statements seems to disappear. But at the same time
an important difference comes into view. A theory that comes
into conflict with observation must be amended or rejected.
In ontology we may choose the corresponding alternative
and reformulate our explanations of terms, but we may also
refuse to accept the conflicting observation by reformulat-
ing *it*. The Cartesian may, for instance, admit that we make
no explicit inferences to the existence of the world in which
we find ourselves. But he can nonetheless refuse to accept
this as a counterexample to the vocabulary he proposes on
the grounds that we need to distinguish between inferences performed explicitly and those that occur but are not explicitly performed. He defends the earlier vocabulary by mak-

ing a further recommendation that takes the teeth out of the proposed counterexample. Interestingly enough, of course, even this move is available in the discussion of scientific theories. But it is not always available. It is available in periods of reexamination of frameworks, when a crisis occurs in the conceptual scheme in a science. Heidegger is content to regard such crises as ontological:

> The real "movement" in the sciences takes place in the more or less radical revision of fundamental concepts that is transparent to itself. . . . In such internal crises in the sciences the very relation of the positive, investigative inquiry to the things investigated is shaken. . . . Insofar as each of these fields is itself taken from the domain of entities, such preliminary research that brings to light fundamental concepts is nothing but an interpretation of this [sort of] entity with an eye to the fundamental condition of its being. . . . such questioning . . . [is] ontology in the most general sense [9–11].

This passage does not show, of course, that the distinction between ontic and ontological discourse cannot be drawn, although it does suggest that the line may not always be clear in actual cases. Ontic statements are made within a given framework. The framework itself, the vocabulary to be used to describe facts, is not in question. Ontology, on the other hand, recommends vocabularies and how we should talk about the world; it recommends concepts and how we should think about it (for this reason we are told that "the explicit execution of designing, especially where ontological concepts are used, must necessarily be a case of constructing" [12]). Ontology need not always recommend a vocabulary other than the one currently in use. It may recommend that we talk the way in which we have been talking. To the extent that ontology gives explanations, it may recommend that we accept established ways of talking and established criteria for concepts and terms, or it may recommend new terms or new criteria. In *S & Z*, ontology makes recommendations for a new vocabulary with new criteria in which to formulate our preontological understanding. *S & Z* needs to be written because earlier vocabularies were unacceptable. For a correct formulation of our preontological understanding, "we not only lack the words needed but also the grammar" [39; see also pp. 310 ff.].

If ontological recommendations concern the framework terms and concepts, no terms are immune to scrutiny and to possible recommendations for reform of their criteria. No terms and concepts remain unaffected by ontological reflection, including those used to state the standards for correct performance of ontological reflection. The ontological recommendations that Heidegger is making in *S & Z* include recommendations concerning the concept of truth. The adequacy of an ontology, as Heidegger envisages it, cannot be judged by standards that are immune to ontological reform. This sort of ontology must contain the standards by which its adequacy is to be judged. With this in mind, Heidegger insists that ontology is circular [e.g., pp. 310 ff.]. It cannot be stated deductively, for valid deductive procedures presuppose that we can validate the formal rules of inference independently of the truth of the premises from which we draw conclusions according to these rules. But this distinction between the formal and material aspects of an inference cannot be drawn in Heideggerian ontology (this point will be developed in Chapter 3).

Where deductive procedures are applicable, we may be able to settle the truth of some statements before we concern ourselves with others. But if ontology is circular, we cannot be sure that any given statement can be made clear and shown to be more worthy of assent than its rivals unless we know a good deal about the remainder of the ontology. Because criteria for an "ontological statement" are an ingredient in a circular ontology, we cannot begin this discussion by provid-

ing a complete criterion of the term "ontological statement."
Nor does Heidegger provide one in *S & Z*. The key terms used
here to characterize statements in ontology, as, for example,
"word," "concept," "truth" and "understand," must be
clarified in the course of the discussions to follow. What has
been said thus far about ontology indicates general features
of Heideggerian ontology. But none of these features will be
clear until we have explicated these concepts a good deal more.

However unclear the concept of circularity itself may be,
it serves at least as a rough index of the difference between
general philosophical clarification of concepts and the more
restricted ontological discussion of different senses of "to be."
Once questions are raised about the senses of "to be," no
statements are immune from questioning. Hence ontology
must be circular. Other clarifications of concepts need not be
circular.

III

Having gained this preliminary understanding of Heidegger's conception of ontology, we shall not approach his text
quite as naïvely as we did at first reading. We shall now be
on the lookout for statements and arguments that appear
either trivial or false, that appear incoherent, or that seem
to fail to respect well-known philosophical distinctions. Such
difficulties indicate the points at which we must attempt to
give explanations of the text. These explanations will consist
in developing the new criteria for terms and concepts that
are suggested in passages that would remain unintelligible if
we used familiar criteria.

We shall not be tempted, as some readers of Heidegger have
been, to take the catch phrases of *S & Z* as statements of Heidegger's doctrines. It is a serious mistake, for instance, to
treat as Heidegger's teachings any of these statements:

The "essence" of dasein consists of its existence [42].
Dasein is being-in-the-world [52].
Dasein is being able to be [143].

Each of these statements illustrates a different type of difficulty. If we take "essence" and "existence" in the familiar senses of each, the first statement is either incoherent or patently false. It may be making claims that are stronger than those made for God by past philosophers. It would then not merely assert that man's essence includes his existence, as defenders of the ontological argument said of God's essence, but that it consists of his existence. This is not a coherent view. Alternatively, the statement may assert that to be human is to be pure act, to have no potentiality at all. This statement is obviously false. Second, it is trivial to say of human beings that they are in the world. Third, to say of them that they are able to be may also be taken to be a perfectly trivial remark (that human beings have potentiality); or, alternatively, it may be taken to be a false remark (that human beings are in no respect "actual"). It is surely false that to be human is to be "potentially" in all respects.

These catch phrases then are not doctrines but warnings to the reader that traditional concepts like "essence," "existence," "world" and "possibility" are to be reconsidered and to be provided with new criteria. They should alert us to expect Heidegger to introduce these new criteria in the course of his analyses in *S & Z*. Heidegger himself insists on this. His statement that "dasein is being-with," for example,

. . . does not make the ontic assertion that I am not, as a matter of fact, present on hand alone, but that other beings of the same species are extant. . . . Being-with is an existential determination of dasein even if no other person is, in fact, present on hand or perceived [120; see also 147].

Being-with is a categoreal feature of human beings, which belongs to being human even if there is only one human being alive. With respect to a human being it is always in order to raise questions or make assertions, albeit perhaps false assertions, about the relations of that person to others. Solipsism may be true but only as a contingent matter of fact. The statement ''Dasein is being-with'' indicates that Heidegger is adding another feature to the criterion for being a person: that human beings, of necessity, have relationships of certain sorts to other persons. But the statement tells us no more than this. The expression ''being-with'' does not make clear what sorts of features of human beings it indicates. It serves as a signal that a new partial criterion for being human is about to be introduced.

We know now, at least in outline, how we must proceed to explicate *S & Z*. A phrase like ''being-with'' points to a partial criterion for being a person. This criterion is meant to replace those which philosophers have given in the past. Heidegger's use of this phrase conveys to us that he wants to bring to light features essentially connected with being a person, features that the tradition ignored. He can show this by discussing examples of what persons do in situations in which they find themselves that could not be properly talked about unless we accept this particular feature as essential. As we in our turn try to develop some portions of the new vocabulary that Heidegger recommends, we need to describe the cases that, according to him, require us to use this new vocabulary. We also need to uncover the sorts of reasons that Heidegger actually does or might give for arguing that the traditional philosophical vocabulary would not be adequate for cases of this sort. I shall provide some detailed examples of this way of explicating *S & Z* in the chapters that follow.

Before I begin, however, an objection to this entire undertaking needs to be examined. Some commentators have argued that examples cannot be used in the explication of Heidegger's discourse in *S & Z* because the subject matter of *S & Z*

defies those thought patterns or language structures that
are geared to the conception or expression of any being.
. . . [Therefore] there is no gradual pedagogy in Heidegger. To fail to make with him the initial leap into
the circular structure of There-being [i.e. dasein] is to
render any sympathetic understanding impossible. . . .
The concept of There-being is a fact. It warrants no justification beyond itself. It needs only to be accepted and
understood.[13]

The thesis here is that talk about being is not, in any sense,
talk about entities. Accordingly the description and discussion of concrete cases can in no way illuminate Heidegger's
statements about being. A particular interpretation of the
distinction between ontic and ontological discourse underlies
this view. Richardson must deny that there is any sense of
"about" in which ontological discourse may be said to be
about entities. But this is a mistake. We have seen earlier that
ontic discourse differs from ontological discourse in that they
are about entities in different senses of "about." The difference between ontic and ontological discourse parallels that
between talk about categoreal concepts and talk about facts.
Categoreal concepts, however, apply to entities, albeit in a
different way from class concepts. We can see this most
clearly in the rare situations in which the reform of scientific
theories becomes indistinguishable from ontological discourse.
Here ontological discourse clearly is about the entities discussed in science.

    If ontological discourse were not about entities, it would
not involve concepts. Concepts determine classes. If the
classes have members, we can point to individuals exemplifying any particular concept. If the classes have no members,
we can still describe what a particular exemplifying the class
concept would be like. (Some of the descriptions would, of
course, not be coherent, as, for example, "square circle.")
Therefore commentators who deny that ontology is about en-

tities, quite consistently deny that it is conceptual.[14] But the arguments brought forward in support of this denial are erroneous. Heidegger moreover makes it abundantly clear that *S & Z* is concerned to recommend new criteria for concepts.

Heidegger tells us that preontological understanding is preconceptual. This statement has been taken to mean that ontological understanding cannot be expressed in a conceptual vocabulary. But we have seen that it means only that one can have preontological understanding even if one cannot give a conceptual formulation of it. In fact, Heidegger insists strenuously that the reforms proposed in *S & Z* concern philosophical concepts for capturing what we understand preontologically. We are told repeatedly that concepts are at issue in *S & Z*. The subject of inquiry in *S & Z*, Heidegger insists, requires "its own conceptual scheme" [6]; what is needed is a "conceptual grasp" of the meaning of being [7]. Phenomenology, the method to be used in *S & Z*, is said to yield concepts [36–37]. The terms coined for use in *S & Z* are said to express concepts [see e.g., 64].[15] Nor does Heidegger retreat from this interpretation in his later works, in which he often gives reinterpretations of *S & Z*, that are, at best, strained. *S & Z* remained incomplete, Heidegger explains in 1947, because the language of metaphysics that it employed is conceptual.[16] Similar suggestions are found in other recent works.[17] There is no doubt that *S & Z* recommends ontological concepts that apply to entities.

2

things

Heidegger makes conceptual recommendations, partly by introducing new coinages and giving them meaning, partly by taking current ones and providing new criteria for their use. The purpose of these recommendations is to allow us to draw philosophical distinctions that we could not draw when using the traditional philosophical vocabulary and to set aside others that the tradition regarded as very important. In this chapter, I shall discuss one such recommendation—the recommendation that we draw a distinction not drawn in the tradition. This is the distinction between objects of use and those things to which questions about use are not applicable.

The distinction is, of course, familiar in ordinary discourse. We have no difficulty in distinguishing tools and other objects of use from other things that are just there, like, for example, the dust under the bed. Nor have philosophers denied that this distinction is validly drawn. But they have not considered it one of any philosophical interest. Objects of

0 0 3 4 4 1

use were thought to be things in the same sense of that term
as all other things. The difference between objects of use and
other kinds of things was thought to be the same sort of difference as that between all other classes of things. This is
what Heidegger wants to deny: The difference between objects
of use and all other classes of things, he holds, is not the same
as the difference between different objects of use or between
classes of things that are not objects of use. To mark the distinction that interests him, he introduces the adjectival term
"ready to hand (*zuhanden*)" for the ontological character of
objects of use and restricts the meaning of the common German word "*vorhanden* (present on hand)" to the ontological
feature of not being an object of use.

Why begin this inquiry into being human by talking about
different senses of "thing"? It is one of the central theses of
S & Z that persons are different from things. But this, of
course, is not a novel view, and it is hardly worth setting
forth once again unless Heidegger can give it a new formulation or support it by arguments not used before. He knows
this and tells us more than once that he is providing a more
adequate discussion than any given by either his immediate
or his remote predecessors on the peculiar ways in which persons differ from things [45–50]. His account is different, for
instance, in that it has different starting points. If we want
to bring out clearly in what ways persons differ from things,
we must begin by asking ourselves what things are. Hence
the analyses of *S & Z* begin with a discussion of objects of
use in order to clarify what it means to be a thing. The relations of human beings to things have, moreover, been an important component of philosophical explications of what it
means to be a person [60]. This fact provides a second reason for beginning the explication of the concept of a person
with a discussion of things, for we cannot be sure that we
understand the relationship correctly unless we have a satisfactory conception of what it means to be a thing. Traditionally, philosophers proceeded otherwise. They thought that

they already knew what to be a thing means and that one
needed only to talk about persons in order to illuminate the
ways in which they differ from things.

I

Examples of the sorts of entities to be discussed in Section
15 of *S & Z* are:

Writing materials, pen, ink, paper, writing pad, table,
lamp, furniture, window, doors, room . . . [68]. . . .
Lanes, streets, bridges, buildings . . . covered train plat-
form . . . street lighting [71].

The explicit purpose of this section is to urge us to adopt a
new vocabulary for talking about entities of this sort. These
entities are very familiar, and we are tempted to describe
them in traditional ways without being at all sensitive to the
ontological commitments implicit in these traditional descriptions. But because these traditional modes of description are,
according to Heidegger, inadequate and need to be replaced:

Gaining phenomenological access to the entities that we
encounter in this way [viz., in our immediate environ-
ment] consists . . . of resisting the urgent and ever present inclinations to interpret the phenomenon so as to
cover it up . . . [67].

If asked what writing materials, pen, ink and paper are, we
are inclined to say that they are "things." Indeed, so "urgent" is this inclination that we are at a loss as to what else
to call them. But this description is by no means ontologically
insignificant. The word "thing" is habitually connected with
explications in terms of "substantiality, materiality, extend-
edness, contiguity" [68]. Once we have said that the objects

of use mentioned, or others like them, are things, we will, if pressed, give a more detailed description of these entities by speaking of them as extended, material substances related spatially to other similar material substances. In these terms, Edmund Husserl explicated what to be a thing means:

> Reality, or what has the same meaning in this context, substantiality and causality, are inseparably connected with one another. Real properties are, by the same token, causal. To know a thing is to know from experience how it behaves . . . in the context of its causal relations.[1]

An analysis of the concept of thing employs concepts like reality, substantiality and, elsewhere, materiality. These concepts are explicated in turn by talking about the extension and the location of things,[2] about their primary and secondary qualities[3] and, ultimately, about the causal relations of the entity. Descriptions of size, shape, location and actual and possible causal relations yield a complete description of a thing. If you want to give criteria for being a thing, you will talk about these features of theirs.

Heidegger's purpose in writing this chapter is to impress on us that we shall "go astray ontologically" [68] if we use this set of concepts to describe objects of use like pen, ink and paper. They "cover up" the "phenomenon" [67]. He rejects the sort of vocabulary used by Husserl, which echoes that used by Descartes and later philosophers. A vocabulary to replace the one that is objected to is being recommended. Instead of answering the question "What are pen, ink and paper?" by saying "Things," Heidegger urges us to reply "Gear (Zeug)."[4]

A philosopher who wants us to adopt a new philosophical vocabulary must explain to us in what respect his vocabulary differs from the one we have been using. Heidegger must explain to us how the criteria for being called "gear" differ from those for being called a "thing" that has a certain function. He is not very explicit on this point. It is our task as commentators to develop his suggestions as far as we can. This task will occupy us for the remainder of this chapter. The second question that needs to be answered about any new vocabulary that is recommended to us—namely, why we should adopt it instead of the philosophical vocabulary we have been using—will be partially answered during this discussion.

It is of no particular philosophical interest whether we make the noise "thing" or the noise "gear" when someone asks us what pen, ink and paper are. Of interest to us are different concepts or the meaning to be attached to words like "gear." If we use the traditional vocabulary, we shall say that pen, ink and paper are things that differ from other things by having special "value predicates" attached to them. They have functions, purposes and uses in addition to being extended, located in a particular spot and subject to specific causal laws. Heidegger rejects this way of talking [68]. But it is not at all obvious that we say anything different about pen, ink and paper when we call them "gear" from what we say when we call them things that possess specific functions. Gear, we are told, "is essentially 'something for . . .'" [68]. Pen and ink and paper are for writing letters, or books, or notes for the milkman. But this would seem to be just another way of saying that the functions of pen, ink and paper are to be used in writing letters, or books or notes to the milkman. For the rest, we would certainly think that the sorts of descriptions we are accustomed to give of things, when we talk about their size, shape, location and causal properties, must also be given of gear. For pen, ink and paper have specific sizes, locations and causal properties. A thing needs a certain extension, location, and specific causal properties, plus a definite function in order to be called "a thing having a function." It seems that the requirements for being called "an item of gear" are no different.

But Heidegger provides another criterion for "gear."

Strictly speaking there "is" never *one* item of gear. A gear context, in which it can be this gear that it is, belongs to being gear [68].

What is meant by "gear context"?[5] Any tool, for example, a pen, is used on certain materials. We use pens to write with ink on paper. The paper lies on something, a table, a desk pad, a board. In unusual circumstances we may write in blood with a pin, or steady the paper on someone's back. But the circumstances are unusual precisely because pins, blood and someone's back do not belong in the gear context of writing. Pens, ink and paper; tables, desk pads and rooms —these do belong. So does the person who is writing, and so do the special skills he possesses and the product—the letter he is writing. These different elements of the gear context all belong together; they are all connected with a familiar set of practices, products and skills. In order for an entity correctly to be called "gear," there must be the requisite gear context in which this item of gear belongs. Hence there never exists one item of gear. For suppose that we find an object that at one time was used for writing, a stylus, let us say, that a Roman used for writing on a wax tablet. It would be utterly misleading to say, "this stylus is for writing." At best, we might say, "This stylus used to be for writing, but now it is not for anything at all." The reason, of course, is that the requisite gear context no longer exists. This fact, in turn, implies that the stylus cannot properly be called "gear" because it is not *for* anything. But it is also true, for the same reasons, that we cannot say of the stylus that it is a thing that has a definite function. For it has no function at all any more [380]. Belonging in a context of other objects of use, materials and supporting objects, together with the requisite skills and practices, is a criterion for being called "gear."

But it is, of course, just as much a criterion for being called "thing having a function."

Thus far we have not succeeded in finding any indication

in the text that talking about "gear" introduces a new concept. It still seems that the criteria for using that word are the same as those for using "thing." Consequently, the difference seems to be merely verbal. Heidegger claims, of course, that the difference is an important philosophical one. We seem to have found one more case in which a claim of his appears false.

Now we recall his earlier remark that it is utterly obscure to speak of a thing, describable in terms of extension, location and causal properties, that, in addition, has a function [68]. But we may well ask whether it is any clearer to say that "gear" (instead of "things") are "for ————." Besides, we might add, the philosopher who, like Husserl, wants to use the traditional vocabulary to talk about things, in general—and about objects of use, like tools or materials, in particular—has the vocabulary in which he can explicate in detail what it means for such a thing to have a function, a use or a purpose. But this contention is precisely what Heidegger wants to deny. The gear vocabulary is not superior to the thing vocabulary in that it alone recognizes that gear is for ————. The thing vocabulary speaks, correspondingly, of things having functions or "value" or "value predicates."

> What, ontologically speaking, does "value" mean? What categories do we need to lay hold of this "belonging" [of values to objects of use] or this having [values] belonging to them? [68]

Is talk about "value" unclear because no one has ever bothered to explicate it, or is Heidegger not satisfied with the explications that philosophers have given of this concept? Or does he perhaps think that it is impossible to give a satisfactory explication of "value" or "function" and related terms as long as one uses the traditional philosophical vocabulary? We must see whether Heidegger's text supplies any answers to these questions.

We shall find some relevant suggestions in Section 16 of *S & Z*. Tools belong in gear contexts. This means that there is a certain place where I look for them. My pen belongs in my pocket or my desk drawer and must be in working order. But it may, of course, be lost. I look for it in the places where it belongs and cannot find it. It may also be broken. Finally, it may turn up in a place where it is in the way because it obstructs the use of other tools. When we say of gear that it belongs in a gear context, we are making an ontological statement: We are not saying that the gear is always in its place and functioning, for this statement would as a matter of fact be false. Gear belongs in a gear context because it is essential, in describing any tool or object of use to say whether it is functioning properly in the place where it belongs or whether it is lost, broken or in the way.

If I look for my pen and cannot find it or discover that it does not work, I discover that it is not usable. The normal practice of reaching for the pen and writing with it is disturbed. Instead I explicitly notice the pen and look for it, if it is lost, or examine it, if it does not work.

> [It becomes] . . . conspicuous. *Being conspicuous* presents gear in a certain way as being not ready to hand. This implies: the unusable is just lying there—it shows itself as gear thing that looks thus and so . . . pure being present to hand makes its appearance . . . [73; italics added].

Gear is characterized by being for something and belonging to a gear context. In view of these peculiar features, gear is said to be "ready to hand." Whether it is broken or lost, my pen is still ready to hand, it is still for writing and still belongs to a gear context. But now it does show certain marked similarities to entities of a different ontological type, namely, those that are called "present on hand." Thus "pure being present on hand makes its appearance." But:

> This character of being present on hand of those enti-
> ties that cannot be used does not lack all characteristics
> of being ready to hand; gear that is present on hand in
> *that* way is not yet a thing that just happens to be some-
> where. If gear is damaged, more occurs than merely that a
> thing is altered or that the properties of something pres-
> ent on hand are changed [73].

Entities that are present on hand "just happen to be somewhere," they have a location in geometrical space. But they
do not belong anywhere. Accordingly, it makes no sense to say
of them that they are lost or that something is in their way,
that something else is where they belong. Entities of such an
ontological type also properly speaking, cannot be damaged.
They are not for anything, thus their functioning cannot be
obstructed by their being damaged. What is present on hand
can merely be changed by having some of its properties replaced by others. Husserl's descriptions of things apply to
entities of this sort: They are extended, located and governed
by causal laws. Gear, tools and objects of use by contrast are
like what is present on hand, when they are lost or damaged,
but this likeness is limited in important ways. Damaged gear
is like entities present on hand in that it appears to be in the
same condition. The ruined pen is "just lying" there like a
pebble on the beach that "happens to be somewhere"; we
look at it and say, "It looks thus and so." But this likeness
must not mislead us into describing the broken pen in the
same terms that we would use in describing the pebble. However useless it may be now, we can still say of the pen that it
is for writing, but is not functioning, and that it belongs in a
definite gear context. Nothing of the sort can be said about the
pebble or about any other entities present on hand. It is never
for anything, it has no place where it belongs.

But none of these thoughts seems very helpful or very
interesting. Of course a tool or object of use, even if it is not
usable, is still different from something that has no function

whatsoever. We cannot describe the broken tool as we describe
a pebble on the beach because the pebble is not a broken tool
at all. It is a different sort of thing. But the pebble on the
beach differs from an item of gear that is lost or broken in
precisely the same way in which it differs from a thing that
is prevented from functioning because it is damaged. So far
we still have found no reason for talking of gear rather than
of things that have functions.

If we discuss pen, ink and paper in the Husserlian vocabulary, we shall speak of their spatiotemporal and causal properties. Having a function is then one of these properties or
perhaps a congeries of properties. If the pen is damaged and
can no longer be used, and if it is necessary to be very precise, we speak of an alteration of the pen in which certain of
its properties are replaced by others. But this, Heidegger
insists, is not an appropriate way of talking:

> If gear is damaged, more occurs than merely that a
> thing is altered or that the properties of something pres-
> ent on hand are changed [73].

If something stops being usable, it does not just lose some
properties and acquire some others. Implicit in this claim is
the further claim that it is impossible to explain what it
means to be usable or not usable by talking about the causal
properties that, according to Husserl, are the only "real
properties." But being usable or not usable can be explained
only in the context of talk about functions. Hence what
Heidegger seems to be saying here is this: The vocabulary in
which we find Husserl discussing things, a vocabulary that
talks exclusively about spatiotemporal and causal properties,
is not adequate for clarifying the peculiar features of gear
such as being for, or belonging in, a gear context. His earlier
claim that talk about "value" was not clear must therefore
be taken in the strong sense that it cannot be made clear as
long as we treat all gear as things, in Husserl's sense of that

term, that is, as entities that are present on hand. The difference between "thing vocabulary" and "gear vocabulary" is in their power to give explications of the terms used. In the thing vocabulary we can use a word like "function," but it is Heidegger's claim that we cannot explain what it means to have a function in the thing vocabulary. But such an explication can be given in the gear vocabulary that he is recommending. The gear vocabulary is needed, therefore, to enable us to clear up notions like "function" or "value" for which no explication can be given if we use the thing vocabulary. In support of these claims, Heidegger must produce two distinct arguments. First, he must give us reasons to believe that the Husserlian vocabulary is not suited for explicating and giving criteria for "function" and all the associated terms. Second, he must show that his own, new way of talking is not open to the same objections.

He does not argue at all for the first of these claims; there are no arguments in *S & Z* showing that we would be unable to give an account, say, of the concept of function if we adopted Husserl's vocabulary. It will be useful, however, to suggest the sorts of arguments that one might try to develop in his support. I shall limit myself to discussing possible explications of "belonging in a gear context." The traditional vocabulary describes things by listing their properties. These properties belong either only to one thing or essentially to more than one thing. The latter we call "relations" or "relational properties." From what has been said about gear contexts it is clear that belonging in a gear context will be described as a relation, if we use the traditional vocabulary. In the Husserlian vocabulary, things have spatial, temporal and causal relations. But belonging in a gear context cannot be a spatiotemporal relation. For gear belongs in its gear context whether it is in any of the places where it belongs, or is lost and is in some other place. Belonging in a gear context is compatible with being located in any place from which things, whether ready to hand or present on hand, are not excluded by the laws of nature or the laws of logic. The range of possible locations of gear is no narrower than that of things present on hand. The difference between entities that may be said to belong somewhere and those to which locutions of this sort do not apply therefore cannot be expressed in terms of spatiotemporal location.

But suppose we say that "belonging in a gear context" is to be explicated as "being most frequently in a certain set of places." Clearly this explication cannot be adequate if applied to individual objects of use. That the hammer belongs in the tool chest is not to say that it is usually to be found there. The question "Why is my hammer never where it belongs?" is perfectly intelligible. Nor can we explain what it means to belong in a tool context by referring to the sorts of places where objects of a certain kind are usually found. Old-fashioned crank telephones are transformed into radios and put in playrooms. The point is, in part, the element of surprise—that the telephone is not used for what it was meant to be used for and that it is not in the context of practices and needs where it belongs. It is certainly possible to say of a certain sort of gear that it belongs in a specific gear context even if most items of gear like it are not found in that context.

A causal analysis of "belonging to a gear context" is no more plausible. With the disappearance of the requisite skills, practices and needs—perhaps because the products of a certain gear context, say, handwritten letters, are replaced by a different product, say, audio tapes—neither the causal laws nor their applicability are changed. The pen still obeys the same causal laws, although it is no longer an item of gear but is, instead, purely present on hand. But perhaps an item of gear may be said to belong in a certain gear context if it regularly undergoes certain changes. This explication is open to objections corresponding to those given in the previous paragraph. Gear that is not in fact used in standard ways, because it is damaged or because it is going out of use or because it is more often misused than used properly, still belongs in a specific gear context but does not undergo the expected transformations.

The defender of the Husserlian vocabulary need not give up yet, however. His next gambit will be to suggest that we can understand what it means to belong to a gear context, if we consider objects of use as things that have a certain extension, location and causal properties about which, in addition, we have certain beliefs. Belonging in a tool context is thus to be construed as an intentional relation, consisting of certain beliefs held by the members of the relevant community. But if we merely require that these beliefs be in the community, our analysis will be inadequate. People hold beliefs about things that do not even exist. Unicorn horns once were thought to possess special medicinal properties. Because unicorn horns do not exist, this belief was not enough to make them belong in the gear context associated with the practice of medicine. If, on the other hand, we insist not only that there be a belief about an item of gear but also that the belief be true, our analysis will fail again. For the belief is true only if the tool in question satisfies certain other conditions that must also be necessary conditions. Having a true belief therefore cannot be a sufficient condition for belonging to a gear context.

Next we must try to say that such a belief is only a necessary condition. But if the belief is true it could not even be that. Its truth entails the idea that the item of gear belongs to a gear context, and that it presumably does so even if we do not believe so. If therefore, we try to analyze "belonging in a gear context" with, as one condition, a belief, it must be a different belief from "this item of gear belongs in——gear context." For such a belief could be neither a sufficient nor a necessary condition. But what other belief would be a likely candidate? No beliefs about spatiotemporal or causal properties of the item of gear in question will remedy the shortcomings of any analysis in terms of such properties alone.

Next one may suggest that an entity belongs to a gear context if we believe that it belongs to it and if it does exist, and along such lines this argument can continue for a long time. Since Heidegger is not interested in developing it, we need not pursue it further. It was sufficient to point out what sort of argument is needed to show that the gear vocabulary differs from the thing vocabulary. Belonging to a gear context, for instance, cannot be expressed in the thing vocabulary, and hence users of the thing vocabulary cannot give an adequate criterion for being an item of gear. But it has not been shown, of course, that this difference exists. In order to give a demonstration, one must continue the argument I have begun here until the conclusion has been firmly established that Husserl's vocabulary is incapable of making clear what to be a tool means. To do so requires not only that we complete the argument concerning "belonging to a gear context" but also that we construct similar arguments concerning expressions like "being for." [6]

But even if we could pursue this argument to a satisfactory conclusion, we still would not know whether Heidegger's proposed vocabulary is not open to the same objections that he raises against the vocabulary he rejects. Nor are we in any position to find out. So far Heidegger has introduced four new terms: "gear," "being for———," "gear context" and "belonging to a gear context." We are still awaiting an explication of them, and it is not at all clear what sorts of terms this explication will use. The language for explicating these terms still remains to be developed. If we may not speak about "being for" as a property of things or a relation between them, what sorts of expressions shall we use to explicate that term and to provide criteria for it? If gear contexts and the belonging of any item of gear in a gear context are not to be clarified by talking about spatiotemporal or causal relations, how shall we clarify them? So far there is no answer to these questions. We notice here what we shall notice again and again in *S & Z* : Heidegger's claims are large and their development cursory. We cannot be sure therefore that his recommended vocabulary is any more apt for talking about objects of use than Husserl's. A problem has been raised that appears to be a genuine one, although we cannot even be quite sure of that, but it is difficult to see whether any steps have been taken toward a solution.

II

Entities present on hand have spatial, temporal and causal properties and relations. We assumed earlier that this is also true of entities ready to hand, except for the special features of gear that the thing vocabulary could not express. But this assumption turns out to be false. Heidegger is defending a more radical thesis. When he claims that the differences between entities present on hand and entities ready to hand are not the same as differences between entities of either one of these ontological types, he insists that an item of gear differs from some present-on-hand entity not only in that gear is for something and is a member of a gear context whereas the present-on-hand is not. The differences are much more extensive. It is not enough to show that objects of use differ from other things in having a feature that cannot be construed either as a property or a relation, as those terms were employed by the tradition. Heidegger wants us to understand that we can give a complete description of objects of use— gear—without speaking of properties and relations at all. It would be incorrect to describe a pen by listing its shape, location and causal properties and then adding that it is for writing. Being for——— is not merely ''an aspect'' added to a thing.

> These entities are in the mode of being ready to hand. This mode of being should not, however, be understood merely as a way of conceiving of them as if the way we talk attached these "aspects" to "entities" as we encounter them originally, as if some world stuff, originally present on hand in itself, were being given "a subjective coloration" . . . Being ready to hand is the ontological-categorial characteristic of entities as they are "in themselves" [71].

The difference between being ready to hand and being present on hand is the difference between different ontological types. Entities belonging to these different ontological types *are* in different senses of that term. Hence the vocabulary applicable to objects of use is different from that applicable to present-on-hand entities. Husserl's thing vocabulary in which we talk about the location, extension and causal properties of entities present on hand is not needed at all in order to say what we need to say about objects of use of all kinds. To talk about gear we require a separate vocabulary.

The arguments outlined so far would, if successful, only have shown that the thing vocabulary will not accommodate such notions as being for ———— or belonging to a gear context. But now Heidegger needs some further arguments that will support his more general claim that the thing vocabulary is not needed to describe those features of gear that remain once we have talked about what a particular item is for and to what gear context it belongs. We need to argue, for instance, that being well balanced is not to be analyzed as a spatiotemporal and/or causal property of the pen, or we need to argue that being high enough is not to be analyzed as a spatiotemporal and/or causal property of the table.

The passage that appears to indicate the sort of line Heidegger wants to take here is quite puzzling.

> Those activities of ours that are adapted to the use of gear . . . do not grasp this entity thematically as a thing

that happens to be there. . . . the less one merely gapes
at the thing that is a hammer, the more actively one uses
it . . . the more undisguisedly one encounters it as what
it is, an object of use . . . however closely we *look at*
things that merely "look to be" of a certain character,
we will not be able to discover what is ready to hand
[69; italics added].

Read in one way, this passage asserts an obvious falsehood.
Read in another way, it renders Heidegger's exposition incoherent. The passage asserts an obvious falsehood if we take
the phrase "grasp thematically" as it is commonly used in
phenomenological writings to refer to one's explicit awareness
of the center of the field of consciousness. We are most attentive to what is grasped thematically whereas we are more
prone to overlook or ignore what occurs at the fringes of the
field of awareness. Heidegger then seems to be saying that we
are not explicitly aware of tools as we use them, very much
as if we might, at times, not even notice it if the tool disap-
peared suddenly. But surely this is not true. For example, a
pianist would notice immediately if someone proceeded to
pull the piano away while he was giving a recital.

Perhaps, however, we should put the stress on Heidegger's
denial that our acquaintance with tools comes from "gaping
at" or "merely looking at." We might remind ourselves that
the typist who looks at her fingers while typing is sure to
make mistakes. The passage now seems to tell us that we are
aware of tools primarily through touch and the kinesthetic
sense of our movements, of the weight and size of the tools,
and of our position. The sorts of properties observed in tools,
while we use them, are not primarily those we see, like shape
or color, but rather those we observe through touch and
muscular sensations. But this thought, of course, instead of
proving that we should not construe the crucial features of
tools as extension, location and causal properties, indicates, on
the contrary, that they are the crucial characteristics of tools,
but that they are felt rather than seen. If this is what Heideg-

ger means, he now asserts what he denied earlier, that the Husserlian vocabulary is adequate to the description of objects of use.

We shall fare better if we remember that Heidegger is doing ontology. This excludes any interpretation of the passage as factual. No assertions are made concerning observed features when using tools. The passage quoted on pp. 46–47 concerns the way we should talk about the features that are already familiar to all of us. Of course, the pianist notices his piano; of course, the typist falters when she looks at her fingers. But when they do so, it does not imply that they observe their own activities through senses other than vision. Heidegger is not telling us that the pianist is not aware of the piano because he does not observe it; he is telling us that it is not useful to use a word like "observation" when describing the pianist's awareness of the piano. It is misleading rather than true or false to speak of the typist as observing her actions through touch instead of through sight. The passage objects to the traditional view that using a tool must be analyzed as observation of the activity and the situation, plus action that is directed by the observation. Using a tool involves its own modes of familiarity with the situation and action. This familiarity cannot be described as the result of observation without misconstruing the facts.

> "Practical" conduct is not "atheoretical" in the sense of being without sight, and its difference from theoretical conduct does not merely consist in this that we look at, in the latter case, while we act in the former. . . . but looking at is as fundamentally a case of caring for, as acting has its sight [69].

The passage turns against traditional views about practical action, where it is held that the information on which one acts is gained by means of "looking at." Heidegger uses this expression "looking at" to designate seeing, and perception by means of the other senses, as it was taken in Cartesian and post-Cartesian philosophy. Seeing was thought to yield knowledge of the properties and relations of things. Heidegger here suggests that there is a way of being acquainted with entities, specifically with objects of use, which does not yield information about properties. Since he believes that knowing how to use an item of gear is not knowing what its properties are, he is here, in fact, supplementing this distinction between entities present on hand and entities ready to hand with a corresponding distinction between two senses of knowing. In order to act, I do not need to know the properties of things because "acting has its sight," acting has its own appropriate manner of access to entities. "Looking at," on the other hand, is "a case of caring for"; it is not as distinct from acting as was traditionally thought.[7]

At this point it might be opportune to observe that it is clearer now why Heidegger begins his inquiry into what it means to be human with a discussion of things. In order to draw the sort of distinction indicated between two senses of "thing," we must also distinguish different senses of "knowing." Because knowing has been traditionally an important concept in the account philosophers have given of themselves as human beings, a reform of our talk about knowing is important for a new account of being human. We are first led to this new sense of "knowing" by our reflections about things.

We must note these claims: Tools in use are familiar to us in ways that are not best described as "observation." Hence the sort of vocabulary that is adapted to descriptions of what we observe is not adapted to the description of tools and other objects of use. How does the vocabulary in which we describe what we observe differ from that in which we discuss tools? Once again we get only the feeblest hints, and it is left up to us to develop them.

In a passage cited on page 46, Heidegger asserted that

> Being ready to hand is the ontological-categorial char-
> acteristic of entities as they are "in themselves" [71].

The expression "in themselves" appears in quotation marks
in order to suggest that the term has one meaning when applied to entities that are ready to hand and a different meaning when applied to entities present on hand. Corresponding
to the two senses of "thing" that are being distinguished are
the two senses of "in itself," which must also be distinguished. If we talk about what a tool or object of use is in
itself, we may not attach the same meaning to that phrase as
when we talk about things present on hand in themselves.

> It is impossible to explicate the "in itself" if we use
> what is present on hand as our primary and exclusive
> paradigm . . . the analyses provided thus far make it
> clear that we can grasp the being-in-itself of entities
> within the world [i.e., gear] only by reference to the phe-
> nomenon of world [75–76].

The distinction between what something is in itself and what
it is for us must be redrawn for objects of use. If applied
there, it is not the same distinction as that between what
things present on hand are in themselves and what they are
for us.

Things present on hand are what they are in themselves
independently of human observers and knowers [202]. In
practice, this means that observation of things is trustworthy
to the extent that it takes place under standard conditions
that assure us that the results of observation are not affected
by any facts peculiar to a particular observer. The truth of
observation statements is not dependent on truths about particular observers. Color-blind people do not observe under
standard conditions, nor do people who are not at the op-
timum or standard distance from an object or in the preferred location for observation. Reliable observation statements about what is observed, made under standard condi-

tions, are dependent only on those statements about particular observers that are true of all observers.

At first, this point seems also to be true of our familiarity with objects of use. We will not trust the man who tells us that a certain hammer is too heavy for a job or that a saw needs sharpening, if we know him to be unskilled in carpentry. The child who is learning to write blames the ink blots on a leaky pen, but we will see for ourselves before we accept his explanation. Our acquaintance with tools, we might say, therefore, is strictly analogous to our observation of things present on hand, for in both cases the statements made are reliable only if they are made under standard conditions and if they are the same for all qualified observers—and to be qualified includes competence in the use of any given tool.

But this similarity is deceptive. Any observed change in the appearance of entities present on hand that is due to a change in the conditions of observation may for that very reason not be regarded as an observed change of the object in itself. We can be confident that a thing has changed its objective, observable properties only if we have assurance that earlier and later observations are made under the same conditions. But this is not true of our familiarity with tools and objects of use. Of course, there is a difference between features that belong to tools in themselves and features that do not belong to them but are mistakenly ascribed to them by users who are not properly qualified. But the criterion for what belongs to a tool "in itself" is not whether the observations have been made under standard conditions. Nor are changes in the features, possessed by tools in themselves, independent of changes in the users. The tool that was not usable for a certain job by the average competent craftsman is put to use brilliantly on that same job by a craftsman of superior skill. New techniques are developed that displace tools, once considered the most suitable for a job, by others that thus far have been considered unsuitable. The job that one man does with one tool is performed by another with a different one. If we switched their tools, neither man could accomplish the job. Whether a tool is suited for a job, is too heavy or too light, and so on depends on the skill and preferences of the users, the techniques available, the materials and all the other elements of a gear context. The sorts of utterances we make about a tool on the basis of our immediate acquaintance with it are therefore not true or false under standard conditions in the same way as statements, say, about shapes and colors of tools. Being properly balanced, being too heavy for ———, being too big for ——— are not properties that tools have independently of truths about one or a selected group of tool users. Yet this does not mean that the specific qualities of tools are "merely subjective" in the sense in which a color-blind person gives us a "merely subjective" account of colors.

The result of observations may claim objectivity if the observation was undertaken under standard conditions. Otherwise observations are subjective. These two terms, "objective" and "subjective," apply only to the colors, shapes, and tactile and other observed properties possessed by entities present on hand that are properly the objects of observation. But the qualities peculiar to gear, such as being for ——— or being well balanced, cannot properly be said to be observed at all, nor are they, strictly speaking, discovered. At the least they are as much invented as discovered. They are not properties belonging to gear independently of all uses and awareness of gear, for they depend as much on our techniques and skills as on the features of the item of gear. Hence they also change with changes in the users as, for example, the development of a new technique or refinement of an established one. Yet, in contrast to the reports of the person who is not competent with the tool, who therefore is in no position to refine or develop techniques because he does not even master established ones, the qualities invented by the master craftsman belong to the tool in itself. There do seem to be two senses of "in itself" distinguishable by the different criteria governing the different senses of the phrase.

Whereas we saw first that "being for ———" and belonging to a tool context cannot be construed as spatiotemporal, causal or intentional relations, this specific thesis has now been extended to embrace a much larger range of qualities of gear. We conclude from the preceding argument—assuming again, of course, that it will stand up under much more detailed scrutiny—that *all* the sorts of things we say about tools while we use them cannot be analyzed into the thing vocabulary because that vocabulary enables us to talk only of those features of entities that we observe under standard conditions. But our familiarity with objects of use as used does not admit the requirement for standard conditions of observation. It would be misleading to say that such familiarity in use either conforms or violates the requirements made legitimately for observation of shapes, colors and causal relations. Hence familiarity in use is not to be analyzed as a kind of observation, and the predicates of objects of use are not observation predicates. We need one vocabulary for entities present on hand, presumably the sort of vocabulary Husserl sketches out, and another for gear.

Once again, of course, it is not very clear what this alternative vocabulary will look like. Heidegger gives us one example. While using a hammer we may say, " 'The hammer is too heavy' or rather 'too heavy', 'the other hammer!' " [157]. The last two of these expressions are not to be taken as elliptical for standard fact-stating sentences based on observation such as "The hammer is too heavy," but as the sort of thing that we say quite appropriately while hammering. An expression that would be elliptical if it belonged to the thing vocabulary is not elliptical in the gear vocabulary. The criteria for correct use, rather than the noises made or the signs written down, distinguish the two vocabularies.

The arguments in the first section of this chapter attempted to show that the Husserlian thing vocabulary is not sufficient for talking adequately about objects of use. The arguments in this section support the conclusion that it is not even necessary for being able to talk about objects of use, insofar as they are used. We are, of course, always free to treat an item of gear as if it were merely present on hand, but then we would simply be ignoring those features that are of interest to its users and instead be attending to features that are of no interest to them. But this point raises a new difficulty: It is one and the same entity that at one time is talked about and used as an item of gear and that at other times is observed and discussed as a thing present on hand. We would seem to be in need of a third, neutral vocabulary to talk about this entity that is, from one point of view, an item of gear, to distinguish it from another present-on-hand entity. But perhaps it is quite misleading to speak of seeing the same entity ''from different points of view.'' We need to ask questions concerning the relations of the different vocabularies. Heidegger has an answer to these questions. I shall discuss it in Chapter 6.

Heidegger's account of gear is cursory, but he devotes more energy to showing that the thing vocabulary is not adequate to the explication of what it means to be a tool or object of use than he devotes to developing an alternative vocabulary. We are therefore not in a very good position to know whether his vocabulary is preferable to the traditional one, and as a result we are not in a very good position to decide whether to adopt it. But we know more clearly what Heidegger considers to be the shortcomings of the Husserlian thing vocabulary. Therefore we have at least one reason for looking for an alternative vocabulary, even if we cannot at all be sure that the one recommended by Heidegger, if developed, would fill our needs.

3

language

Ontology, as Heidegger understands it, recommends that we talk and think in ways to which traditional philosophy has not accustomed us. The preceding chapter set forth one such recommendation. Heidegger is not the only philosopher, however, who thinks that his task is to change our linguistic habits. In order to determine Heidegger's position more specifically, we need to examine some other recommendations of his, namely, those that concern language. To do so will enable us to distinguish the nature of his recommendations for a new vocabulary from that of the linguistic recommendations that are made explicitly by philosophers of orientations that are otherwise very different. (If we interpret the term "linguistic recommendations" with sufficient latitude, we may note that both W. V. Quine and Rudolf Carnap regard such recommendations as an important if not the major task of philosophers. Although his reasons would differ from theirs, Heidegger would agree with them that actual uses of language are not philosophically

sacrosanct.) We must know what Heidegger thinks language
is, in order to understand what it means for him to reform
the language of ontology.

In the course of his career, Heidegger held at least three
distinct views of language. I shall not concern myself with
his views in such books as *Unterwegs zur Sprache* and *Gelassenheit,* most of which were written after World War II.
My main concern here, of course, is the conception of language
in *S & Z.* But it will be easier to understand this conception
if we begin with a discussion of the views that Heidegger held
on language at the time of World War I.

I

In 1915, Heidegger submitted his *Habilitationsschrift, The
Doctrine of Categories and Meaning of Duns Scotus.*[1] This
book bore the clear imprint of Edmund Husserl's early work,
particularly his *Logical Investigations,* a second edition of
which had appeared in 1913.[2] A good portion of Heidegger's
book on John Duns Scotus is devoted to showing that many
of the distinctions for which Husserl had recently argued
could be found in Scotus' writings.[3] Central is the distinction
between thinking, or any other mental act, and what is being
thought or is the content of these other acts. Mental acts are
psychological events. They occur in time; they are known
empirically and are the subject matter of psychology. Contrary to earlier logicians—John Stuart Mill, for instance—
Husserl had argued in *Logical Investigations* (first volume)
that the contents of mental acts, thoughts, judgments or
beliefs must be differentiated from the acts of thinking, judging or believing because the laws governing contents are not
known empirically and are therefore not the objects of an
empirical science—psychology—but of the a priori science
that we call "logic." The burden of that extended polemic

had been to assert the independence of logic from psychology. Heidegger finds Scotus insisting on very similar distinctions.

> Scholastic thinking showed a maturity of insight for the peculiar features and independence of the logical domain that we must not ignore or underestimate and that is in sharp contrast to the formulation of solutions for logical problems in the manner of psychologism [an approach to logical problems], which has only recently begun to lose favor.[4]

"Psychologism" designates the doctrine that logic and psychology are not distinct. Clearly, Heidegger approves of Scotus' antipsychologism and thus, indirectly, of Husserl's views on logic.

Logic, on Husserl's view, has two parts. One contains rules governing the correct formation of sentences. These rules are designed to separate sense from nonsense, to eliminate from the language sentences that are gibberish, like "This irresponsible is green" [*LU* II, 319–20]. The second part of logic concerns rules that separate sentences that are free from contradiction from those that are not; both kinds of sentences make sense. "This circle is square" is self-contradictory, but it is not nonsense like "this irresponsible is green" [*LU* II, 326]. (In *FTL* Husserl insists that "truth" is not at issue in either of these parts of logic and adds a·third discipline to logic, which he calls "logic of truth." It seems to correspond to what we might call "semantics.") The first part of logic is called "universal grammar" and also "doctrine of meaning (*Bedeutungslehre*)"; the latter is called "logic proper." In spite of its name, the "doctrine of meaning" does not correspond to what is now often called "semantics." Husserl calls "doctrine of meaning" that part of formal logic that provides the formation rules of any language. He insists on this in his later work on logic.[5] The name "universal grammar" renders much more precisely what he has in mind. The formation rules in logic provide nothing less than certain essential and universal features of any language. Hence universal grammar is the a priori part of empirical grammar.

> With respect to empirical-grammatical forms, they [viz., the a priori laws of meaning] are prior and are comparable to an absolute and fixed "ideal framework" that is more or less explicit in empirical manifestations. One must have this framework before one's eyes in order to be able to ask significantly how German, Latin, Chinese, etc. expresses "the existential statement," "the categorical statement," the hypothetical antecedent" [*LU* II, 339].

The study of empirical grammar requires a conceptual framework that can be provided only by that part of formal logic that yields the formation rules of any language. Universal grammar consists of analytic a priori statements [*LU* II, 333 ff.]. The criterion for analyticity for any given sentence is that it "permits formalization . . . *salva veritate*" [*LU* II, 256]. A sentence is analytic if we can substitute required variables for its noun and adjectives, and constants for the logical connectives, without affecting the truth value of the sentence. It is then analytic because the meaning of the words in the original sentence does not affect its truth or falsity, because that depends exclusively on the logical constants.[6] Universal grammar is a part of formal logic as we know it. It begins with a set of basic sentence forms and develops more complicated formations deductively [*LU* II, 328 ff.].[7]

Of crucial importance for our inquiry is the view that the formation rules for purely formal systems constitute the " 'ideal form' " of any language [*LU* II, 336]. Of course, these formation rules are not premises from which the grammars of all possible languages can be deduced, but they provide a priori knowledge of features that all languages must possess [*LU* II, 340]. If challenged, Husserl would no doubt enter the customary disclaimer that his discussion is restricted to those parts of natural languages that consist of "descriptive," "fact-stating," or "informative" discourse. So-called emotive uses of language do not fall under the forms of formal logic. The disclaimer suggests that the formation rules of systems of formal logic provide the necessary features of only parts of natural languages, and who would want to quarrel with that?

But the disclaimer is disingenuous. Consider what is not thought to fall under the rules of purely formal calculi. Insofar as we make true or false statements about our own or other peoples' emotions, such statements must obey the purely formal formation rules just as all other statements do. It is only the "expression" of emotion or what Husserl calls *"Kundgabe"* that is eliminated from formal consideration. This term *"Kundgabe"* applies to all those linguistic phenomena that can not be classified as statements. Expression, if we look closely, is construed as a causal relation. My face expresses my anger; so does my tone of voice and its loudness. The relation between these manifestations and the anger manifested is the same as that between the smoke that manifests fire and the fire itself [*LU* II, 23–35]. The relation is causal, not intentional. The anger that you see on my face is not to be construed as a proposition, for I do not mean to tell you anything when I make an angry face. One does not usually make faces or gestures on purpose [*LU* II, 31]. They are caused by inner states and for that reason are not to be counted as instances of communication. If, on the other hand, one does make faces or gesticulates on purpose, we can, presumably, take these acts as propositional, as asserting facts about oneself. Any disclaimer that formal systems represent only the form of fact-stating discourse is therefore disingenuous because it turns out that all discourse is fact stating: There is no other discourse. Phenomena that are usually counted as linguistic or as cases of communication are analyzed either as statements or as the effects of bodily states or of some kind of affect. If of the latter sort, they are not regarded as cases of communication at all; thus phenomena that are apparently linguistic, that might resist analysis according to the model of formal logic, are reinterpreted in order to show that they are not really linguistic at all. Hence formal logic does indeed specify necessary features of all linguistic phenomena, on this view.

This discussion shows that Husserl belongs with all philosophers who believe that formal logic and formalized languages are essential to remedy certain defects of ordinary language. Their motto is "Formalizing clarifies." [8] This statement implies that natural languages are defective to the extent that they are at variance with the forms of formalized languages. Formal logic contains necessary conditions for any set of sounds or marks to be a language. This assumption is made wherever a philosopher believes that the use of formal notation improves on the use of informal notations, that is, wherever the "ideal-languages" approach is used. A philosopher may regard the choice of a formal system as, in some sense, "arbitrary," but as long as he does not regard it as "arbitrary" whether we choose to transcribe unclear statements into a formalized language rather than into, say, music, painting or movement, he is committed to the view that formal logic provides necessary features for any natural language.

A definite conception of language is implicit in these claims about the relation of formal logic to language. Logic is, in Husserl's scheme, analytic a priori. Other philosophers may want to take a more moderate stand. But it is generally agreed that logical statements are not contingent, empirical truths. In the end they may not turn out to be true of all possible worlds, but they are certainly true of more than this actual world. Accordingly we must think of language in such a way that its empirical features are sharply separable from those nonempirical features that are the concern of the logician. (At least Husserl must think of language in this way because he wants to hold that logical statements are true or false and that they can be said to be true or false with regard to something.)[9] These nonempirical features Husserl calls "meanings"; we might also use the term "concept." At least some statements about meanings are supposed to be true of all natural languages. But each of these languages uses different sound patterns and inscriptions to convey these meanings. Statements about the sound patterns of any given language are true only for that language. Statements about these sound patterns and written marks must therefore be logically independent of some true statements about meanings. Statements about meanings must also be independent of statements about the psychological states of persons while they use language or about the objects that language is used to talk about. For statements about the psychological states of language users and about the world about which we make true or false assertions are not true for any world but this one. They must therefore be distinguishable from statements in logic. Similarly, statements about what an expression means are not statements about what that expression refers to for it is an empirical question whether an expression refers at all. Finally, the empirical circumstances surrounding any particular uses of language are not relevant to meanings. It is possible to talk adequately about meanings, and to do so while not saying anything about speakers, listeners or the conditions under which language is being used. Meaning is logically independent of use.

Once we accept Husserl's conception of the relation between formal logic and natural languages, we can show that natural languages must be as he conceives them. A language whose necessary structural features are contained in a formal system must have the other features that have been mentioned. What is more, we can state the relation between Husserl's conception of language and his view of the relation of logic to language in perfectly familiar, formal logical terms. We can also explicate key terms in his description of language, like "independent," in the same formal logical terms. What we cannot do, however, is to give a deductive argument in support of his claims concerning the relations of logic to language. It would be circular to describe language, as Husserl describes it, and then to conclude that formal logic and language are related as he says they are related, for we would have to appeal in turn to his account of that relation to support his description of language. More to the point, any attempt to construct a deductive argument to prove Husserl's views about the relation of logic to language would presuppose its conclusions by applying rules of formal logic to gauge the validity of the argument. We can develop his conception of language deductively, but we cannot prove it correct in the same way.

The central features of Husserl's conception of language are set forth in these two passages:

> I understand that repeated acts of entertaining an idea [*vorstellen*] and judging intend identically the same concept or proposition. I understand that where, for instance, we speak about the *proposition* or the *truth* "π is a transcendental number" we have nothing less in mind than the individual mental event or aspect of a mental event of any particular person. . . . I understand finally that what I intend in the sentence mentioned is identically what it is, regardless of my thinking or existing or of any person's existence or acts. The same is true for all meanings. . . . [*LU* II, 100].

and

> There is no necessary connection between the ideal entities which, in fact, function as meanings and the marks to which they are tied, i.e., by means of which they have reality in the human mind [*LU* II, 104–105].

The central points in these passages can be stated in five theses. The first and second thesis are expressed in the second passage:

1. *Meanings are distinct from marks.*

The assertion itself is not as interesting as the sense given to the key terms in it. The term "meaning," as the first quotation suggests, may be taken to stand both for "concepts" and for "propositions." But it must be clearly understood that concepts are not psychological entities, not entities in anyone's mind, but are what a (categoramatic) word means; similarly, it must also be clearly understood that propositions are not linguistic entities, are not sentences in any particular language, but are what such sentences mean. By "marks," on the other hand, we must understand the configuration of sounds or of marks on paper, that is, the material objects that can be exhaustively described by mentioning their acoustical or geometrical properties.

The first thesis presupposes that what is commonly called a "word" or a "sentence" consists of two parts; one of them, the meaning, is definitely not a material object; the other, the mark, definitely is. The first thesis insists on this distinction, formulated in this way.

2. *Meaning and mark are mutually independent.*

Husserl points out that whereas marks are individuated by spatiotemporal position—this occurrence of "word" is distinct from that occurrence of "word" by virtue of their different placement on the page—both marks have identically the same meaning. Meanings, he says, are "general objects" [*LU* II, 101 ff.]. The true description of the meaning of "word" is not affected by its being associated with the first, second or third token of this word type in this paragraph.

Nor is the description of the meaning affected by being associated with "word" (in English) or with *"Wort"* (in German) or with any other mark. The mutual independence of word and mark means that any mark or any meaning, if each changes its associations to a meaning or a mark, respectively, alters only one property : that of being associated with some specific mark or meaning. One might also state this thesis by saying that, according to Husserl and the early Heidegger, marks and meanings are externally related.

It follows from the first two theses, as stated, that we are sometimes able to talk about the difference between meaningful and nonmeaningful statements without talking about the marks used to express meanings in any given natural language. This suggests that it may be possible to say something about the conditions for meaningful statements about all languages, for one of the differences between languages— their marks—turns out to be logically independent of meanings. The two theses also show that some empirical statements that may be made about languages—namely, those that refer to marks—are not necessarily relevant to discussions of what makes or does not make sense. Here we have the first step toward showing that we can make a priori statements about conditions of meaningfulness for all languages.

3. The meanings of words are distinct from the mental states of a speaker or listener.

Among the logicians whom Husserl had been attacking in the first volume of *Logical Investigations,* the opinion had been widespread that images or ideas are what we mean by "the meanings" of words. To say that a word means ———— is to say that when one hears or uses that word, one has the image of ———— in one's mind or else fails to understand the word. Husserl holds that such identification is mistaken, as the second quotation shows. This eliminates one more reason for regarding logic as an empirical discipline. Statements about the psychological states of language users surely are empirical. But we do not need to talk about such states when we talk about meanings.

4. *The meanings of words and expressions are not determined by their referents.*

Meaning and referent obviously cannot be completely unrelated. Sentences are true or false depending on what is referred to in them and this is determined by the meaning of words. Hence the meaning of words determines what sorts of referents words and sentences can have. But there is no converse relation between referent and meaning. What a word or an expression means is not determined by any referents they may have. Husserl's example is "the victor at Jena" and "the vanquished at Waterloo"—two expressions with different meanings referring to one and the same individual [*LU* II, 46–47]. The meaning of an expression is independent of any features that an existing referent may have. The meaning of "the victor at Jena" is not affected by the fact that the man to whom it refers lost the battle of Waterloo. In fact, its meaning would remain unchanged even if no one had ever fought, lost or won the battle of Jena.

We can therefore talk about meanings of expressions without talking about any existing entities to which these expressions refer by virtue of their meaning. Truths of logic are in this respect independent of talk about facts. An apparent exception to this consists of those cases in which a word is used to refer to its own meaning. (Because, for Husserl, words consist of marks and meanings, to mention a word may be to employ it to refer to its meaning, to its mark or to both mark and meaning together. Only the first form of mentioning a word is relevant in the present context.) When a word is used to refer to its own meaning, meaning and referent are apparently identical and hence cannot be said to be independent of each other. But Husserl denies this identity by pointing out that when an expression is being mentioned, it is being used with a different meaning. In " 'The earth is round' is a statement,'' the meaning of the statement ''The earth is round'' is not the proposition that the earth is round. That statement functions here as its own name and this involves a ''change of meaning'' [*LU* II, 322]. An expression does not refer to its own meaning by virtue of that meaning. An expression that is mentioned must therefore be sharply distinguished from an expression that is used. It remains true that talk about meanings of expressions does not commit us to asserting the determination of meanings by referents. I may use the expression ''the meaning of 'gruly' '' to refer to the meaning of ''gruly,'' but the fact remains that ''gruly'' has no meaning.

5. *Meanings are objective.*

The term ''objective'' is Husserl's:

> We call an expression objective if . . . it can be understood without any reference to the person using the expression or the conditions under which it is being used [*LU* II, 80].

The first of the two Husserl quotations given on page 62 makes the same point without using the term ''objective'': Statements about meanings are true or false regardless of whether anyone entertains, believes or knows the expressions that have these meanings. No contingent statements about persons or their uses of language are needed for making true statements about the meanings of words and expressions.

Husserl is aware that this thesis needs defense and he tries to defend it. For one thing, egocentric particulars like ''I,'' ''there,'' and ''today'' cannot be understood, one might say, unless one also knows some contingent statements about the identity of the speaker and about his spatiotemporal position. Husserl does not regard this as a decisive objection to his thesis that meanings are objective, because the changes of meaning [viz., of the egocentric particulars used by different persons at different times] are, strictly speaking, changes in the acts of meaning [*LU* II, 91].

The distinction between act and content is once again called upon to save the day. It does not matter for our purposes that the solution, at least as stated, is anything but convincing or that Husserl admits that it will never, in fact, be possible to replace egocentric particulars with purely objective expressions [*LU* II, 91]. Ideally, he continues to maintain, meanings are objective. Even if natural languages do not fully conform to the requirement that meanings be objective, this apparently does not invalidate the fifth thesis; it merely shows a shortcoming of natural languages.

The implications of this thesis are important. If the meaning of statements and other expressions is independent of facts about the speaker, then the meaning of expressions is independent of the use to which they are put by the speaker. We do not need to know what someone is doing when he is uttering a certain expression—for instance, whether he is trying to deceive or tell the truth—in order to understand what is being said. But, we might ask Husserl, suppose the utterance is not a statement but a question, a request or an order. In this case it would seem that we must know what the speaker is doing—for instance, that he is asking a question—in order to understand what he is saying and to be able to respond to it properly. If someone says to you "I am thirsty" and you say "Is that so?" instead of giving him a glass of water, you have not understood him. Husserl meets this objection by using the distinction discussed earlier between what an expression means and what it expresses. "I am thirsty" makes a statement about the speaker. It tells us something about his sensations. To that extent, "Is that so?" is a perfectly appropriate response. But insofar as saying "I am thirsty" is asking for water, the utterance expresses the feelings of the speaker, that he wants water. "I am thirsty" expresses a desire—just as a red face expresses anger. His wish for water causes him to make a statement about himself. If I am properly acquainted with the relevant causal laws, I may make the needed inference in order to understand "I am thirsty." I need to make the inference only in order to understand the wishes of the other person, which are expressed by "I am thirsty" [LU II, 32–33, 78–79]. What the statement "I am thirsty" means and what it expresses are again independent. I may utter it when I do not want water, for example, if I am thirsty but have taken a vow to drink no water before sundown. On the other hand, I may express my wish by sign language without using any expression whatsoever. Hence one need not know what the expression is meant to accomplish in order to be able to understand what it means.

It is implicit in this argument that what an utterance means is what it asserts, and it follows that all meaningful uses of language assert something and are therefore to be construed as statements. On Husserl's view of language, statements are the paradigms of language. All uses that appear to be different from statements—for example, wishes—are construed as statements plus something else, which may be, for instance, an expression of an inner state of the speaker.

If all uses of language are statements, so are explanations of what we mean by particular utterances. Explanations of language are also statements, and this, in turn, tells us something about the sorts of entities that meanings are. Husserl speaks of them as "objects," but not, of course, as objects known by experience. Theses three and four eliminate that. Instead we should think of meanings as "general" or "ideal" objects. But they are objects nonetheless. Nor is this merely a careless way of using terminology. Objects are what statements are about. Statements are true or false. They are true or false in relation to something. We may say that they are true or false with respect to facts (Husserl calls them

"Sachverhalte") [*LU* I, 227 ff.]. But in order for any particular statement to be true or false with respect to any particular fact, the statement must be connected with the fact in some other way because for any given statement that is true of a fact, there is a second statement, contradicting the first, that is false. Statements therefore are not merely true or false of facts; they also refer to facts. Statements refer to facts by virtue of the names of objects occurring in these sentences. This view, that meanings are objects of a certain sort, follows from thesis five together with the further assumption that truth consists of some sort of correspondence between statements and states of affairs. Husserl does make this assumption; hence he is committed to speaking of meanings as objects [*LU* II, 107–108 ff.]. Because meanings are objects, statements about them are true or false, even if they are purely formal. Husserl thus rejects the notion that a formal calculus does not consist of true statements but rather of the logical consequences of axioms and definitions adopted by us.[10] We are not free to adopt any system of logic that appears most useful to us.

In the Scotus book, Heidegger subscribes to these five theses. We are told that marks and meanings are distinct.[11] Discussion of marks and discussion of meanings are mutually independent.[12] Meanings are not to be identified with mental entities[13] or with the physical objects to which they may refer,[14] and, finally:

> the doctrine of meanings . . . must exclude all problems, in themselves by no means unimportant, that have to do with factual matters, and processes, and with questions about the purposes of the use of signs.[15]

Meanings are objective. Like Husserl, Heidegger concludes therefore that the doctrine of meaning belongs with logic because it deals with the "logical structure of meanings."[16] He quotes Husserl when he characterizes this doctrine of meaning.[17] It deals exclusively with "meanings in themselves."[18]

If one accepted this Husserlian account of language, one would not be inclined to describe the philosopher's talk about words and concepts as "making recommendations." To be sure, a philosopher might recommend that we use a different mark for a particular meaning (or concept) from the one we have been accustomed to use; he might do so because in the course of the history of philosophy the familiar mark has been associated with so many different meanings that to use it now would be to invite misunderstanding. This would be a purely verbal maneuver. We saw in Chapter 2 that Heidegger's recommendations are not of this sort. He did not merely recommend that we use the mark "gear" where before we used the mark "thing"; instead he recommended new concepts to us by providing new criteria for new marks or old established ones. In Husserl's scheme such recommendations for new criteria would come out as statements about meanings, not about marks. But statements about meanings are true or false, and to make presumably true statements about meanings is not most aptly described as "making conceptual recommendations."

In his polemic against psychologism in the first volume of *Logical Investigations,* Husserl argued that it is a mistake to identify the meaning of a word with, for instance, a mental image. That "meaning" and "mental image" have the same meaning is, according to him, a falsehood. He does not merely recommend that we draw a distinction here. He asserts that a distinction exists whether we draw it or not, and he tells us how we must on pain of irrationality use our words. It is inappropriate to recommend that one speak according to true rather than false rules of meaning. For this reason Husserl's reflections about concepts must be aimed at providing careful descriptions and clarifications of meanings. The philosopher knows

> that he does not *create* the objective validity of thoughts and their connections, of concepts and of truths . . . but that he *understands and discovers* them [*LU* II, 94–95].

As long as Heidegger shared Husserl's view on language, he would not have thought of talking about the philosopher's work as making recommendations about concepts. But by the time he comes to write *S & Z*, he has changed his views. Now philosophy recommends new criteria for concepts.

The truth or falsity of statements about concepts, however, is still of some importance. As we saw in Chapter 1, Heidegger will cite as one of his reasons for being extremely critical of a certain concept, that the explication of the concept implies false statements. Thus Descartes' explication of "world" implies that we know by inference from evidence what the world is like and whether it exists. Similarly, Descartes' explication of knowing on the paradigm of mathematical knowledge has the consequence that sensory qualities—for instance, hardness—are not real [97]. But, as we also saw in Chapter 1, these difficulties can always be evaded by introducing other distinctions and reforming other concepts. If any explication of a concept implies a falsehood, we are not thereby obligated or even authorized to regard the explication as false because the implications can be transformed into true ones by altering the language. For Husserl, truth consisted of the correspondence of our statements about meanings to these meanings themselves and was, therefore, a property of single statements. For Heidegger, the concept of truth has become more complex. The truth of any given statement depends on the particular language to which it belongs and not only on its relation to facts. Hence we can either reject a conceptual explication or adjust our language to accommodate it.

Although one can always evade awkward consequences of conceptual explications, the need for adjustments is a sign of strain in a language, and often the strain is not removed convincingly by changing the explications of other terms. The language as a whole must meet our demands for truth, in a different sense of that term in which truth is not relative to a specific language. Whatever adjustments a philosopher may make in his vocabulary to meet technical objections in the

terms of technical philosophical discourse, we are always entitled to be skeptical with respect to these changes on the
grounds that his vocabulary does not do justice to what we
consider the world to be like before we have begun to give a
·philosophical explication of our ordinary understanding.

There is then a second appeal to truth, namely, to a prephilosophical, commonsense view of the world according to
which hardness, for instance, is real (whatever that term may
mean precisely), and we are sure that there is an external
world although we have no evidence for its existence. Appeals
to common sense weigh heavily, even for Heidegger. We have
seen him appeal to ordinary, prephilosophical facts about our
use of tools, and in section II we shall give examples of other
such appeals in his discussion of language. Such appeals,
however, do not possess ultimate authority for him. As I shall
show at the end of Chapter 5, Heidegger is certainly willing
to cast doubt on our everyday understanding of the world.
Philosophical explications may be attacked and supported by
appeals to ordinary experience and understanding. But this
understanding is itself subject to philosophical scrutiny and
criticism. Even between ordinary everyday understanding
and more articulate, precise philosophical understanding we
move in a circle.

Heidegger leaves no doubt that he has changed his mind
about language since writing the book about Scotus. In the
tradition, which he is now attacking at every turn, "Grammar sought its foundation in this 'logic' . . ." [165]. A few
lines later he speaks of the "task of liberating grammar from
logic." If this phrase means anything, it means that Heidegger now wants to present a view of language in which grammar does not have an a priori foundation in purely formal
logic. He has now become intensely distrustful of the *Bedeutungslehre* whose beginnings he had earlier admired in Husserl and had therefore looked for in Scotus [*ibid.*]. A new
conception of language is needed, but this can be discovered

only in the course of the sort of ontological inquiry undertaken in *S & Z*.

If we are to understand what Heidegger is doing when doing ontology, we must understand this conception of language. But his suggestions concerning language are so brief that we must keep clearly in mind the views that he now disavows. In contrast to the conception of language outlined in this section we can state the alternative views in *S & Z*. These views, in turn, will make clearer what sorts of recommendations ontology makes and will also provide examples of such recommendations; after all, Heidegger's discussion of language is itself ontological.

II

We begin with these two sentences:

Meanings grow into words [*Den Bedeutungen wachsen Worte zu*]. It is not true that word things are equipped with meanings [161].[19]

The passage can be understood in at least three different ways, depending on where we locate the central points in the two sentences.

For instance, we may notice the contrast between meanings that "grow into words" and meanings with which words are "equipped." This thought surely looks like an attack on the view that it is up to us to choose what meanings to give to words. Heidegger now seems to prefer to account for the connections between words and meanings by an analogy to a process of natural growth, a process that in the main is not under our control. Thus he seems to contradict flatly what we have seen him assert repeatedly: that we recommend what meanings words should have and thus, in some way, choose what words should mean. This interpretation of the passage cannot therefore be correct.

Another analysis of the passage indicates an agreement between the first sentence, which seems to attribute priority to meanings—they are there first and then "grow into words" —and the second sentence, which denies the priority of words over meanings. It is not true that there are words first, which are then "equipped with meanings." Heidegger seems to tell us that a Platonic realm of meanings exists. But if this were true, statements about meanings would certainly be objective, and then it would not be possible, as we saw, to think of ontology as recommending criteria for concepts. This second reading must therefore also be rejected.

A third analysis of the passage indicates a contrast between "words" in the first sentence and "word things" in the second. An obscure contrast, to be sure, but not one that is altogether unfamiliar to us. We encountered a parallel locution to "word thing" in the preceding chapter, in which we quoted Heidegger as saying

the unusable is just lying there—it shows itself as gear thing that looks thus and so . . . pure being present on hand makes its appearance [73].

A "gear thing" is something that, although usually a tool or object of use, is now just there, to be examined for its objective properties. We treat gear as gear thing if we ignore that it is for a specific use, or that it belongs in a tool context, and instead look at it as something present on hand. Correspondingly, a word thing is a word taken, not as an integral part of the complex sets of practices and gear that we call "language," but as an object present on hand, describable as what it is in itself, independently of human users, in terms of physical properties. The distinction is between, on the one hand, words as full-fledged parts of language and, on the other, marks, as Husserl thought of them, as physical objects. It might be objected that this distinction assumes that language is also a gear context. But Heidegger insists that language (*Sprache*) is one form of discourse (*Rede*) and discourse is an existential, that is, a feature of being human. This objection assumes that being a gear context is incompatible with being an existential. Heidegger does not seem to think so [see, e.g., 161]. It is not at all clear, of course, what sort of entity a gear context is. I shall suggest in the final chapter that this is not accidental but an indication of a serious gap in the Heideggerian conceptual structure as he develops it in *S & Z*.

This third interpretation—that a distinction is drawn between words as full-fledged parts of language and marks as physical objects—is confirmed if we consider the Husserlian view of language that Heidegger had shared but now rejects. Then he distinguished between marks, as physical objects exhaustively describable by physical object predicates and meanings. This thesis not only affirmed a distinction but gave it a particular formulation, by claiming that marks are physical objects or material things in the way in which Husserl regarded things, to which nonmaterial entities, called "meanings," were associated. Words thus fell apart as it were, into two incommensurable pieces, one a physical object, the other an ideal entity. Together they constitute˙ what we call a "word." Heidegger of course, does not reject the distinction altogether. Nobody could reasonably do that. But he does reject this particular formulation of it. We can certainly ask for the meanings of given words, and our questions can be answered. But from this observation alone it does not follow that there are physical entities, completely devoid of meaning, that are left over when we subtract the meaning from the word. It is a misleading picture of a word to think of it as a physical object, a "word thing," which we then "equip" with meaning, in the way in which we put a name tag on a box or attach a flag to the flagpole. Instead, Heidegger suggests that we should think of meaning as growing into words.

We shall not find it easy to give a full explication of this expression, but we can get a preliminary sense of it. Words—not now as physical objects plus meanings, but simply as words as they are familiar to us before we engage in philosophical reflection—are related to what they mean, what we ask questions about or explain to ourselves or others, just as a full-grown plant or animal is related to its seed or to itself before it reaches maturity. The man is not a distinct entity from the child he was; instead he brings to completion what was not fully articulated and developed in detail in the child. If you look at a child, you do not know clearly what sort of person he will be, but there is a fair indication of what sort of person he will not be. The outlines of the future adult are given, but the details remain to be elaborated. In the same way, what we mean reaches articulation and fruition only when it is put into words. We cannot know with certainty what the explication will say until it has been formulated. Heidegger recognizes the distinction between words and meanings but refuses to explicate it as a distinction between physical objects and immaterial meanings, as was done in Husserl's first and second theses.

There are two related considerations for rejecting Husserl's first, and with it, his second thesis about language. Marks and meanings, Heidegger points out, are not easily distinguished. Ordinarily,

> . . . what we hear in the first place are never noises or sound patterns, but the creaking wagon, the motorcycle. We hear the column on the march, the tapping woodpecker, the crackling fire. A rather artificial and complicated attitude is needed if we are to hear a "pure noise" [163, 164].[20]

It is not true that we hear a noise of which we can give, however roughly, a purely physical description from which, in conjunction with empirical generalizations, we infer that there is a woodpecker in the vicinity or that some army is on the march again. The same observation can be applied more specifically to words. One must make a special effort to hear only the sounds made by a speaker, and one needs much practice to succeed in doing so. It takes considerable skill to make a phonetic transcription of someone's speech. Ordinarily we hear what someone says rather than the phonetic characteristics of his speech. We ask, "What does this word mean?" and not "Is this noise associated with a meaning (and therefore a word), and, if so, what is its meaning?"—because we know only dimly what specific noises someone makes when he speaks.

Even if marks were perceived as distinct physical entities, we would have to deny that they are independent of the meanings with which they are associated. Heidegger reminds us that we pronounce words and phrases with all sorts of variations of "intonation, modulation and speed" [162]. All these are clearly physical aspects of speech; they are properties of the mark. But they are not independent of the meaning attached to the marks. What someone means, what he is telling us, is certainly affected by the way in which he says it. Whether "Fire!" is a request for a match or a warning that fire has broken out depends on how I pronounce the word. Certain meanings cannot be associated with certain physical objects. I could not just be asking for a match if I yelled "Fire!" agitatedly, at the top of my lungs. The conclusion to be drawn from these two remarks is this: Those sound features that do not contribute to the meaning, that are independent of what someone is saying to us, often are not noticed at all. In cases in which someone's accent does not contribute to the meaning of his speech, we usually do not notice its peculiar phonetic features. The aspects of marks that we do notice are those that are not independent of what is meant— for instance, when racial prejudice is expressed not by what is said but by an imitation of the speech of some Negroes. In

cases in which we respond to a recognizable physical object,
it is not independent of the meaning; when such independence exists, we do not know the physical object to which we
respond unless we have acquired the specialized skills of the
phonetician.

Heidegger, I should think, considers these to be strong arguments against Husserl. It seems false, in a fairly down-to-
earth and familiar sense, that there are physical marks to
which we respond because a certain meaning is associated
with them. But of course Husserl would not be moved by
these observations. He would reply that they show only that
marks and meanings are usually so firmly joined by our linguistic habits that it requires an explicit reflection to separate
them. But because we know that meanings are objects, albeit
ideal ones (thesis five) and that marks are physical objects,
we also know that marks and meanings are distinct and mutually independent, even if this is not usually apparent to the
users of a given language [cf. *LU* II, 1st ed., 360–361]. Heidegger, on the other hand, believes that his observations are
telling blows against the views attacked. This is not a mistake
on his part but, instead, shows that he does not share Husserl's fifth thesis either. Husserl's five theses are not mutually
independent, and one cannot refuse to accept one of them
without possibly rejecting some of the others. If Heidegger
wants to make plausible his criticism of the distinction between mark and meaning, he must give us reasons for believing
that meanings are not objective and are not objects, as Husserl had maintained.

Quite consistently, Heidegger does attack this fifth thesis.
He writes:

[In discourse we] assent, refuse, invite, warn; we speak
out, bespeak, speak for someone, "make statements,"
and make speeches [161].[21]

We are here reminded of the very different uses we make of
language. But why is it important for us to remember them?

To be sure, we use statements for all sorts of purposes. Nobody would deny that, but these uses, one usually thinks, and
Husserl thinks so, are independent of what these statements
say, of what they are about. But the reminder that different
uses exist is designed to deny just that: that use and what a
statement is about are independent. For Heidegger continues
in the same passage,

> Discourse is discourse about . . . What discourse is
> about is not necessarily and not [in fact] very often
> like the subject matter of an assertion ascribing a prop-
> erty to something. An order that has been given also was
> about something, a wish is about something. When we
> speak for someone we speak about something [161–162].

Different uses are about something in different ways or, if
you will, in different senses of "about." The different uses
are thus not to be construed as different employments of statements, for all statements are about facts in the same sense of
"about": They are true or false. Not all uses of language are
to be regarded as statements precisely because, in the different
uses of language, the relation of what is said to what it is
about is very different. But, as we saw earlier, Husserl's thesis
five, that meanings are objective, entailed that statements are
the paradigm of all uses of language and that we need not
know for what someone is using an utterance in order to understand him. We need merely to understand what he is asserting.

Heidegger turns against this view by emphasizing the very
different uses we make of language.

> Reports [*Aussagen*] about what is happening around us,
> descriptions of objects of use, "on-the-scene reports,"
> recording and establishing "the facts of the case," de-
> scriptions of a state of affairs, recounting what has hap-
> pened—these "statements" cannot be reduced to theo-
> retical statements without seriously distorting their
> meaning [158].

Heidegger does not tell us in any more detail in what ways these different sorts of utterances differ. I shall make some suggestions in order to clarify the passage and the point it makes.

Notice, to begin with, that Heidegger gives us a series of examples of uses of language that in ordinary usage are called "statements." The point of the examples is to make us see that we should not slide from the ordinary to the philosophic use of "statement" without some reflection, for the various cases are not best and most properly construed as "statements" in the technical philosophical sense. Consider these cases:

Reports about what is happening around us might be pointers like "There is a fat lady over there" or expressions of distress like "I've been robbed!"

Descriptions of objects of use are given when we explain to someone how to use a tool; for example, we say, "One holds it here . . . like this . . . , then one moves one's hand like this. . . ."

On-the-scene reports are found, for instance, in a newspaper. They do not merely report the facts but attempt to convey the emotional impact of an event on the participants or the mood that pervades a place.

A police report records and establishes the facts of a case. It tells you about an accident, which car was traveling in what direction and at what speed. The format of such a report is preestablished by police procedure.

I might be giving a description of a state of affairs when asking a lawyer for advice. I tell him what he needs to know about a situation so that he can appreciate my particular problem. The point of my telling him is to set forth that problem.

When I recount to someone what has happened, I am perhaps trying to entertain him, or to impress him with the exciting life I have led, or to appeal to his sympathy for my suffering.

One may grant that all these are different uses of language

and yet hold that they exemplify only different ways of making statements or what Heidegger, in the passage quoted, calls "theoretical statements." If, like Heidegger, one wants to reject this contention, one may argue, for instance, that in each of these cases the listener must give a very different response from that appropriate to someone's making a statement before we are willing to say that he has understood it. To statements he may respond with assent to, denial of or doubt about the truth of what is stated. Any of these responses indicate that he has understood the statement. But if he were to respond to "I've been robbed" with "Yes, that's true" or if he were to say "Is that so?" to someone who shows him how to hold a tool, we would not be sure that he understood what was said. If someone tells us that he has been robbed we call the police (if we believe him) ; one responds to instructions by trying to do what has been demonstrated. If one is doubtful whether any robbery did take place, he does not merely ask for evidence but tries to get the whole story after trying to calm the victim. If one has no confidence in one's instructor, one asks for his credentials or says something like "I thought one held it there . . . like this." Similarly, a person has failed to understand an on-the-scene report from a hotel fire if he says, "It is false to say there are scores of victims, there are only thirty-nine." The proper response is one of horror or indifference. Similar observations can be made about police reports, descriptions of states of affairs or one's retelling his experiences. In none of these cases are questions about truth irrelevant, but no one who understands these different kinds of utterances would respond with assent or dissent or doubts about their relationship to the available evidence.

Not all utterances that are ordinarily called "statements" are statements in the technical philosophical sense in which philosophers like Husserl took "statements" when they regarded them to be the paradigms of all uses of language. Moreover, one and the same utterance may sometimes be a statement in this technical sense and may sometimes be used very differently. Heidegger uses the example of the cabinet-maker who lays down a tool with the words "too heavy" [157]. If he is being watched by someone who is not a cabinet-maker, the statement may explain what he is doing. It points out that he put down the hammer because it was not adequate for the job. If the cabinetmaker has an assistant who gave him the hammer, "too heavy" may be a reproach or a request for a lighter hammer. "Too heavy" may also be a reminder to himself that he had found the hammer too heavy before but had forgotten. "Too heavy," finally, may be elliptical for the statement "This hammer is too heavy" or for "This hammer is too heavy to be used for this job."

In response to Husserl's first two theses, which distinguished marks from meaning, we found Heidegger interested not in denying them and asserting their contrary or contradictory, but in showing that there are many cases in which the distinction between what a word means and what it looks or sounds like cannot be drawn in the terms Husserl proposed. Here, similarly, Heidegger's reaction to the fifth thesis does not consist in his asserting that statements about meanings are dependent on statements about the conditions under which the statement is uttered. If statements mean what they assert, then it may well be true that one can understand what a statement asserts without knowing who actually uttered it and where and at what time. It is true then that meanings of statements are objective. The point of the preceding cases is to show that understanding what a statement means is not paradigmatic for understanding what any utterance means, for not all utterances are statements. As a consequence, a philosopher may very well refrain from asserting or denying that meanings are objective. For most utterances the question whether their meanings are objective or not does not apply or is not interesting. If "too heavy" is meant as a reproach or a reminder, it does not assert anything; it reproaches or reminds. Hence, the question whether one can understand what is asserted without knowing the circumstances does not arise. Nor does there seem to be any point in arguing that one can or cannot feel reproached or register a reminder without being aware of the circumstances, because reproaches and reminders of course have their context, which one must understand to appreciate what is being done.

Even with respect to statements, the controversy loses interest. If "too heavy" is sometimes a statement, sometimes a pointer, at other times a reproach or a reminder, we certainly need some extraneous information to help us decide which it is in any particular case. In the larger sense of "knowing what an utterance means," in which sense this phrase includes knowing whether someone gives me information about the hammer or is scolding me, knowing what an expression means requires knowing a good deal more about the occasion than what is being asserted. In a narrow sense of "meaning," in which a statement means what it asserts, Husserl is probably right when he says that meanings are objective. From Heidegger's point of view, Husserl's fifth thesis is true, but within such narrow limits that it is more interesting to show, not that it is false, for it is not, but in what respect it is incomplete and unilluminating. We shall see in the next section that Heidegger does not even consider Husserl's view on meaning as suitable for all statements.

The same oblique treatment is given to the third thesis: that meanings are distinct from mental events. In response to this thesis Heidegger certainly does not assert that meanings are identical with images or ideas. Instead he continues his attempt to replace Husserl's vocabulary in which it is an important question whether or not meanings are mental states or events. If we distinguish the "real act" from the "ideal content" of a judgment,

> is the actuality of knowing and judging not being broken into two modes of being and two "levels" in such a way that we can never grasp the ontological type [*Seinsart*] of knowing by sticking these two levels together? Is psy-

chologism not justified in its objection to this separation?
[217].

The distinction between real psychological events and the
"ideal" contents of these events is not acceptable. The rejection of that distinction is foreshadowed in the preceding reflections about meanings and uses and about meanings and
marks. But the rejection of Husserl's distinction is not of
course an endorsement of psychologism. Heidegger wants to
reject both alternatives, psychologism and antipsychologism.[22]
He wants to make us see that the question "Are meanings
real or ideal entities?" is not the right sort of question to ask,
because Husserl altogether misconstrued what sorts of entities "meanings" are. Heidegger suggests that it is very misleading to speak of meanings as "objects" as Husserl had.

What then are meanings? I suspect that Heidegger would
not like the question in this form. He would prefer to answer
a question like "What are we saying and doing when we say
'What I meant was . . .'?" Instead of talking about meanings in a way that sounds as if one were talking about objects,
Heidegger talks about meaningfulness (*Bedeutsamkeit*) [87].
When he does use the expression "meaning (*Sinn*)" he does
so in the context of talk about explication. "We call 'meaning' what can be articulated in understanding disclosure"
[151]. Meanings are not objects, for meaning is what we explain.[23]

But is "Meanings are not objects" incompatible with
"Meaning is what we explain"? One would think, on the
contrary, that it is meanings we explain because they are objects of some sort. We explain what a word means when we
tell someone what meaning or concept is habitually associated
with a particular mark—for instance, when a foreigner asks
us what a particular English expression means. He will repeat
the sounds that he has heard but not understood, and we tell
him what concepts are associated with these sounds by produc-

ing synonymous expressions in English or, better yet, by translating the expression into his native language. In this case we
convey to him the meaning that is connected with this particular sound. By translating we establish the connection between a sound in a new language and the meaning that the
person, because he associates it with certain sounds in his
native tongue, already knows. Once we have explained this
to him, he understands. If meanings were not distinct objects,
we could not explain sounds that someone does not understand
by referring to meanings that are familiar to him through
their association with the sounds of a different language. We
can explain meanings only because they are objects.

Once again we find unclear the distinctions between Heidegger's views and those that are more familiar to us. In order to clarify the difference between his views of meaning and
Husserl's,[24] we must ask what Heidegger has in mind when he
talks about "explication." To begin with, it is clear that the
sorts of examples that Heidegger has in mind when he talks
about "explication" do not involve translation from one language into another or explanations of the meanings of unfamiliar sounds. The examples that Heidegger takes as paradigmatic are probably those in which, for example, I explain
(make clear to) myself something I understand vaguely but
now work out in more detail—for instance, when I work out
a philosophical thought that I have grasped in outline but
have not yet developed fully. In this case, I am not making
statements about something that could be considered an independently existing object (my thought), but I clarify that
thought by articulating it. The thought is not already fully
formed and now merely put into words; it is articulated and
developed by being put into words. What I articulate is not
something existing full-fledged in some ideal realm but is
rather a "hunch" or "a feeling" that this is the way things
are. In this case, I can know explicitly only what it is I think
after having made it clear, and the thought is only as clear

as I make it. In some way, I have already laid hold of the thought, I understand it, but I do not understand it clearly until I have explicated it. For this reason Heidegger writes:

> We call it "explication" [*Auslegung*] when we develop what we understand. In explication, understanding appropriates what it has understood. Understanding does not become something other than itself in explication but comes to be itself. In the order of existential concepts, understanding does not come to be by virtue of explication, but explication rests on understanding. Explication is not taking cognizance of what has been understood but is the working out of the possibilities traced out [*entworfen*] in understanding [148].

It is not true that I understand only after an explanation has been given. On the contrary, my giving an explanation presupposes that I already understand what I explain. This is true even if I explain something to myself, as in the case in which I try to make my ideas clear. I have already laid hold of these ideas; I have them. Heidegger calls this *"Vorhabe."* Furthermore, when I explain something to someone, I am answering a question, and that again is true if I explain or clarify something to myself. If someone says to me, "Explain this to me," I begin by asking him what he does not understand and what he wants explained. For anyone to ask that sort of question, he needs a prior understanding of some sort, a *Vorhabe,* and having asked his question he broaches the matter in a certain way, in the light of his particular question. Heidegger calls this *"Vorsicht."* In this way, when I explain what, in one sense, I already understand, I do not merely rehearse to myself or convey to the other the understanding I already have—"Explication is not taking cognizance of what has been understood"—but I work out this understanding by trying to answer a particular question and by putting it in a particular vocabulary to which I have committed myself or to which perhaps another person who wants an explanation from me has committed me. This, Heidegger calls *"Vorgriff."* [25] These three terms—*Vorhabe, Vorsicht, Vorgriff*—refer to three features of the explication of meaning, and meaning is what we explicate in this particular way [150].

This account of explication presupposes a distinction between two different senses of understanding. We encountered this distinction in Chapter 1 in the form of the distinction between preontological understanding and explicit ontological knowing, and again in Chapter 2 when we discussed knowing tools by using them. Preontological knowledge involves an understanding of the world for which the ability to formulate what one understands is not a necessary condition; this understanding is inarticulate.[26] There is a second sense for which ability to formulate is a necessary condition. This is the more familiar sense in which we say of someone, for instance, that he does not understand the political situation because his account of it is rudimentary and ill informed. I shall discuss this distinction between two senses of knowing and of understanding in Chapter 5. But we must notice one consequence of drawing this distinction. If meaning is what we understand, and if we can understand without being able to formulate what we understand, it follows that not only linguistic entities can be understood and have meaning. The concept of understanding is applicable in contexts that do not involve language at all. Meaning is therefore also attributable to entities other than those belonging to language. Hence Heidegger applies both the terms *"Bedeutsamkeit"* and *"Sinn"* to all entities, not only to linguistic entities [87, 151]. The importance of this point will come to light in the next section.

In explication, my inarticulate understanding becomes transformed into understanding in a different sense of that term: by being put into words. It is transformed in a very particular way by being put into a very particular set of words. If we put the same inarticulate understanding into different words, the transformation is different. Heidegger insists on this when he introduces the term *"Vorgriff."* For the same reason he tells us that "meanings grow into words." A child grows into a man and is thereby transformed. Had he grown into a different man, he would have undergone a different transformation.

Heidegger proceeds here as he did in the earlier cases. He does not deny, in opposition to Husserl, that meanings are objects but tries to suggest that this way of talking applies with ease only to a very restricted range of cases. In Husserl's vocabulary, objects are what we make statements about; statements are true or false with respect to states of affairs. The claim that meanings are objects thus implies, at the least, that our explications of what something—a word, an expression, a statement or a long passage—means are either true or false. Different explications are to be adopted or rejected in the light of their truth or falsity. But in the sort of examples that Heidegger regards as central, this account is unconvincing. In the cases considered earlier in this section, I explain something to someone else or to myself that I understand to some degree, sufficiently to feel unsure and to want a more detailed and lucid explanation. What I have to say, for instance, about a concept leaves me feeling dissatisfied. I have the sense that my explication does not do justice to that concept. Therefore I try to do better. The difference between the original statements that did not satisfy me and the later ones that seem much more illuminating cannot be captured merely by contrasting the truth of the later ones with the falsity of the original statements—or by saying that the earlier and the later explications were both true, but that the later one was more explicit and complete.

Consider the discussion of things in the preceding chapter. Heidegger claims that Husserl's vocabulary is unable to explain to us what we mean when we ascribe a function to a "gear thing." This is a much weaker claim than saying that Husserl's explications are false. They certainly are not false, and we may well agree that they are true. But neither statement has much bearing on the disagreement between Husserl and Heidegger. If we restrict our talk about things to the spatiotemporal and causal properties of things, we have no answer to the question of what sort of property a function is. If Heidegger is right on this point, a Husserlian must regard functions as unanalyzable. Now this is a perfectly respectable philosophical answer, but not a satisfying one. Heidegger thinks that if he uses different terms he can say more about those aspects of objects of use that are indicated by the word "function." Suppose that he does give us a fuller account of what it means for an object of use to be for something. We have then learned something and feel enlightened. We are no longer dissatisfied. There are many ways in which we might describe the difference between the Heideggerian and the Husserlian accounts. Only in rare cases, however, would we compare them with respect to their truth values.

Even in the cases that concern translation, talk about meanings as objects is not uniformly felicitous. Heidegger, we saw earlier, insists that an explanation consists of words, not noises. By the time someone asks us what a certain word means, he has at least understood this much: that it is a word that he does not understand, which thus has a certain place in the economy of the language.[27] The Husserlian account of translation as providing a link between the sounds of one language and the meanings, which are shared by the speakers of different languages, applies only in the fairly artificial case in which we take it for granted that we are asking questions and giving answers about words. This initial understanding can be ignored in that case, and we can concentrate all our attention on the difference between the noise, of which we know only that it has a meaning, and our understanding of that meaning. Only under these conditions can one regard a word as a noise that has a meaning.

If it is not useful to think of what expressions mean as objects, it is no longer clear what we mean when we ask whether meanings are ideas or images. If meaning is what I articulate

when I talk to you, then what I say may be about images or
ideas, but it is not an image or an idea. So far one may seem-
ingly agree with Husserl and, at the same time, accept Heidegger's way of talking about meaning. But of course Husserl
asserts that neither ideas nor images are identical with meanings. If we talk like Heidegger about what expressions mean,
we do not deny this identity but talk in such a way that it
makes no sense either to assert or deny it. If you want to
know what an expression means, I may tell you by talking for
awhile or perhaps by making a gesture, drawing a picture or
pointing. Any of these actions explicate the expression you
did not understand. If someone comes along now and wants
to know whether my gesture or what I said was an image or
an idea, we would not know what to reply, except that it is
not a sensible question. Once we stop talking about meanings
as objects, the controversy, in which Husserl's third thesis
takes a stand, has lost relevance.

Meaning, according to Husserl's fourth thesis, is not determined by the existence of, or facts about, the referent. This
thesis applies to all words and expressions. It presupposes
that we may always ask about any given word or expression
what its meaning is and what it refers to. Sometimes the answer will be that the word has no meaning because it is a
proper name; at other times it may have a meaning but no
referent, because nothing exists to which it might refer. The
two questions are always applicable. But it is clear from all
that has gone before that these questions are not always applicable, on Heidegger's view of language, and when they are,
they are not quite the same sort of questions that one asks
about language in Husserl's scheme. As Heidegger talks of
language, meaning is articulated in explication. Not only
words but also things, as we understand them, for instance,
preontologically, can be said to "mean" something. This unformulated meaning is put into words and is articulated in
different ways depending on the initial questions asked and
the vocabulary used. There is then not much point in talking

about *the* meaning of an expression. On Heidegger's view of language, it is not at all clear what one asks for when one asks for *the* meaning of an expression. One only knows what is asked for in requests for explications that raise specific questions and make use of a specific vocabulary.

Once we deny, on the other hand, that all utterances are genuine statements or can be rephrased as statements, unless they are illegitimate uses of language, it is not at all obvious that one may inquire after the referent of every linguistic expression. As soon as we are willing to say that warning someone is not making a statement, but is using language to perform a certain action, questions about referents are no longer universally applicable. One can always ask to what a statement refers, although sometimes there is no referent. But it does not even make sense to ask what a warning, a command or a promise refer to, in the sense of "refer" that Husserl employs.

Heidegger, therefore, does not deny Husserl's fourth thesis. In his vocabulary the temptation to either affirm or deny it would never arise. This has some important implications. As long as we think of language as composed of words each of which is capable of having a fixed meaning and a referent, we must, as we saw earlier, be careful to separate cases in which words are used to refer to something other than themselves from cases in which they refer to themselves. We invite confusion unless we recognize that the same mark may be used in both cases but that the meaning is not the same. But if we reject the Husserlian view of language, we no longer have any reason for insisting on a strict separation of use from mention for all uses of language, although, of course, the fact remains that "Cicero has six letters" is nonsense in all but the most unusual cases.

If, in addition, we think of meaning as what we understand, as Heidegger does, so that it is perfectly acceptable to speak of the meaning of things and events—and if using language is one way of deepening our understanding of some-

thing or, put differently, articulating the meaning of something—then there may well be cases in which talking about
language serves to develop and enrich our understanding of
the entities that are talked about. In this case, talking about
language is not clearly distinguishable from talking about
nonlinguistic entities. (This throws light on the difficulty encountered at the beginning of Chapter 1, where Heidegger
seemed to talk indiscriminately about being and ''being.''
We understand now that he has no reason for insisting on the
distinction.) Specifically, philosophical explications of concepts may then, with equal justice, be regarded as discussions
of the world, of those entities to which the concepts are meant
to apply. Also, a discussion of alternative vocabularies for
talking about things is not exclusively concerned with language but develops alternative ways of understanding things
themselves. Similarly, one commits oneself to a particular
view of the world by using a particular language. All explication involves a *Vorgriff,* a particular conceptual scheme in
which to frame the explication. A given language is an example of such a conceptual scheme, which determines (to some
extent) what we can or cannot say in that language. ''Any
language already contains a well-developed set of concepts''
[157].

Most commonly discourse speaks out and has always
already spoken out. It is language [*Sprache*]. But what
has been spoken already contains understanding and
explication. Language . . . contains an explication of
our understanding of dasein. . . . it regulates and assigns the possibilities of our average understanding. . . .
[it] is the guardian of an understanding of the world
disclosed and, equally originally with it, an understanding of the other's being-with and of one's own being-in
[167–168].

We have seen a number of very different examples of the
way in which any given language ''regulates and assigns the

possibilities of our average understanding.'' If we use Husserl's thing vocabulary we are unable to explicate the concept of function. Our inability to do so leads us to claim that the concept is unanalyzable. Here the use of a certain language not only affects what we say as philosophers, but it also has implications for our conception of what we do as philosophers. A Husserlian needs the concept of function. Its unanalyzability cannot be used to eliminate the concept from the language. We are thus constrained to say that some concepts are essential even though philosophers are unable to say anything about them. Philosophical explication of terms thus comes to be something of a luxury for it makes no contribution to our effective use of our language. If this state of affairs has no other effects, it will certainly encourage philosophers to separate sharply their uses of language, as ordinary men, from their philosophical talk about language. Their talk as philosophers is genuinely professional, in that it has a more restricted domain than their daily talk, but it is also more technical. Philosophy comes to be a profession, and it is possible, as Hume did to shrug off the conflicts between one's convictions as a man and one's results as a philosopher. If we think, furthermore, of the sort of concepts that philosophers have regarded as unanalyzable (e.g., ''the Good'') and the areas they have declared outside their competence (e.g., ''normative ethics''), one can see perhaps that committing ourselves to a concept of language in which some concepts cannot, in principle, be analyzed is making very momentous philosophical stands possible. (Husserl himself did not take any of these stands. We shall see the reasons for that in Chapter 4.)

We can give other examples of the implications of certain uses of language for what one says and also for what one does. Thus, most obviously, the rejection of the Husserlian conception of language—and with it the requirement that use be sharply differentiated from mention—affects the practice of the philosopher by altering his standard of what are clear statements. Husserl is committed to the maxim that ''For-

malizing clarifies''; Heidegger is not. For many philosophical
uses of language, a Heideggerian would not dream of using
formal notations or of expecting others to use formal notation. Commitment to this maxim obviously has a considerable
impact on philosophic practice and even affects the curricula
of graduate departments of philosophy.

One's explication of the concept of understanding has extensive implications for practice. On Husserl's view, understanding what is asserted in a threat or a wish is a perfectly
genuine case of understanding, even if one does not respond
appropriately to the threat or wish because one does not know
that he has been threatened or asked for something. A man's
ability to be receptive to the intention with which an assertion was made is regarded as an accomplishment that is distinct from understanding what an utterance asserts. One need
not be aware that he is the object of demands or threats in
order to prove that he understands the language in which
they are made. In Heidegger's view, on the other hand, knowing what a person is doing when he says, once again, ''too
heavy'' is necessary in order to understand the language.
Hence Heidegger tends to regard responsiveness to the uses
of language as a much more elementary accomplishment. One
would expect therefore that in Heidegger's view failure to be
sensitive to the actions people perform when they speak is
regarded as a graver defect than it is in Husserl's view. To be
deficient in such sensitivity is to lack the skill that separates
men from brutes, the skill to speak and to understand.

We have outlined Heidegger's view of language as it is
developed in fairly self-conscious opposition to Husserl and
to his own Scotus book. The view culminates in wiping out
the distinction between talk about the world and talk about
language by substituting for that distinction the contention
that we talk, think and act differently if we use different
languages. In different languages ''meanings grow into
words'' in different ways.[28]

III

The expression "Meanings grow into words" still seems to need explication, however.

Clearly, we say, Heidegger uses a metaphor here. We need to render its literal meaning to the greatest extent possible. To do so seems the most obvious step to take next, but, precisely for that reason, it must be considered carefully. To ask Heidegger to provide us with an explication in literal language is, in fact, to ignore his warnings that in using established vocabularies we take over the philosophical commitments that have been built into them. If we apply the distinction between literal and metaphorical uses of language to *S & Z*, we are committing ourselves to a view of language that is not his and that is therefore not appropriate to explicating *S & Z*. Traditionally, an expression is said to be used metaphorically if it violates existing rules of language. This statement is, of course, an oversimplification. Established metaphors like "keeping a project under wraps" are used according to definite rules and yet are felt to be metaphors. But this complication may be ignored here; Heidegger's phrase is not one that is familiarly used in established ways. A characteristic of a violation of rules of language is that a statement is either false or nonsensical if it is interpreted literally. Meanings, for instance, are not living matter. They cannot therefore be said to grow into words. If we take its component terms in their literal meanings, this statement makes no sense at all. But literal meanings determine the conditions under which the statement is true. Unless we can replace the metaphorical uses with literal ones, we are in no position to determine whether Heidegger is making a true assertion.

This standard view of metaphorical uses presupposes that correct uses of language conform to certain rules, that one can make oneself understood and can understand others only if one knows and observes these rules, and that departures from these rules result in failures in communication which can be remedied only by replacing the offending expressions with others that do observe the rules—the so-called literal uses—of language. It seems quite clear, however, that Heidegger does not see language in this way. He does not deny, of course, that language in most cases is used in ways that are formulable in rules. But clearly he does not believe that communication is impossible unless rules are known and observed. It is perfectly possible to communicate fully while ignoring or violating rules of language.

The evidence for this comes from Section 35 of *S & Z*, entitled ''Idle Talk *(Gerede)*'':

> By virtue of the average intelligibility of the language we use in expressing ourselves, communicated discourse can, by and large, be understood even if the listener does not take up an attitude in which he understands anew what discourse is about [*sich in ein ursprünglich verstehendes Sein zum Worüber der Rede bringt*]. One does not so much understand the entities talked about but merely listens to the talk itself. That is what we understand; we understand only in a way, and from the outside, what the talk is about; one means to say *the same thing,* because one understands what is said in common in *the same* average way [168].

The passage seems to vacillate between talking about language and about what we use language to say. Toward the end of the passage, Heidegger certainly seems to be saying that ordinarily we understand each other because we all say more or less the same things. Communication rests on shared opinions and common beliefs. But earlier in the passage we are told that everyone understands language without taking up "an attitude in which he understands anew what discourse is about." We can understand what someone says without knowing anything about the subject he is talking about. This means that we understand only the traditional ways in which language is used, that is, we share in the "average intelligibility possessed by . . . language." We have a superficial and unthinking understanding of what we say and others say to us. Ordinarily we understand each other, even if we are not familiar with what another person talks about, because we all use the same rules of language.

In the light of what I said at the end of the last section about Heidegger's refusal to differentiate sharply between talk about language and about what one talks about by using it, this vacillation is not surprising. Insofar as he does recognize that language ordinarily is used in standard ways, he insists at the same time that people ordinarily see the world in the same way. The shared rules of language go hand in hand with common views about the world and about the sorts of disagreements about it that are at all intelligible. The central point of the section about "idle talk," however, is that not all uses of language are standard, although admittedly most of them are [169]. Heidegger denies that one must obey the rules of language in order to communicate. Presumably he does not merely mean that we can guess what someone says even if he violates rules of language. The contention is rather that we communicate at least as fully as with standard expressions, and certainly more richly and satisfyingly, in many instances, by using linguistic expressions that violate or ignore established rules of language. Accordingly, there are cases in which it is not legitimate to ask us to restate uses that violate established rules by using language that does not violate them.[29] Heidegger's talk about language in particular and about dasein in general is presumably one such case. To ask us to restate the novel expressions and uses in *S & Z* in language conforming to standards of ordinary English (or German) usage would be to misunderstand the project.

The task is to propose a new philosophical vocabulary so that we may be able to talk about the world and about ourselves in essentially novel ways. One example of novel ways of talking is Heidegger's "Meanings grow into words." This is not a metaphor to be restated in nonmetaphorical language. To explicate it is to present Heidegger's views of language as I have done. No other kind of explication is needed.

But Heidegger does not merely deny that observing rules is necessary for communicating. To the extent that idle talk is one aspect of "falling away from (*Verfallen*)," rule-governed speech must be regarded as derivative from speech that is not rule governed. What were at one time new ways of talking and new ways of seeing the world have now become established as conventional uses. What we now call literal uses were, then, startling innovations. The new ways of letting us see the world that were made accessible in these new expressions have become as familiar and conventional as the expressions themselves [cf. 166, 167].

But here Heidegger seems to hold a view that is clearly too extreme. We might take his claim seriously that the sorts of rules of language that are embodied in dictionary definitions (and in the more sophisticated versions of dictionary definitions given by philosophers) are not necessary for communication. But no language, we would insist, can function unless it observes the elementary rules of logic. All language must conform to some rules.

This, however, is what Heidegger wants to deny. Knowing and observing rules, whether formal logical or rules of meaning, is not a necessary condition for communication. This does not mean, of course, that Heidegger does not recognize the elementary distinction between coherent and incoherent utterances, between conclusions that do and do not follow from utterances and, in general, between rational and irrational discourse. At issue is the traditional claim that any account of rationality necessarily involves reference to rules and to standard ways of using language. Heidegger rejects this claim. He therefore rejects, *a fortiori,* the Husserlian position that rationality must be defined by reference to formal rules [159, 165]. Formalizing does not always clarify, and the formal patterns of logic do not have any clear relevance to many important uses of language.[30] This thought is implicit in the preceding section.

When I discussed Heidegger's reaction to Husserl's way of talking about meanings as objects, it turned out that Heidegger does not restrict terms like "meaning" and "means" to linguistic entities; he also speaks of the meaning of things, events and other entities in the world. This way of talking deprives us of the traditional means for distinguishing language from things; in other words, we cannot say that words are the only things that possess meaning. "Explication"—the central term in Heidegger's explanation of the concept of language—is not restricted to talking or writing. In fact, it refers to a much more pervasive phenomenon and Heidegger pointedly illustrates what he means by "explication" by talking about nonlinguistic acts.

> Our original practice of explication does not consist of a theoretical statement, but in circumspectly and carefully laying down or changing the tool "without wasting any words" [157].

In its primary sense, "explication" refers to actions instead of talk. Our everyday use of gear and of the things in our immediate environment, in which we elaborate our understanding of uses, techniques and practices, is an example of explication as Heidegger uses that term [149]. He regards it as a fundamental feature of our acquaintance with the world that the understanding we have of things, objects of use, conditions and practices is capable of further elaboration. He uses the technical term "discourse" to mark this feature of our acquaintance with the world as one of the equiprimordial features of that acquaintance (the term "equiprimordial" will be discussed in Chapter 5). Language is just one form of discourse. Language, in other words, is one of many different ways in which we explicate our preontological and preverbal understanding of the world. Words, expressions, phrases are "ready to hand"; they are objects of use as are tools, materials and products of our practical activities [161].[31] Heidegger wants to stress the analogies between language and these practical activities. Less clear is his plan to formulate the differences between, for instance, speaking English and being a cabinetmaker. Obviously he does want to draw the distinction: Of the various forms of discourse and explication, language is only one, but it is distinguished from others by having its own name. There are some suggestions for ways of providing a clear meaning for the name "language" in Section 17, which deals with signs.

But if we stress the analogies between language and other common practices, we shall not insist that what an utterance means is what it asserts; instead, as we saw in the preceding section, we shall focus attention on what a person does when he makes certain utterances in a situation. To do so will yield useful points about many utterances; the fact remains, however, that in many situations it is at least as important—for an understanding of language—to know what a man is saying as to know that he is making a statement, giving a description, producing an argument or making a prediction. In all these cases, we would say, people are making statements. Statements are true or false by reference to states of affairs. The relations of statements can be formulated in terms of their truth and falsity. Statements are subject to rules of formal logic.

Here again Heidegger dissents. The analogy between practical activity and language not only serves to remind us that we must understand what a person is doing when he speaks, if we are to understand what he is saying; it also presses the claim that the traditional concept of a statement is applicable, if at all, only in a small number of cases. For example, in many instances, when one makes statements, describes, argues or predicts, it is not appropriate to conceive of what one says as a public replica of the thought in one's mind or of a state of affairs. We saw Heidegger argue this point in the previous section. When one says something, one lets something be seen in a certain way [154].

Statements are also cases of explication [157]. In a statement or description, prediction or argument, the entity talked about is often presented to us in a way in which we had not seen it before. What we say, in many cases, throws new light on what we talk about. Here the analogy with other practices will again be helpful. Earlier we stressed the analogy between using language and using tools. Now we may point to the analogy between the products of practical activities and the products of speaking (statements). One might be tempted to see, for instance, an actual chair as a replica of the type chair, just as statements traditionally were thought to be replicas of facts. This may be appropriate when a chair reproduces a pattern executed many times before. But suppose someone makes a new chair. Perhaps his chair is simply a variation of a familiar pattern: The three spindles in the back of a Hitchcock chair are replaced by an urn-shaped slat. Perhaps the departure is more radical as, say, in the first bentwood chair or the first cardboard chair. In all these cases, we can as readily say that the actual chair shows in a new light what a chair can be as we can say that it is a reproduction of an established type of object of use. The new chair uncovers new possibilities either in a familiar chair pattern or in chairs, in general, by inventing new forms of chairs. Similarly, we may think of sentences in many cases not as reproducing facts or thoughts but as illuminating them. ''Is it true?'' is not the most appropriate question about sentences of this sort. Before we ask it, we want to know first whether the sentence fits the subject, whether it does justice to it or whether perhaps it provides a very one-sided view.

These analogies are important because they reinforce the insight that in many cases coherence or rationality in language cannot most suitably be construed in terms of formal logic—that is, in terms of the truth values of statements. When we are interested in the actions performed by means of language, for instance, making promises, demands, or giving warnings, we must talk about coherence in terms appropriate to the coherence of actions. When we must pay attention to what is said in language (for instance if we say something novel or unfamiliar about a topic), we shall nevertheless not always speak most readily of statements in terms of what is true or false in familiar traditional senses. None of this implies that significant discourse may not be incoherent and, to that extent that it is, unsatisfactory. But we are being urged to recognize that there are many different sorts of coherence, even in language, and that coherence explicable in terms of the truth or falsity of statements is only one of them.

4

phenomenology

We need to reform our philosophical vocabulary if we want to ask lucidly what we usually put obscurely as "What is the meaning of 'being'?" But as we saw in Chapter 1, a reform of talk about being involves a reform of talk about human beings. We need new ways of talking about ourselves. Such a reform however, cannot be undertaken unless we have some indications of what in the current vocabulary needs to be reformed. First, therefore, we must consider the shortcomings of current ways of talking about human beings. For Heidegger these shortcomings emerge from his conflicts with Husserl over the phenomenological program.

It is clear from the outset that Heideggerian phenomenology differs radically from Husserlian. Section 7 of *S & Z* is entitled "Phenomenology." Although it is quite long, it is peculiarly uninformative; it seems very much as if Heidegger were taking some pains to minimize the differences between himself and Husserl. But in the light of the preceding chapter on language we can see some sharp disagreements. Heidegger's ontology presents us with a new view of the world through the use of a new vocabulary in which to articulate our understanding, until now inarticulate, of ourselves and our world. This enterprise presupposes that there are alternative ways of articulating this understanding. One may prefer one way of articulating to others. Heidegger certainly recommends his vocabulary to us. He prefers it to traditional vocabularies. But one cannot simply claim that one's own account is true and all others false. "Letting the world be seen" in a certain way through a particular vocabulary is not the same as describing the world as it is as a matter of objective fact or, put even more strongly, as a matter of a priori necessity. Heideggerian ontology does not describe objective reality, the world as it exists independently of ourselves and the language we speak; Heideggerian ontology exhibits it in a particular, favored perspective.

Not so phenomenology as we have encountered it thus far. The enterprise that Husserl had called "doctrine of meaning" in the first edition of *Logical Investigations* turns out, in the second edition of that work, to be a part of phenomenology. Phenomenology claims objective truth for its statements. It clarifies concepts. Concepts, or "meanings," as Husserl calls them, are said to be objects. Meanings also are said to be objective; they are what they are independently of the specific uses we make of them. Statements about concepts, phenomenological statements, are therefore, if true, objectively so. They describe something whose existence and characteristics are not affected by being described. Phenomenology in this sense is descriptive. It does not recommend a way of viewing the world; it shows us aspects of the world as it is in itself.

Ontology and phenomenology seem to be very different enterprises. Yet Heidegger insists that "ontology is possible only as phenomenology" [35]. He obviously does not use the term "phenomenology" in the same sense in which it appears in Husserl's *Logical Investigations*. In this chapter I shall explain what Heidegger means by "phenomenology" and the connection between his use of the term and Husserl's.

We must begin with a fuller discussion of Husserl's conception of phenomenology.

I

Science consists of truths, but it is more than a collection of true propositions. In order to count as a science, a set of true propositions must be connected with one another in such a way that some propositions are premises for others and other propositions are evidence for the truth of the premises. Not all knowledge, therefore, is scientific; it is scientific knowledge only when supported by evidence. True propositions are expressed in true statements, but are independent of anyone's uttering or thinking the statements. Truths are truths "in themselves." They are true by reference to what exists in itself. Individual and, Husserl thinks, therefore contingent truths [LU I, 232] refer to individuals as they exist in themselves. General truths refer to ideal entities that also exist in themselves, although of course in a different sense of "exist" [LU I, 228 ff.]. Science is rigorously objective in that no inferences concerning knowers or anyone's knowledge can be drawn from the existence of facts or of ideal objects, such as, for instance, propositions.

The connections between truths, which make them into a science, are not of the same kind as the connections between facts or other real objects. The relations between propositions are described either in the terms of formal logic or by means of nonformal, epistemological terms like "evidence" or "probability." The connections between facts on the other hand are, for instance, causal. In order to feel confident that our knowledge is genuinely scientific, we need the assurance not only that our individual assertions are true, but also that the truths are connected validly. Before we can have this assurance we must show the objective validity of our principles of inference and of our epistemological principles. To provide this added assurance is the task of phenomenology [*ibid.*].

In *Logical Investigations* the terms "phenomenology" and "epistemology" are almost synonymous. Epistemology or phenomenology

> is prior to all empirical theories, also of course to all metaphysics, furthermore also to all factual sciences which explain phenomena, that is to natural science on the one hand and to psychology on the other. It does not try to *explain* knowledge as an event in time, either from a psychological or from a psycho-physical point of view. Instead it wants to *elucidate* the idea of knowledge with respect to its constitutive elements and/or laws. . . . it wants to render the pure forms and laws of knowledge clear and distinct by means of a return to an adequately fulfilling intuition. This elucidation requires . . . a phenomenology of the experience of getting to know and knowing, of perception and thinking, a phenomenology which is exclusively interested in a merely descriptive analysis. . . .
>
> This metaphysical, physical and psychological presuppositionlessness . . . [*LU* II, 21].

The term "theory" is used in an extended sense in this passage to refer to the orderly connections of truths that constitute a science. Phenomenology, also called the "theory of theories," is the science, then, of the necessary conditions that human knowledge must satisfy in order to be scientific. The central features of this phenomenology are all mentioned in the foregoing passage. They require some elucidation.

Phenomenology is said to be "presuppositionless" in the last line of the quotation. Earlier portions of the passage explain what this means. Phenomenological statements are logically "prior" to statements of fact in the empirical sciences and "prior" to statements in metaphysics. Empirical or metaphysical statements are therefore not premises from which phenomenological statements can be inferred. The truth of statements in phenomenology is independent of the truth of statements in the empirical sciences or in metaphysics. This implies that unlike the factual sciences—for example, psychology or the natural sciences—phenomenology does not make existential statements, nor does it make use of existential statements as premises. Empirical statements have no place in phenomenology. The reference to metaphysics furthermore eliminates nonempirical, existential statements (e.g., "God exists") from the scope of phenomenology. In this respect, phenomenology is like mathematics. It deals with concepts without asking whether anything corresponding to them exists at specific times and places.

But phenomenology is not, for all that, a branch of mathematics. Its methods for the treatment of concepts are very different from those used to construct mathematical theories. Phenomenology does not lay down definitions and axioms in order to derive their logical consequences. Before proceeding with the main theme of our discussion, we might note that this last statement is actually an oversimplification: Husserl's relevant views are unclear. On the one hand, he explicitly claims synthetic a priori truth for statements in phenomenology [*LU* II, 252]. But the doctrine of meanings already mentioned in the preceding chapter is certainly to be elaborated on the model of other mathematical disciplines. Its statements will be analytic a priori [*LU* II, 335]. There are some suggestions that the analytic statements presuppose others that are not analytic but synthetic a priori [*LU* II, 328], but perhaps the same is true of mathematics proper, on Husserl's view. The relation between mathematics and phenomenology needs further discussion.

But to return to our main theme: phenomenology does not merely define terms; it "elucidates" concepts and defends its elucidations by reference to an "adequately fulfilling intuition," which it describes. Phenomenology does not stipulate and deduce; it intuits and describes.

These descriptions must be distinguished, of course, from the descriptions of matters of fact given in the sciences and in everyday life. Phenomenology differs from most sciences as well as from everyday discourse because it reflects about just those mental (or intentional) acts that we leave out of account in ordinary life or in science. This means that

> while we perceive, think, relate objects or look at them under the ideal aspect of law, etc., we [viz., as phenomenologists] must not direct our theoretical interest to these objects and to them as they appear in the intentions of those acts, which so far had not been the objects of our attention at all. It is these acts, on the contrary, which we must now look at, analyze, describe [*LU* II, 10].

The sciences and our day-to-day discourse deal with what we perceive, think and know. Phenomenology deals with our thinking, perceiving and knowing. As Husserl uses the term "intentional act," it refers to mental acts like thinking, perceiving or knowing, as well as to the thought, the percept or the knowledge. It does not refer to what one is thinking about, what one is perceiving or what one knows; in other words, it does not refer to that by reference to which my thinking may be said to be clear or confused, my percept veridical or illusory, my knowledge genuine or mistaken [*LU* II, 386 ff.]. Phenomenology is reflective. It reflects about the intentional acts through which we perceive, through which we think and through which we know the world. Ordinarily we do not attend to these acts because we are exclusively interested in their objects. The acts are, in Husserl's jargon, "anonymous." They lose this anonymity in reflection.

This distinction between reflective and nonreflective awareness is important in order to establish the characterization of phenomenology, but it does not separate phenomenological statements clearly from other kinds of statements. Reflection occurs both in the course of scientific inquiry and in ordinary affairs. Besides, it is the task of psychology to deal with certain kinds of characteristics of thinking and of other mental acts. But unlike reflection in science or everyday life, phenomenological reflection does not yield statements asserting or denying existence. Phenomenology does not deal with existents *as* existents. It describes our mental acts without making or using existential statements about them. It deals not with the existence of individual intentional acts or with facts about them, but with the "essences (*Wesen*)," the essential features of these acts [*LU* I, 241]. Phenomenological description is not the description practiced in the sciences or in everyday life, for phenomenology describes essences given in the "intuition of essences (*Wesensschau*)" as we reflect about the mental acts through which we have access to the world and to ourselves.

By "essences" Husserl means something very much like "concepts"—not, of course, in the sense in which we think of concepts as psychological entities but in the sense in which we say of someone that "he has the concept of '*x*'" if he knows what something must be like in order to be rightly called an "*x*." To describe the essence of any particular entity is to set down the crucial conditions for being an entity of that sort. The "intuition of essences," which has gained considerable notoriety, merely refers to the attempt to get a clear grasp of concepts, particularly those needed for formulating a theory of science. The enterprise that Husserl describes in *Logical Investigations* as the "intuition and description of essences" is not essentially different from what is often called "conceptual analysis." [1] The task is not, for instance, to "*explain* knowledge, as an event in time . . . [but] to *elucidate* the idea of knowledge" [*LU* II, 21].

Like any other conceptual analyst, Husserl wants to differentiate his enterprise from lexicography. Phenomenology does not deal just with the meanings of words. A clear distinction

must be drawn between the phenomenological clarification
of concepts and the explanations of what the words mean in
any given natural language.

> We definitely do not want to concern ourselves with
> "mere words." . . . Meanings which are only animated
> by remote, vague and indirect intuitions [*Anschau-
> ungen*] cannot satisfy us. We want to return to the
> "things themselves." We want to . . . fix the meanings
> in their irrevocable identity by comparing them repeat-
> edly with reproducible intuitions [*LU* II, 7].

Husserl insists for two reasons that phenomenology does not
concern itself with "mere words." What a word means ordinarily is in many cases quite vague, at least by philosophic
standards. We cannot be satisfied with dictionary meanings
of words, because they are often "only animated by remote,
vague and indirect intuitions." The explication of a term in
the dictionary does not come up to philosophic standards of
explication. Besides, natural languages are individual existents. Statements about them are contingently true. But the
statements in phenomenology are a priori. Statements about
language are, if true, "individual truths" (i.e., truths about
individuals), truths about this or that aspect of a particular
language, and "individual truths are contingent" [*LU* I,
232]. But statements about essences are a priori.

The reflections in which these essences will come to light
are reflections about consciousness, the totality of intentional
acts [*LU* II, 324 ff.]. It is easy to see why. In order to provide
the firm foundations for scientific knowledge that Husserl's
epistemological undertaking is meant to provide, we need to
investigate the meanings and interrelations of concepts like
knowledge and perception; we must investigate what it means
to say that someone knows, that he is perceiving or thinking.
We must be able to say, for instance, what the difference is
between my thinking, my perceiving or my knowing that it is
raining. In these three acts, not only is the object the same, the

fact that it is raining, but also the "content" (i.e., the proposition "that it is raining") is the same. They differ only with respect to what Husserl called their "act quality." To clarify this difference is one of the important tasks of phenomenology—a task for which Husserl later introduces the term "noetic analysis." For this reason phenomenology is said to describe consciousness.

But, of course, phenomenology does not study consciousness empirically. It addresses itself to consciousness as essence and thus, as we might say, to the concepts of thinking, perceiving and knowing. Consciousness as studied in phenomenology is generally referred to as "pure" consciousness. Empirical psychology, on the other hand, studies consciousness as an existing individual, as a consciousness that is someone's and is individuated by some "I." This "I," Husserl insists in *Logical Investigations* (first edition), is "an empirical object . . . like any other thing" individuated by an empirical body and by the unity, most probably of a causal nature, of the different mental events in any consciousness [*LU* II, 331–332]. What we refer to with the word "I" thus does not appear in our phenomenological studies because the "I" refers to certain empirically observable and hence contingent connections. Like the phenomenology of the later works, phenomenology in *Logical Investigations* deals with pure consciousness. But unlike the transcendental consciousness that makes its appearance later, pure consciousness does not contain an absolute ego or subject in this early version of phenomenology. Husserl does not merely omit any reference to such an ego; he also explicitly rejects the Kantian and neo-Kantian claim that there is a nonempirical ego that would have to be studied in the nonempirical study of consciousness that he calls "phenomenology" [*LU* II, 340 ff.]. The only "I" recognized in the first edition of *Logical Investigations* is an empirical "I."

This, in outline, is phenomenology, the new science that will provide us with a reliable theory of science by means of presuppositionless descriptions of the essential features of pure consciousness revealed to us in the intuition of essences. With this characterization, Husserl tries to differentiate phenomenology from psychology and linguistics, on the one hand, and mathematics, on the other.

These features of phenomenology are required by the original formulation of the task to be fulfilled. Phenomenology is to be a science. Science consists of a system of true propositions. Propositions are true if they correctly represent independent existents, whether they are facts or essences or themselves true propositions. The objectivity of any science depends on the objective validity of the connections between its statements. A science about the requirements for objectivity of all scientific knowledge thus must deal with the connections between the propositions in any science. Phenomenology, Husserl concludes, must therefore be distinct from all existing sciences. The various features of phenomenology establish this distinction.

This account of phenomenology in the first edition of *Logical Investigations* contains, with one exception, all the essential features of phenomenology mentioned by Husserl in his middle period. The exception is the "transcendental subject" or "pure ego," which appears only in *Ideas*.[2] The other features, of course, undergo all sorts of changes. Some are merely terminological; others affect the substance of Husserl's conception of phenomenology. The "transcendental-phenomenological reduction" exemplifies both changes. The expression itself does not appear in *Logical Investigations*. But, in part, the introduction of this term only represents a change in Husserl's terminology. Much of what Husserl tells us about the reduction amounts to a description of the transition from nonreflective to reflective thinking.[3] The new term thus refers merely to a feature with which we had already become acquainted in *Logical Investigations,* that is, that phenomenology is reflective. But, on the other hand, the transcendental-phenomenological reduction is intimately associated with the newly discovered transcendental ego. This ego, we are told, can be discovered only after we have performed the reduction. Not any sort of transition from reflective to nonreflective thinking will achieve this discovery, and to that extent the addition of the reduction adds a new aspect to the earlier account.

All the other key terms in Husserl's repeated discussions of phenomenology undergo corresponding changes. If one followed these changes in detail, one would find oneself retracing the route that Husserl traveled so laboriously through a maze of connected philosophical problems. I cannot do this here. I must present the differences between earlier and later versions of phenomenology schematically, focusing attention exclusively on the changes following the introduction of the transcendental ego as if this were the only respect in which phenomenology in 1913 differs from phenomenology in 1900. But this oversimplification will enable us to explain why the later phenomenology is so elusive. However elaborate Husserl's descriptions, we are left with the feeling that we have not understood what we are expected to do as phenomenologists. Husserl himself never lost this feeling, the feeling that he did not fully understand what it meant to do phenomenology. This is one of his reasons for describing himself as a "perpetual beginner." Phenomenology is supposed to be a science in which many researchers contribute to increasing our knowledge. But as a cooperative enterprise, it seems, it cannot get started. Husserl's beginnings turn out to be false starts; instead of tackling concrete tasks in phenomenology, he feels again and again compelled to turn to reconsiderations of what constitutes a phenomenological problem and the proper way of tackling it. These failures stem from deep conflicts within Husserl's philosophical strivings. Much of the phenomenological program can be stated with considerable precision and detail. But there are other intimations and philosophical concerns that try to find expression but that do not fit properly into the framework of the program. It is they that disrupt the orderly development of phenomenology as a science. These conflicts account for the aura of desperate struggle and defeat that surrounds Husserl's writings. They also account for the startling divergence between Husserl's descriptions of phenomenology and those given by Heidegger and other philosophers who profess to have been deeply influenced by Husserl, as, for instance, Maurice Merleau-Ponty.

II

In *Logical Investigations* Husserl denied that phenomenology dealt with any self or ego on the grounds that the self is an empirical entity. Subsequently he changed his mind on this point. In *Ideas* he claims to have discovered the transcendental ego. Phenomenology is now occupied not only with the description of a pure and, as such, nonindividuated consciousness but with a consciousness that is always someone's because it contains an ego. This ego, falling within the scope of phenomenological reflection, is not an empirical ego; it is a "pure ego." Husserl also calls it a "transcendental subject."

This view does not just represent a change of a single doctrine. Conflicts that had been in Husserl's thought all along now come to the surface. He had made a good case for claiming that there are objectively true statements about the conditions for objectivity and that these statements are neither empirical nor true merely by stipulation. But his argument is not conclusive, of course, and one may well continue to wonder whether there are nonempirical, nonanalytic statements as Husserl claims. But the discovery of the transcendental ego and the concomitant changes in the meanings of the other key terms, particularly of the "reduction," will not serve to establish phenomenology's claims more securely. The claim that there exists for each person an absolute subject whose existence is known only a priori will not shake the convictions of the philosopher who is still inclined to assimilate the clarification of concepts to mathematical logic, and who holds that statements in mathematics are true by stipulation; nor will it shake the convictions of the philosopher who continues to insist that our clarification of concepts is, ultimately, making empirical statements about actual uses in our language. For it is precisely the possibility of such a priori knowledge that is not stipulative that these philosophers question. Husserl's early account of phenomenology is not strengthened by the "discovery" of the transcendental ego.

Quite the contrary. This discovery sets up intolerable strains within the account of phenomenology. Phenomenology had been regarded as a science, more specifically a science of essences, and was for that very reason not an empirical science, for empirical sciences deal with truths about individuals. "Truths about individuals are, as such, contingent" [*LU* I, 232]. Similarly, we were told that phenomenology cannot lay hold of whatever is individual. "For it [viz., phenomenology] the singular is forever the ἄπειρον" ["Strenge," 318].[4] But now we have discovered a transcendental ego that is an individual. Everybody has one [*Encyc.*, 294].[5] A distinction is introduced between the "eidetic reduction," which lays bare the realm of essences—this is the reduction that had been referred to in fact, if not in name, in the *Logical Investigations*—and a new kind of reduction called the "egological reduction," which reduces the world to the transcendental ego and its intentional acts [*Encyc.*, 245–246]. Husserl now asserts what, in the light of the earlier account, would have been a contradiction, namely, that phenomenology is a science that treats of individuals but nonetheless does not produce contingent truths. Earlier he had said that phenomenology could not deal with individuals because statements about individuals were merely contingently true. But now it would seem that, having bracketed the world and discovered the transcendental ego, we will make an existential statement.

This ego is said to have "absolute existence," which *"nulla 're' indiget ad existendum,"* and this itself is a statement in phenomenology [*Id.* I, 115]. As a consequence the introduction of the transcendental ego tends to blur the distinction between phenomenology and the empirical sciences, a distinction that Husserl regards as indispensable in philosophy.

More specifically, the distinction between the phenomenological descriptions of essences and the existential statements about individuals, made in the course of empirical studies, was used to differentiate reflection in phenomenology from empirical reflection. This is of particular interest to Husserl because he believes that there is a branch of psychological research that consists of reflection about one's own psychological phenomena, not of observation of subjects other than the psychologist—a discipline that is not the same as phenomenological inquiry, although it is sufficiently like it to merit the name "phenomenological psychology." In the framework of *Logical Investigations* phenomenological psychology could have been said to differ from phenomenology proper because this psychology reflects about individuals whereas phenomenology reflects about essences. But once we admit that phenomenology makes existential statements about individuals, we take back the distinction between empirical and phenomenological reflection and thus make it impossible to differentiate phenomenological psychology from phenomenology proper. In fact Husserl repeats often that in these two fields

the same phenomena and essential insights appear . . . but, as it were, provided with different operators [*Vorzeichen*], that alter their sense radically [*Encyc.,* 247–248].

In what way do they alter their sense? The reader will look in vain for any further light on the difference between phenomenological psychology and pure phenomenology. The reason for this difficulty is clear: Husserl is trying to draw a distinction that his vocabulary does not admit.

Once he has committed himself to speaking of phenomenology as a science dealing with individuals, he finds himself differentiating between "eidetic" phenomenology—the study of essences, which was all that phenomenology was concerned with in the early version—and "egological" phenomenology, which deals with the individual intentional acts of the individual "pure" consciousness. The first subject matter of phenomenology is now the "stream of consciousness" [*Id.* I, 106; see also 69 ff.]. This consciousness always has the prefix "pure," which suggests that it is not the object of sensory experience. But we now find that we have a nonempirical object that is subject to change and in fact has its own temporal determinations [*Id.* I, 72]. One of the hallmarks of the empirical, temporal position is now ascribed to nonempirical, pure consciousness.

These are some of the difficulties that suddenly come to plague Husserl when he introduces the transcendental-phenomenological reduction as the key to revealing the transcendental ego. Before this addition was made, the description of phenomenology may not have convinced everybody, but it was not beset by any obvious inconsistencies. Once the reduction has been used to introduce the pure ego, the description of phenomenology seems in various ways incoherent.

Because Husserl continued to struggle with apparently conflicting philosophical intimations without giving them clear formulations, it is not easy to see what sorts of problems and thoughts moved him to introduce the utterly disruptive doctrine of the transcendental ego into an otherwise coherent and promising outline of phenomenology. We must gather together some of the other indications of philosophical conflict if we are to guess the direction his thought was taking.

We are told in the preface to *Logical Investigations* that Husserl had been led by his doubts about the validity of his psychologistic orientation in the earlier work, *Philosophy of*

Arithmetic, to reflect critically on "the nature of logic and, specifically, about the relation between the subjectivity of knowing and the objectivity of the content known" [*LU* I, vii]. Similarly, he raises the question "how the 'in itself' of objectivity can be presented to us, that is, become in some sense once again subjective" [*LU* II, 9]. He asserts in a series of lectures given in 1907, entitled *The Idea of Phenomenology,* "that we do not understand in what sense something could be both *in itself* and yet *known to us*" [*Idee,* 29];[6] again, ten years later, he repeats in his article for the *Encyclopedia Britannica* that

> all existential statements are true for us. The evidence
> supporting them, whether it be empirical or deductive,
> has force for us. . . . This is true of the world under
> every description, even the self-evident one that what
> belongs to it is *"in and for itself"* as it is, regardless of
> my or any other person's awareness of it [*Encyc.,* 288;
> italics added].

We can sense some connection between these different formulations of a problem and the introduction of the transcendental ego. In both cases it is something called "the subject" that seems to elude his grasp. But it is difficult to specify what that connection is. It was not clear what, precisely, Husserl thought he had discovered when he discovered the transcendental ego. In the present context it is not at all clear what problem he is trying to bring up. It seems either trivial or self-contradictory to say that whatever is, in itself, is what it is for us. It is trivial if we are saying that we know what things are in themselves only insofar as we know them. It is self-contradictory if we are saying that the existence of things, independently of human knowers, depends on our knowing them.

In a different way, the role of the subject is brought within the purview of phenomenology when Husserl reiterates again and again that "the object constitutes itself in the process of coming to be known (*in der Erkenntnis*)" [*Idee*, 75]. The subject or ego, Husserl seems to be saying, has a place in the phenomenological sphere because objects are "constituted" by reference to a subject. Objects, whatever is in itself, are in some way dependent on this subject. But Husserl also takes it to be analytic that knowledge is objective, that is, that the existence of objects and their possession of determinate properties allows no inference as to their being known or as to the existence of any knowers. It seems very odd, therefore, for him to claim that objects are constituted by a knowing subject, for that would allow us to infer from the existence of the object that some constituting knowing subject must exist.

In all of these instances, Husserl is groping for a clearer apprehension of the role and nature of the subject in the context of theoretical knowing. We must now turn to one other manifestation of internal strain in Husserl's thought, which, at first, seems to have no connection with problems concerning the cognitive subject. In 1910, Husserl published a long paper "Philosophy as Rigorous Science" in which he repeats his earlier polemics against psychologism and then turns against Wilhelm Dilthey's "historicism," which he considers, like psychologism, to be inconsistent with the objectivity that is an essential feature of all scientific knowledge. Historicism denies that philosopher's statements are synthetic a priori and, as such, eternally true. The philosophical verities of one generation may well be ridiculous errors from the viewpoint of a later age. According to the historicist:

If someone claims an idea to be valid, he means that it is an intellectual product which exists, as a matter of fact and is regarded as valid and . . . determines how people think ["Strenge," 325].

The historicist denies that a distinction can be drawn between a view that is generally accepted and a view that is true. Such a conception of philosophy, Husserl believes, leads to skepticism and thus eventually undermines the objectivity not only of philosophy but also of the sciences. Historicism must for that reason be rejected.

But, on the other hand, Husserl can well understand why anyone would embrace a historicist view:

> . . . [Our] philosophical misery, the poverty of our world view, overwhelms us. The extension of the range of the positive sciences only aggravates it. The tremendous wealth of scientifically "explained" facts, which positive science presents to us, cannot help us since these facts and all the sciences bring with themselves necessarily a dimension of perplexities, whose solution becomes for us a matter of life and death. The sciences have not resolved the riddles of reality in any respect, of that reality in which we live and work and are ["Strenge," 335–336].

This is a new problem. The earlier inquiry was begun to remedy deficiencies in the existing sciences. The key concepts used there needed clarification. But this is no longer the only or even the main problem.

> If it were only the lack of theoretical clarity concerning the sense of the "realities" investigated in natural science and the humanities . . . instead our misery infects our whole life. But to live is to take a stand and doing that is subject to certain obligations ["Strenge," 336].

The difficulties now are not merely theoretical; they are moral and practical: We no longer know what justification to give for living and acting in certain ways. We live

> in a world which has become unintelligible, in which we ask in vain for purposes and for the meaning which formerly was recognized unquestionably both by the understanding and the will [FTL, 5].

We are uncertain about practical matters—as, earlier, Husserl believed us to be uncertain about the foundations of our theoretical pursuits—because we have lost the certainties possessed by other generations. This uncertainty may well move us to accept as true what is generally believed: in other words, to embrace historicism.

One of the causes of our loss of certainty is precisely the advance of the sciences, the "tremendous wealth of scientifically 'explained' facts." If we look more closely, however, we see that the crisis is not caused by the advance of science; instead the advance is itself a symptom of an underlying cause. Scientific progress was made possible by a transformation of science. Science has become entirely a theoretical pursuit:

> The great philosophies of the past were undoubtedly philosophical world views, insofar as their creators were animated by the desire for wisdom; but they were to the same degree scientific philosophies insofar as the goal of rigorous science was alive in them. Both of these aims were either not distinguished at all or not distinguished sharply. They came together in practical striving. But all this has been changed thoroughly since the timeless totality of rigorous science came into existence ["Strenge," 332].

The current crisis in morals is the result of our distinguishing sharply between science and the pursuit of wisdom. The difference between the two, as Husserl sees it, is twofold. Scientific statements are, if true at all, eternally true. They are also "impersonal." The wisdom of one age, on the other hand, is the folly of the next. Wisdom is a personal possession ["Strenge," 339]. If we reflect on these two differences and develop them, particularly the second one, beyond the few hints Husserl gives us, we can begin to grasp the quandary of which this passage is an expression.

Science is impersonal. This means that science is a cooperative venture. No personal traits are needed for participating in scientific research other than a certain intelligence and training. In all other respects, scientific researchers may differ enormously. Some are religious, some are not; some are gentle, some violent; some love their bodies, some hate them; and so for all other differences of personality and moral character. These differences do not affect the outcome of their scientific endeavor. The physics of the tyrannical man does not differ from the physics of the lover of freedom. But wisdom is a personal possession precisely in the sense that a man cannot be wise no matter what his character or temperament may be. It is difficult to conceive of a man who is both violently destructive and wise. But different wise men are, for all that, still very different sorts of persons. For this reason the wisdom of one is very different from that of another. Their wisdom is expressed in very different ways, and the forms of expression are integral to what is expressed. The wisdom of Socrates could not be expressed in homely parables or dark sayings without being completely changed. There is no universal language for the expression of wisdom as there is for science. There is no universal wisdom of which the wisdom of this man and the wisdom of that man are parts, corresponding to the universal science of which one science—say, geology—and another science—say, zoology—are parts.

There is only one science. But each wise man has his wisdom and his style of expression. Each learner, moreover, requires a particular variation of this style. For to be wise is not just to know that certain statements are true. To be wise one must act in certain ways. One must be a certain sort of person. To gain wisdom, then, is not just to learn and assimilate a doctrine. To acquire wisdom is to learn to be wise, and to do so is to change one's way of life and to change oneself. To teach wisdom is to change persons. To the extent that persons differ when they come to the wise man for instruction, his instruction must address itself differently to different men. He must vary his mode of expression and instruction with the different needs and powers of understanding of different individuals. Wisdom cannot be learned from textbooks; it is taught only in a very personal relationship between teacher and learner ["Strenge," 338–339].

But Husserl thinks it analytic that "knowledge is objective." What I know is true; moreover, it is true whether anyone knows it or not. The truth value of what I know is unaffected by my knowing it or anyone else's knowing it, or by any other fact about myself or others as knowers. Hence when we discuss knowledge, for example, in science, we need to talk about evidence and the validity of arguments, but we need not talk about the man who discovered this particular item of knowledge, let alone about his other discoveries, his way of life or his character. The biography of Sir Isaac Newton is not relevant for understanding or assessing the truth of Newtonian physics. The life of St. Francis is essential for understanding and feeling the persuasiveness of his teaching. A man's wisdom is not his product but is the man himself. Wisdom is intimately tied to individuals. It cannot possibly be called "objective." It is therefore not an item of knowledge.

But this view raises a serious problem. We do want to speak of moral knowledge and of knowledge of how to live. The point of insisting on these locutions is that we want to recognize a difference in the moral realm between knowing and believing and between true and false beliefs. We want to be able to say that some moral beliefs are false. Not all moral notions are justified merely by the fact that they are held sincerely by someone. If possessing wisdom is not the same as possessing knowledge but knowledge can be had in morals, then the wise man is no longer qualified to give moral guidance. Husserl accepts this conclusion. He also holds that empirical science cannot yield moral knowledge because statements about norms of any kind cannot be derived from statements about facts ["Strenge," 336]. Hence for moral guidance we must look to an a priori science of value: phenomenology.[7]

But this conclusion conflicts with the original description

of the moral crisis in which we find ourselves. Husserl had blamed our lack of moral certainty and the loss of all sense of the intelligibility of the world on the separation between science and the pursuit of wisdom. Due to this separation the wise man had lost the authority of the sciences and thus had lost his credibility. Because we see clearly that he does not possess knowledge, we have become very uncertain about his credentials. We do not trust him any more. But, equally important, since having parted from the wise man, the scientist has rigorously refrained from making any claims about possessing wisdom. Science has become strenuously theoretical. It does not raise questions about values and, to even less an extent, offers to answer them for us. Notice, moreover, that this withdrawal from the concern of the wise man, from the moral realm, is not limited to sciences insofar as they are empirical but insofar as they are sciences of any sort—in other words, insofar as they claim to produce objective knowledge. What invalidates the wise man's claim to knowledge is the fact that knowledge is objective, by definition, but wisdom is not. But if this is the source of our great "philosophical misery"—that wisdom deals with moral questions but no longer has our confidence, and science, which has our confidence, does not deal with moral questions—then surely all our hopes for finding illumination about moral questions in phenomenology must be in vain as long as phenomenology remains, as Husserl insists it must remain, vigorously scientific. Husserl's solution of the moral crisis must fail if we consider it in the light of his own diagnosis of that crisis.

This is not a careless inconsistency on Husserl's part but the sign of a deep difficulty. We have already seen his reasons for insisting that the distinction between knowing and believing and between believing truly and falsely applies to morals. Knowledge, however, is by its very nature objective. Known facts are independent of being known. Being known in no way affects or alters them. When I come to know something, in this sense of knowing objectively, the world is altered in only one way: A fact is added to the totality of facts: I know something that I did not know before. Knowing objectively can therefore provide guidance for acts of making, but an act of knowing cannot be identical with an act of making. It does not alter any existing objects, except the person who knows now what he did not know before. Objective knowledge is not, in itself, productive. Nor is it, in itself, practical. An act of knowing objectively is not identical or logically connected with an action.

Because my act of knowing alters the world only in that it adds the fact that I know to the totality of facts, any act of knowing—even if what I know is a moral imperative—is compatible both with my performing and my failing to perform the action required by the imperative. It is morally wrong not to do one's duty, but it is not a logical error. (Some philosophers, for instance Kant, seem to deny this. They want to say that a man who acknowledges a duty but does not will to perform it is making a logical mistake. His assertion of his duty is logically incompatible with his statement that he will not do it. But Kant, of course, did not therefore deny that it is logically possible that men make self-contradictory assertions and act on them. In fact, his entire analysis of duty rests on the recognition that men do not always do what they know to be their duty. Saying that one ought to x and that one will not x is logically incoherent. But saying that one ought to x and then refrain from x-ing is logically possible.) Moral knowledge is also theoretical and that means that it is neither productive nor practical.

The knowledge of the wise man is of a different sort. It is not his knowledge alone that earns our respect and admiration but his acting on that knowledge. He not only knows what is good or what his duty is, but also acts in ways that seem to us exemplary. We might still admire what he does, however, but admire the man less were his knowledge and what he does not most intimately connected. If a man does what is good, although he believes it to be bad, or because he meant to do something else that he thought, perhaps correctly, to be good, we do not hold him up to ourselves as an example of a wise man. Exemplary is the man whose knowledge of good and evil is evinced in his conduct. He does what is good because he knows what is good; for him, to know the good is to do it. The knowledge that makes a man wise involves, unlike theoretical knowing, both knowing and doing.

Nor is the wise man's knowing altogether distinct from making. If we suppose someone to possess the sort of synthetic a priori knowledge of good and evil that Husserl expects to gain from his phenomenological reflections about morals, we would not expect him to be wise by virtue of that knowledge alone. In addition to possessing this knowledge, the wise man must know how to apply it. But knowing how to apply it is not an item of theoretical knowledge; instead it is much more like a skill (I shall discuss the difference between theoretical knowledge and skills in the next chapter). Knowing how to apply his knowledge of good and evil cannot in itself be treated as an item of theoretical knowledge, perhaps in the form of a rule or an imperative, for that would require further rules to tell us how to apply the first set of rules. Besides, the wise man's virtue consists not merely in his unshakable cleaving to the good he knows but also in his unexpected and admirable applications of this knowledge. We hold him up as an example not only for his unwavering good faith but also for his understanding of the good that seems so much deeper and superior to our own. What we share with him is the knowledge of the good, but what we miss in ourselves and admire in him are the novel applications of this knowledge that show the good in a very different light. Not being items of theoretical knowledge, these applications cannot be said to be discovered. The wise man's greatness does not lie in moral discoveries as much as in inventions. He invents new ways of giving body to our intellectual apprehensions of the good. His knowledge is productive. He is superior to us by virtue of his ability to create new moral demands and standards for conduct.

But what he invents are not merely new techniques for applying general moral principles. What we admire in him is not merely individual actions but the consistent depth of his understanding as evinced in actions. We call not only his actions good; we call the man himself good. The wise man's wisdom is productive not only by creating new standards of conduct; insofar as his person exemplifies and embodies his wisdom, his person is what he produces. He makes himself. Using the figure of the moral hero as their paradigm, philosophers have therefore said that a man must know himself in order to be a good man. The sort of knowing these philosophers demanded is not exhausted by knowledge of facts about oneself, but is the sort of knowing that makes one into what one is. The sort of knowledge one needs in order to gain wisdom is not theoretical and objective knowledge about oneself. It is, instead, knowledge that transforms.

It is for such reasons that wisdom is said to be personal. Exemplary wisdom is the creation of a certain man who does something that in some ways is like discovering, and in other ways, like inventing, and who thereby makes himself into a model for men. But men differ and so, therefore, does wisdom. Wisdom is always some particular individual's wisdom, and when we want to learn, not only do we learn the teachings of someone, but also we learn from him. We must know not only what he said; we must know what he did. Learning in this instance, however, is not merely by imitation. My wisdom cannot simply be a copy of another man's. I must transform myself in the light of what I have learned. I do not acquire objective knowledge when I learn to be wise. I become a different person. When I learn from a great model, I do something that is in part discovering and in part inventing.

The inconsistency between Husserl's diagnosis of the causes

of our moral disorientation and his prescription for its cure results from the conflict between his inclination to hold that there is objective knowledge in morals and his conviction that objective knowledge cannot make men wise and exemplary. This conflict springs from concern for a proper account of what it means to be a subject—in the present context, a moral subject. On the one hand he is content, indeed eager, to claim that knowledge is objectively true. This is one of two conditions for its being scientific knowledge, the other being that individual items of knowledge are connected in specific, systematic ways. On the other hand, he is uncertain whether the moral subject can be the object of such knowledge (whether the knowledge is prescientific objective knowledge or full-fledged scientific knowledge) or even whether its relations to moral value and action can be described in terms of knowing in this sense. The wise man's knowledge both of the good and of himself did not seem to be the sort of theoretical knowledge involved in scientific knowledge because for him to know the good is to do it, and the knowledge he has of himself is knowledge that transforms. Hence the relationship of his action to what he knows cannot be described by saying that his actions are guided by theoretical knowledge. We can begin to see what it is about the subject that concerned Husserl.

Corresponding strains developed in his thought about the cognitive subject. Here we can begin to see why Husserl thought that the "discovery" of the transcendental ego would ease these strains. While he continued to think of phenomenology as a science, he also tended to talk about the cognitive subject and its role in ways that made it seem certain that this subject was not known as the objects of science are known. Its relationship to the world was not to be accounted for in terms of objective scientific knowing or of prescientific objective knowing. This thinking comes to light quite clearly in a series of lectures he gave in 1928, a year after the publication of *S & Z*, in which he summarizes many of the results of the *Ideen* of 1913 and the work that had been done in the intervening years. Husserl writes:

> Objective entities are entities merely in a peculiar, relative and, with that, incomplete sense, due, as it were, only to the fact which is not noticeable in the natural attitude, that the transcendental constitution is concealed.[8]

The objective existence of objects and facts about them is here compromised by the suggestion that this objectivity is only half the story; it is not full-fledged objectivity but is relative to a constituting subject. The same suggestion is made concerning that subject itself:

> I, who am in my absolute and ultimate being, in no way an objective entity but the absolute subject-ego, find in my life which constitutes all objective being, myself as validity-correlate [*Geltungs-korrelat*] . . . valid as object.[9]

The subject itself is not an object except in relation to itself; it counts as (*gelten*) an object only for itself, under the aspect of transcendental ego. Objectivity of self and world has been relativized to the transcendental subject. The relation of that subject to itself as well as to the world is therefore no longer to be described as one of having objective knowledge or corresponding beliefs. The sense of "knowing" that we must use here is like the one we were forced to use when talking about wisdom, a sense in which knowing is also doing and making.

> The life of consciousness is always a life which constitutes meaning in itself as well as meaning from meaning: in ever new steps takes place a creating and transforming of "objectivities [*Gegenständlichkeiten*]." [10]

The awareness of the objects of consciousness is creative as was the wise man's awareness of himself and of the good.

Husserl then has serious doubts whether objective knowing exhausts our noncausal relations to ourselves and the world and whether, particularly, we can understand what it means to be a subject if we assume that "to be" is always to be the object of actual or possible objective knowledge, that is, to be independently of being known. Yet, on the other hand, he still maintains that phenomenology, whose task is to unveil the transcendental subject, is a science. It is apparently a matter of objective knowledge that there is a transcendental subject that is not to be known objectively.[11] The conflict between the inclination to claim that knowledge is by definition objective and his doubts as to whether a man is wise by virtue of his objective knowledge, although wisdom is a case of knowing in some sense, is here repeated as a conflict between the claim that phenomenology, in which we reveal the transcendental ego, is a science and the claim that what we know in phenomenology is not an object of scientific knowledge.

This conflict also finds expression in the difficulties mentioned earlier. On the one hand, Husserl outlines a new philosophical discipline that will give us objective knowledge of the conditions for objectivity. On the other hand, he speaks of objects being "constituted" in experience. The term "constitution" suggests that the world is not there, in itself, a world of which we discover various features, but that, instead, in some way we make the world by virtue of experiencing and knowing it. The word "constitution" suggests a relation to the world that reminds us of the wise man's relation to himself: It is neither pure, objective knowing nor simply the act of making (we obviously do not make the world; it is there already), but a relation that should be described, in some ways, as an act of making and, in other ways, as knowing. Husserl's introduction of the term suggests that in some moods at least he is not so sure that all knowing is objective.

Similarly, discordant tendencies come to the surface in his frequent use of the term *"Leistungen* (achievements)*"* to refer to intentional acts, which suggests that knowing is in some way productive. These tendencies also appear in his insistence that whatever is, is "in itself, for us," thereby claiming both the objective existence of facts and entities and their relativity to the transcendental ego.

The originally promising and unproblematic program of *Logical Investigations* is disturbed by the "discovery" of the transcendental ego and all the concomitant alterations in the meanings of key terms in phenomenology. We can see now what moved Husserl to take this step and to persevere so stubbornly although his enterprise was now beset by difficulties at every turn. He not only failed to resolve these difficulties but also, as a consequence, was never able even to state very clearly his worries about subjects. From what we have seen, his thinking is propelled by some deep-seated uneasiness about the concept of a subject, but he does not manage to give a very specific account of the content of that uneasiness. Only very slowly did the complexion of his problem become clearer to him. A footnote in "Amsterdamer Vorträge" suggests the direction his thinking is going to take:

Rigorous science—that concept certainly undergoes transformation in the course of the entire enterprise of phenomenology in the light of the reduction. The will to be ultimately responsible . . . leads to the insight into the inadequacy, in principle, of all "rigorous science" on account of its being positive science, etc.[12]

Much later he writes, rather wistfully,

The dream of philosophy as a science, as serious, rigorous, even apodictically rigorous science—this dream will never be realized.[13]

Here hope ends that philosophy will become a body of objective knowledge like the natural sciences.

Husserl never quite realized the full import of this concession. It never did become completely clear to him what his problem was, what he felt science could not tell us about subjects, or even that he was committing himself to two incompatible positions. His attempts to resolve his difficulties failed because they were of the wrong sort. Neither the "discovery" of the transcendental ego nor of its "constitutive accomplishments" were appropriate remedies for his philosophical ailment. What was needed were not discoveries of new facts about ourselves or of entities whose existence we had not previously suspected. The difficulty was conceptual and required conceptual reforms. It concerned the thesis about the meaning of the concept of "knowledge"—whether it does make any sense at all to speak of knowledge that is not objective. Husserl's philosophical intimations about the nature of the subject or about persons should have led him to reexamine the claim that it is true by virtue of meanings (and in that sense "analytically" or "necessarily" true) that knowledge is objective.

We have here, however, a question not merely about "knowledge" but also about "objective." Very roughly, statements about "knowledge" want to specify with precision our prephilosophical determination to differentiate statements about the world as it is, from statements about the world as we imagine it to be, or wish it were, or think it ought to be. The object of true belief is, in some sense, independent of ourselves in ways in which my imaginings, wishes or demands are not. The serious issue raised by Husserl's philosophical conflicts concerns the precise specification of this independence from ourselves of what we know. It concerns therefore the concept not only of a subject but also of the object and the correlative terms "objectivity" and "subjectivity." Husserl had assumed that the independence of the object of knowledge from the fact of its being known could be stated in terms of one-sided entailment for all senses of "knowing." (Knowing something entails the truth of one's knowledge but the truth of the statement does not entail that anyone knows it.) It is this assumption that Heidegger questions. For this reason his reexamination of the notion of a subject, his "fundamental ontology of dasein," is largely concerned with a reexamination of the contrast that traditionally was designated by the terms "objective" and "subjective." More specifically, the distinction between what is ready to hand, what is present on hand and what is neither because it is an aspect of dasein amounts to a suggestion that the terms "objective" and "subjective" have much more limited application than philosophers have traditionally believed. Entities that are present on hand may be said to exist, whatever they are, objectively or subjectively. This distinction, however, applies neither to objects of use, as we have seen already, nor to subjects, as we shall see in Chapter 5.

III

Heidegger formulated his agreements and disagreements with Husserl in his comments on Husserl's article for the *Encyclopedia Britannica*. Heidegger wrote these comments in the same year in which he published *S & Z*.

We agree that the transcendental constitution of what exists in the sense in which you speak of "world" cannot be made clear by going back to entities of the same ontological type.

This is not to deny, however, that the locus of the transcendental is some sort of entity—but here precisely arises the problem: What is the ontological type of the entity [or: In what sense of "exist" does the entity exist] in which "world" constitutes itself? That is the central problem of *Being and Time* [*Sein und Zeit*], i.e., a fundamental ontology of dasein. The task is to show that dasein is of an altogether different ontological type from all other entities and that the ontological type of dasein, being what it is, conceals within itself the possibility of transcendental constitution.

Transcendental constitution is the central possibility of the existence of the factual self. This concrete human being is, as such, never a "real fact in the world" because human beings are never merely present on hand [*vorhanden*] but exist [*Encyc.*, 601–602].[14]

The passage raises several questions: (1) Heidegger seems to agree with Husserl that the world is "transcendentally constituted." But we would look in vain for any reference to "transcendental constitution" in *S & Z*. Heidegger does insist several times that "being is *the* transcendens without qualification" [e.g., 38; italics added] and speaks in that connection of "transcendental knowledge" as another name for ontological knowledge. But he does not talk like Husserl of "transcendental constitution." It seems clear that Heidegger and Husserl agree on something; it is not at all clear what it is. (2) What is meant by saying that the locus of the transcendental is some sort of entity but not an entity of the same ontological type as (what Husserl calls) "world"? (3) What, finally, is the ontological type of those entities that Husserl calls "world"? We notice that Heidegger encloses the term in quotation marks. He obviously wants to suggest that Husserl's use of "world" is rather special and, what is more, open to argument.

The final paragraph of the passage answers the last question. Dasein "is, as such, never a 'real fact in the world.' " Heidegger's use of quotation marks here, one would think, serves in part to acknowledge that this is indeed a very odd statement. Can it be that dasein, that is human being, is not a real fact in the world? Unless Heidegger attaches some special meaning to "real fact in the world," that is a gross falsehood. As the end of that same sentence, the last sentence of the quotation, indicates, he does restrict the word ''fact'' to entities that are present on hand. To say of something that its existence is or is not a fact presupposes that the entity spoken of is an entity present on hand. To say that dasein is not of the same ontological type as what Husserl calls ''world'' is to say that dasein is not present on hand. Dasein is thus not known objectively because Husserl construed all entities, and also their totality, which he called ''world'' in such a way that ''to be'' meant ''to be knowable objectively.'' Implicit in Heidegger's refusal to treat dasein as an entity present on hand is a criticism of the meaning that Husserl gives to the concept of world and, with that, the way in which Husserl thinks the world is known (see Section 14 for several meanings of ''world'').

The locus of the transcendental is an entity, but not of the same ontological type as Husserl's ''world.'' The phrase ''the locus of the transcendental'' refers to what Husserl calls the ''transcendental subject'' and what Heidegger calls ''dasein.'' Heidegger overstates the extent to which he and Husserl agree. To be sure, Husserl insists that the transcendental subject is a different sort of entity from those in the world, including our empirical selves. Husserl recognizes that we cannot make sense of talk about ''constituting'' as long as we think of whatever does the constituting as the sort of thing of which empirical science gives us an account. This is one of the results of the rejection of psychologism. Besides, ''constituting'' is not a word in the scientific vocabulary or one without which it would be incomplete. But Husserl does not draw the distinction between what does the constituting and the constituted in the terms that Heidegger thinks are needed to state it. For Husserl draws the distinction in epistemological terms. The constituting agent is not the sort of entity known to empirical science. It is said to be a ''pure'' ego. But Heidegger, as our passage suggests, believes that the distinction is not between what is known empirically and what is known a priori, but between what is known in the sense in which the scientist knows and what is known in some other sense. The transcendental subject of Husserl's is not known in the sense of "knowledge" in which knowledge is necessarily objective. Hence the "locus of the transcendental," although an entity, is not an entity of the same ontological type as facts and whatever else we know objectively. There is agreement then that what does the constituting and what is constituted are, in an important respect, different. But Heidegger does not approve of Husserl's statement of that difference.

His next remark, that the locus of the transcendental is, of course, an entity, leads to an explanation of this disagreement. In his own way Husserl did agree that transcendental constitution cannot be made clear by "going back to entities of the same ontological type" as those constituted. He had recognized this necessary distinction by speaking of the transcendental subject and its constitutive functions as "discovered." This seems to imply that the transcendental subject is numerically distinct from empirical subjects. We have always known that there are empirical selves. Any other self that needs to be discovered by a special technique, the reduction, would seem to be a distinct entity. Similarly, it would seem that besides all the familiar activities of human beings like perceiving, believing, naming and describing, Husserl has also discovered one more, again numerically distinct activity that is called "constituting."

But he is, of course, of two minds about this. There are times when he does not want to draw the distinction between the transcendental and the empirical subject in this way. At such times he insists on the numerical identity of empirical and transcendental subject.[15] Heidegger agrees with him here but sees, perhaps more clearly than Husserl, that this view involves considerable difficulty. "Here precisely arises the problem": What is meant by saying that subjects, as we know them, "constitute" the world? If the transcendental subject is not numerically distinct from the empirical subject, we must also deny that constituting is a newly discovered activity distinct from all those activities of ours that are familiar to us. (Any discovery of a new kind of activity performed by empirical subjects would surely be an empirical discovery.) Heidegger attempts to solve the difficulty by reconsidering traditional descriptions of mental activities in such a way that talk about constituting is no longer talk about a distinct activity but now comes to be, instead, talk about a new way of considering the activities that we have always performed. To talk about our ordinary activities like perceiving, thinking, naming or describing as ways of constituting the world is (as we saw in the preceding section) a way of suggesting that they are in some ways like theoretical knowing but in other ways like doing or making. But we cannot even make, let alone develop, this suggestion and hence clarify the talk about "constituting" unless we deny that all knowledge is by necessity objective. Insofar as Husserl never seems fully prepared to make this denial, Heidegger refuses to follow him. In this lies the core of their disagreement.

Husserl tried to clarify "constitution" as a distinct "accomplishment (*Leistung*)." Heidegger reexamines familiar mental activities in order to show that they are indeed constitutive, because our acquaintance with the world is not always an instance of objective knowledge. The meaning of "knowing" in the sense in which it is necessarily true that knowledge is objective is only one meaning of that term and not the primary one at that. A meaning of knowing must be developed for which objectivity is not a necessary feature. In this meaning of "knowing" an act of knowing is at the same time also an act of doing and/or of making something. This in turn calls for a rather different conception of the subject. For if "knowing" in the primary sense is not objective knowing, then subjects are not related to themselves as objects and subjects of objective knowledge. This means that subjects do not exist, as they are, independently of their knowledge of themselves. Instead, subjects are dependent on their knowledge

of themselves. In order to be a human being, I must know that
I am one and what it means to be a human being. This is the
knowledge that Heidegger calls "preontological." Furthermore, if we thought very differently about ourselves, we
would be very different sorts of people. The concept of the
subject that Heidegger hopes to develop is one in which it
makes perfect sense to say of a person that to know the good
is to do it. It also makes perfect sense, given a proper explication of all the terms, to say that human beings are what
they conceive themselves to be. For this reason, Heidegger,
early in *S & Z*, produces the phrase "the essence of dasein is
its existence" and then proceeds to explicate "existence" as
something like "understanding" or "knowing," and these
terms as "determining real possibilities (*entwerfen*)" [Sec-
tion 31]. But to determine what is really possible for me is to
determine what I am.

A subject, in this sense, would presumably also know the
world in that sense of "knowing" in which knowing is at the
same time practical and productive. For such a subject it
would therefore also be true that, if it conceived the world in
radically different terms, it would itself be radically different.[16] This is what Heidegger takes to be the philosophical
insight in Husserl's talk about transcendental "constitution"
and "transcendental subjects." He thinks the insight is genuine and terribly important.

We have had instances of Heidegger's development of this
insight in the preceding chapters. Preontological understanding, discussed in Chapter 1 and to be discussed in more detail later, exemplifies the new sense of "knowing" that Heidegger regards as essential for a workable transcendental
philosophy. The point of denying in Chapter 2 that there is
ever "*one* item of gear" was to make the existence and nature
of objects in the world relative to human practices and skills.
This illustrates one respect in which our knowing the world
also transforms it. In very different ways Heidegger tries to
develop the transcendental motif in the discussion of language

in Chapter 3. A particular language contains a particular way of explicating the world, and thus people who speak different languages must, to that extent, live in different worlds. [See also *S & Z*, p. 47, *n* 1, and p. 139.]

To the extent that Heidegger considers insightful Husserl's talk about transcendental constitution and transcendental subjects, there is real agreement between the two. Because Heidegger also thinks that Husserl never made clear what his insight was, and for the reason that Husserl never developed the philosophical vocabulary that would have clarified it, Heidegger does not use, in *S & Z*, the jargon that proved unhelpful for Husserl. Hence he does not use Husserl's term "transcendental constitution," although he does agree with Husserl that something exists that is like what Husserl had called "transcendental constitution."

Now we can explain why Heidegger calls his own enterprise "phenomenology" although he makes no reference to some of the most famous features of phenomenology and rejects others outright.

It has often been remarked that Heidegger does not accept the transcendental-phenomenological reduction, which is an essential element of Husserlian phenomenology. Heidegger apparently ignores it. Nor do we find any mention in Heidegger of essences or of the intuition or description of essences. He makes no clear declaration about the general character of his statements, whether or not they are a priori. It is even less clear whether he would want them to be regarded as analytic or as synthetic a priori.

"Descriptive phenomenology," we read, is a "tautological expression."

> The character of the description itself . . . can be determined only in view of what sort of "thing" the "subject" is that is to be "described" [35].

What we mean by "describe," according to Heidegger, depends on what we are describing. Husserl had insisted that

we are speaking about objectively existing entities in phenomenology, which are not, of course, entities that exist contingently. These he calls essences. Description thus consists of
enumerating or summarizing the properties of these objectively existing entities. Because Heidegger, on the other hand,
explores the possibility of a language in which not everything
has objective existence, he does not find the concept of an essence useful. Therefore he does not use the term. "Description" accordingly does not mean what it means for Husserl:
making objectively true statements, as firmly supported as
possible, about the abstract entities to be described. Instead,
Heidegger informs us, "phenomenological description means
the same as 'explication' " [37].

We have seen in the preceding chapter that in *S & Z* the
term "explication" refers to the activity of putting what we,
in some way, understand into words, and to do so in such a
way as to gain a more adequate understanding. This may
mean giving a formulation to understanding that so far is unformulated, as we do, for instance, in the case of preontological understanding. It may also mean using a precise philosophical vocabulary in order to demarcate clearly distinctions
whose meanings are vague in ordinary usage. In view of the
most familiar senses of "to describe," it would have been misleading for Heidegger to refer to what he thinks we do in
ontology as "description." For explication involves some
measure of transformation of our understanding; it involves
letting something be seen as something. The most illuminating
analogies for illustrating the term are not taken from scientific inquiry but from artistic expression. Explication is faithful to what it concerns—in the way in which De Kooning's
nudes are faithful to female nudity rather than in the way in
which a statement of fact is faithful to the facts. But the
terms "description" and "intuition" fit the latter model more
naturally than the former. Heidegger therefore uses them
only in his discussion of phenomenology to establish contact
between Husserl's vocabulary and his own.

On Husserl's view of language, for which statements are paradigmatic, the truth and falsity of statements is determined by what the statements assert, but the facts are not affected by being asserted in a statement nor are objects or events in any way affected by being named or described. Here one can draw a clear distinction between a priori and a posteriori discourse by distinguishing between the sorts of entities that determine whether statements in the different types of discourse are true or false. Objects of actual or possible observation determine the truth of a posteriori discourse. Ideal entities determine the truth of a priori discourse. (Other philosophers may say that words and the rules governing their use are what determine the truth of a priori statements.) Once we reject the Husserlian view of language and the view that truth is objective, we find not only that our utterances are dependent on what they are about but also that, conversely, the world is affected by being talked and thought about in particular ways. From one point of view, all language may be said to be "prior" to what we talk about. Any utterance may therefore be called "a priori." The distinction between utterances that are clearly subservient to specific facts and others that are not must therefore be redrawn under suitable circumstances. Under such circumstances any statement may be regarded as a priori. The same statement may be a posteriori elsewhere. The primary question for the philosopher is now what explication to give to the "priority" of utterances.

How must we understand the character of this "pre-"?
Is it sufficient to use the formal term "a priori" [150]?

Heidegger rarely uses the term "a priori" because the distinction it indicates has become problematic.

Heidegger does not merely ignore but rejects outright Husserl's claim that phenomenology is reflective [115]. He not only doubts whether it is self-evidently true, as Husserl had thought, that we have direct access to ourselves via reflection, but thinks that it is false. Reflecting is like intuiting and describing except that here the subject and object are one and the same individual. Reflective knowledge is merely a special case of objective knowledge. If we knew ourselves primarily by way of reflection, we would be what we are independently of our knowledge of ourselves. Because Heidegger denies this, he is also committed to deny that the most ready access to ourselves is provided by reflection.

Insofar as the transcendental-phenomenological reduction describes the transition from nonreflective to reflective thinking, Heidegger's distrust of reflection leads him to leave the reduction aside in his account of phenomenology. Commentators have been quick, perhaps too quick, to point this out.[17] But Husserl's views are never unambiguous. Different philosophical intimations find expression in each of the major doctrines. Thus also in the reduction. Husserl contrasts the "natural attitude" of the ordinary man and the man of science with the special attitude that is taken in practicing the reduction and the new realm of being, unsuspected in the natural attitude, which is revealed by it. This contrast has nothing to do with the difference between nonreflective and reflective thinking but echoes the distinction between philosophy, which goes against the grain of common sense, and the ordinary understanding of the world, a distinction first suggested in the story of Thales falling into the well while looking at the stars. It is found again much later in Hegel's reference to philosophy as *"verkehrte Welt,"* where philosophy is the world stood on its head. The tradition is continued by Heidegger's distinction between men's average understanding of the world and of themselves—which is said to be not "authentic (*eigentlich*)"—and the authentic understanding, which militates against plain sense and accepted opinions, which is rarely reached and then only with difficulties. Although here Heidegger once again avoids the Husserlian terminology, he takes over one of the thoughts that animated Husserl's talk about the transcendental-phenomenological reduction.

These are Heidegger's reasons for ignoring or explicitly rejecting the most familiar features of Husserl's phenomenology. They are all features that are intimately connected with Husserl's commitment to objectivism.[18] But Heidegger uses the term "phenomenology" in order to indicate his connection with the motifs in Husserl's thought that disturbed his objectivist views: the concern about the subject, the notion that the complexion that the world turns toward us in some way reflects our own, and that we are, in some sense, what we conceive ourselves to be. Heidegger pursues Husserl's philosophical tendencies that tend toward a transcendental philosophy. He calls his ontology "phenomenology" inasmuch as Husserlian phenomenology was transcendental. Neither Kant nor Husserl, he believes, succeeded in formulating a tenable transcendental philosophy, because of their objectivist bias. He sets out therefore to reformulate the transcendental philosophy that Husserl failed to state clearly, and, like Husserl, he calls his transcendental philosophy "phenomenology." [19]

At first glance this interpretation seems at odds with Heidegger's remark that "The expression 'phenomenology' refers primarily to a concept of method" [27]. I have argued that Heidegger adopts the term "phenomenology" to indicate the continuity between his and Husserl's transcendental philosophy in spite of serious disagreements about the explication of key concepts. The concept of phenomenology therefore seems to be a substantive one. It is used to indicate that there is a common problem, namely, "What is the ontological type of the entity in which 'world' constitutes itself?" (The disagreement may be said to concern the meaning of "ontological type.")

But if we look at this passage carefully, we can see that there is no conflict between Heidegger's statement and the preceding account of phenomenology. Heidegger explains why he insists that "phenomenology" is the name of a method. In the first place, he wants to forestall any misunderstanding that might be engendered by the verbal analogy between "phenomenology" and, say, "theology." Phenomenology is not to be thought of as a discipline that differs from others by having a special subject matter, phenomena, as theology in turn differs from, say, geology by dealing with God rather than with the earth [34]. What is more, Heidegger is at pains to dissociate himself from the phenomenological school. Although freely acknowledging his debt (and more guardedly his objections) to Husserl's thought, he does not want to be regarded as one more member of the Husserl circle or of the wider phenomenological movement [38].

More important, the characterization of "phenomenology" as the name of a method is less informative than one might think at first. The description of a philosophical method must be firmly "rooted in the analysis of the things themselves" [27]. Contrary to a widespread notion that one can discuss methods, at least in some areas, without discussing the problems to be solved by means of these methods, or that discussions of methods do not prejudice the results to be obtained by them, Heidegger, in consonance with his claim that ontology is circular, asserts that we can develop a method only while using it, that to choose a certain method at the beginning of an inquiry will prejudice its outcome, and that we can talk about method only by talking at the same time about the problems to which the method is to be applied. Hence to talk about phenomenology as a method is to talk about the transcendental problem that he and Husserl hold in common.

The development of the method goes hand in hand with its application to the problems that it is designed to solve. Hence Heidegger's own discussion of "phenomenology" in Section 7 of *S & Z* is quite uninformative. He recognizes this by saying that this section will provide only a "preliminary concept (*Vorbegriff*)" of phenomenology [28]. Heidegger is in no position to give an account of "phenomenon" or of the criteria of adequacy of phenomenological analyses as long as he has said nothing about the different senses of "to exist" and nothing about "knowing" and "truth." Like any other philosopher, he cannot give a detailed account of his method until he has used it extensively. The main function of Section 7, besides simply making a declaration of the continuity between *S & Z* and Husserl's work, is to forestall possible misunderstandings and to indicate the directions in which later analyses will have to move to clarify Heidegger's sense of "phenomenology."

The better part of the discussion of "phenomenon" is taken up with differentiating "phenomenon" from "appearance" and justifying that distinction by explicating "appearance." "To appear," he argues, refers to something being manifested by means of something other than itself; for example, diseases appear by virtue of their symptoms, Gods appear to us in clouds or burning bushes, the unity of a nation appears in a patriotic symbol. What appears in this way is never seen directly as such [29]. "Appearance" may also refer to that through which something, which we do not confront directly, manifests itself [30]. Phenomena are not in this sense appearances. They are never "something, 'behind' which there stands something else 'which does not appear' " [35–36]. On the other hand, phenomena are not something that does not confront us directly but appears to us by virtue of something else [31]. This serves to differentiate Heidegger's from Husserl's sense of "phenomenon"; Husserl often had spoken of phenomena as "appearances" in which the world manifests itself to consciousness [see e.g., *Encyc.*, 279]. Heidegger also tries to show that the sense in which he uses "phenomenon" is not the same as Kant's.

As we would expect, what Heidegger tells us about "phenomenon" in this preliminary section is extremely meager and unilluminating. A phenomenon is "that which shows itself as itself (*das Sich-an-ihm-selbst-zeigende*)" [28]. But what that means, of course, is quite obscure. He gives us one hint concerning the meaning of this phrase by equating it with "what is revealed (*das Offenbare*)," thus clearly linking his conception of phenomenon with his conception of truth. But at the moment this only serves to put us off until we have found how he explicates "truth." His formulation of the meaning of "phenomenon" is deferred until we have an explication of "truth."

The impossibility of explaining what is a phenomenon in this early part of *S & Z* is suggested more forcefully in his final statement about the term:

> What is it that must be called "phenomenon" in a primary sense? What is, in its very nature, *necessarily* the subject of *explicit* exhibiting? Obviously whatever primarily and ordinarily does *not* show itself, . . . what is . . . hidden . . .
>
> But what remains in a primary sense *hidden* . . . is . . . the *being* of entities [35].

I do not think that it is altogether accidental that Heidegger once again states his views in such an apparently paradoxical form. What was earlier called "that which shows itself as itself" is now introduced to us in a different guise, namely, as "what does not show itself, what is . . . hidden." Both of these phrases supposedly refer to the concept of phenomenon. One could not possibly take both as an explanation of what "phenomenon" means unless one had a very low opinion of Heidegger's ability to be consistent or to explain himself. Instead we must take the second passage, like the earlier one, as an attempt to defer the clarification of "phenomenon" by giving only some brief indications of what other concepts must first be examined before we can return to explicating it. In the published portions of *S & Z*, of course, this explication is never given explicitly.

These are the points that need to be cleared up before we can understand the second version of "phenomenon" and before we can see why he wants to formulate it in just that way: Being, as we saw earlier, is known by us preontologically. In other words, we understand and know being without necessarily having formulated this understanding or knowledge. But when Heidegger talks here of "phenomenon" as what is "hidden," he means more than that it is something that we understand without being readily able to talk about it. We shall see in Chapter 5 that Heidegger holds that we may be preontologically mistaken and that to be preontologically mistaken is the common and average condition of men. What is thus commonly not only not formulated, but also mistaken, in our unformulated understanding, which is called "preontological"—this is what Heidegger wants to call "phenomenon." Chapter 5 will throw some light on these notions. But we can see, at least in outline, how Heidegger connects the terms "phenomenon" and "being" if we keep in mind his repeated remarks that "philosophy has traditionally put truth together with being" [212], a juxtaposition of concepts of which he clearly approves. The first formula given for "phenomenon" connected that term with truth. If truth, in turn, is closely allied with the concept of being, we can see the connection between what we ordinarily mistake, even preontologically, and what is to be called not only "phenomenon" but also "being." The meaning of "phenomenon" as well as the plausibility of giving the term that meaning hangs on Heidegger's explication of "truth" and of "knowing," particularly of "preontological knowing" and its companion term "being preontologically mistaken."

Heidegger needs to reform the vocabulary in which we talk about ourselves so that he can begin to do ontology. But in what respects and in what directions our talk about human beings must be reformulated cannot be inferred, of course, from any concept of ontology because that concept is, on the contrary, what we are still looking for and will not be able to formulate satisfactorily until we understand the concept of being better than we understand it now. But such understanding will not be ours until we have a more suitable language in which to talk about human beings. Heidegger therefore had to take his leading suggestions for a reform of such talk from some other source. He chose to begin with the problems that were very close to him, not only as a result of his association with Husserl but also because they had in various ways been discussed by other philosophers of the day, particularly by Dilthey and Max Scheler.[20] He let himself be guided in his reform of our way of speaking about human beings by the problem about human subjectivity. His general attempt is to oppose the Husserlian tendency to construe human beings on the analogy of the objects of the natural sciences, objects that do not depend on knowers for their existence or essence, a view in which being, but not entities, depends on us because there is being only where there is dasein [183, 212]. This general line of thought seemed wrong to the later Heidegger, who insists, on the contrary, that men are dependent on being, and who tries to reinterpret *S & Z* in that sense.[21]

5

understanding

Husserl's discussion of consciousness was deeply disturbed by the conflict between assumptions that shaped his vocabulary and an insight that would not let itself be expressed in that vocabulary. Consciousness was always thought to be a case of knowing, and by definition knowing was objective. In the language permeated by these assumptions it was impossible to give voice to the insight that, in some very important cases, there is no sharp distinction between apprehending what the world and the self are like and transforming world and self. The conflict, as well as its resolution, sought but never found, bears directly on the question of what it means to be a human being. Here Heidegger makes contact with Husserl. With Husserl he asks what being human means. He also shares with him the conception of what would be a satisfactory answer to that question, namely, a detailed account of how human beings constitute themselves and the world.

The key concepts that Heidegger introduces in order to provide such an account are "being disposed," [1] "understand-

ing" and "discourse." These three concepts are said to be
"equiprimordial"; the phenomenon of being equiprimordial,
Heidegger complains, has often been neglected in ontology
[131]. But we are not told what "equiprimordial" means. Because the concepts are introduced separately, each in a section
of its own, and Heidegger insists, for instance, that "understanding is always in a mood (*gestimmtes*)" [142], readers
of *S & Z* have concluded that the three concepts refer to distinct phenomena, which, however, always occur together.

But this explication of "equiprimordial" is not correct. It
would fit the views of a philosopher like Franz Brentano,
whose account of emotions Heidegger opposes, much more
readily than Heidegger's own views. Brentano held that there
is no emotion without an idea or a belief about the object of
the emotion and that, conversely, there is no cognitive act
without emotional reverberations. Are we to believe that Heidegger's term "equiprimordial" is merely an obscure reference to this constant association of emotional and cognitive
phenomena? In that case he would be complaining about the
neglect of a relationship that has been widely recognized and
that he, as we shall see, wants to reject.

S & Z's recommendation of a new set of concepts amounts
to a suggestion that we draw philosophical distinctions where
none were drawn before or that the distinctions that the tradition has considered most important either be ignored or be
given less prominence in favor of other distinctions that Heidegger wants us to draw. For instance, we are urged to draw
a distinction between the instruments in the laboratory and
the entities that these instruments are designed to measure,
in other words, between entities ready to hand and entities
present on hand. Heidegger here introduces a philosophical
distinction not drawn by his predecessors. The distinction between mark and meaning, on the other hand, which Husserl,
for instance, had regarded as important, is simply dropped.
In the present discussion of the concept of understanding we
are urged to make less of the distinction between cognitive

and emotional phenomena and to replace it with a distinction between senses of "knowing."

Traditionally, thoughts were regarded as phenomena separate from emotions. A typical case of thinking was, for instance, entertaining a statement, speaking to oneself subvocally. Running away from a charging bull was the manifestation of a typical case of fear. The meaning and truth value of the statement made subvocally were independent of the emotions of the person talking to himself. Conversely, it was thought that I know that I am running away from the bull not by virtue of my fear but by virtue of an associated idea of the bull. As Brentano, for instance, asserted the constant association of emotions with ideas and the emotional concomitants of beliefs, he presupposed that all beliefs and emotions are like those in the typical cases and that, therefore, thoughts and emotions are mutually independent. I could still know and believe what I know and believe now, even if for some reason my beliefs no longer came with an aura of emotion. I could, on the other hand, still be afraid, if emotions were no longer attached causally to beliefs (because, say, they were caused directly by events). I would simply no longer know what the cause of the emotion was. The traditional scheme attests the constant association of thinking and feeling, which are thought of in very specific ways, namely, as separate in the ways indicated.

When Heidegger urges us to make less of the distinction between thinking and feeling and instead to put the distinction between two senses of "knowing" into a prominent place in our philosophical vocabulary, he denies that the typical traditional cases are indeed paradigmatic. Traditional conceptions of thinking and emotion are therewith relegated to a restricted range of cases; they are no longer thought to yield the primary meanings of the relevant terms. His claim that "being disposed" and "understanding" are equiprimordial, therefore, does not assert the concomitance of the traditionally understood concepts of thought and emotion but in-

stead suggests a new concept wherein emotion and thought
are not separate as they were in the tradition. Emotion and
thought, in this new version, cannot exist one without the
other. To have an emotion is to know, but not to make statements to oneself subvocally. To know in this sense is to feel,
but not quite in the sense of reacting to a fact in the world.
For the traditional distinction between feeling and thinking,
Heidegger substitutes a distinction between a traditional sense
of knowing and a new one, in which to know is to feel.

The new distinction is marked terminologically by contrasting *"erkennen* (knowing)" with *"verstehen* (understanding)."* This new concept is the subject of this chapter. I shall
begin with those aspects of it for which Heidegger uses the
expression "being disposed."

I

Section 29, on moods, opens by contrasting the "possibilities of disclosure" of moods with those of theoretical knowing
(*"erkennen"*). We are told that much that is not accessible
to theoretical knowing is capable of being disclosed in moods
[131].[2] The comparison indicates that moods are thought to
be like theoretical knowledge in the sense of being instances
of what Heidegger calls "disclosure." In important respects,
moods are like theoretical knowing: We may say that they
are cognitive. At the same time we are told that the sort of
knowing found in moods is different from theoretical knowing.
The claim that moods are cognitive thus remains quite unclear unless we can specify the difference between theoretical
knowledge and knowing as it occurs in moods.

Heidegger's recommendations are more readily clarified if
one knows the philosophical issues that they are meant to resolve. For that purpose it is helpful, as it has proved helpful
in earlier chapters, to know who his opponents are as he de-

velops his new concepts. In Chapter 5 of *S & Z* now under discussion there are clear indications who the opponents are. In a brief survey of the history of philosophical treatments of emotions we are told that

> affects and emotions end up among psychic phenomena; as the third class of such phenomena they function side by side with having ideas and willing. They are reduced to being concomitant phenomena [139].

The phrase "third class of psychic phenomena" reminds one strongly of Brentano.[3] But the tripartite division into acts of cognition, of feeling and of willing is not Brentano's but Kant's.[4] In conscious opposition to Kant, Brentano saw two distinct classes, having ideas and judging, where Kant saw only one, cognitive acts. Kant's two classes of feeling and willing are, in Brentano's scheme, fused into one. Other philosophers, as, for example, Hume, regarded cognitive phenomena as one class and emotional phenomena, to which belonged willing, as another; thus they ended by saying there are only two classes.

Heidegger distinguishes the sense in which emotional phenomena, specifically our moods, reveal the world to us from the very different sense of awareness of the world that we have in theoretical knowing.

> If one identified what moods disclose with whatever dasein, in this mood, knows theoretically "at the same time," one would completely mistake the phenomenal characteristics of *what* moods disclose and *how* they disclose [135].

Whatever we are aware of by virtue of our moods is not to be thought of as a theoretical belief concomitant with the emotional state. This suggests that neither the number of major classes nor the distribution of the wide variety of psychological phenomena into these classes is the primary target of Heidegger's polemic, but rather certain common views held by all the traditional philosophers about the relations between phenomena of different classes. All agree that emotional phenomena, however classified, are dependent on cognitive acts. An emotion is always said to be tied to the idea of the object that inspires the emotion and, in some cases, also tied to further beliefs about the object. A woman's beauty gives me pleasure because I have an idea of her. If in addition I believe, for instance, that she is my daughter or my wife, her beauty will fill me with pride.[5]

These are not empirical generalizations about feelings like pleasure and pride, but conceptual analyses. They are supported by arguments from the meanings of terms, not by reports of observations. They rest, to begin with, on the distinction between bodily sensations like itches and tickles, and emotions, like fear and pride. Bodily sensations have causes, but there is nothing odd if a person does not know the causes of an itch. Emotions, by contrast, have objects, and ignorance of objects is possible but requires explanation. A man is proud of something; something gives him pleasure. To feel pride without knowing its source is peculiar, and so are pleasurable feelings that appear to have no object. (It matters little, therefore, whether we say that emotions too have causes or whether we say that they have objects; the crucial difference is that bodily sensations are not incomplete without my knowledge of their causes; but emotions are incomplete if I do not know what occasions them.) This distinction, however, is not sufficient to support the claim that all emotions require cognitive acts. Brentano, for one, regards all emotions as intentional in themselves. Being afraid, for instance, has an object, as such; it is always fear of something. The intentional relation is not, as it were, contributed by the concomitant cognitive acts. Nevertheless, Brentano insists, as Hume and Kant do, that there can be no emotional act that is not accompanied at least by an idea and sometimes also by a relevant belief. Why is Brentano so certain of that?

Suppose we thought that to be is to be independent of human knowing or, more generally, to be independent of awareness. Philosophers have thought this and have, for that reason, been much troubled by all those properties—as, for instance, perceptual qualities—that objects do not seem to possess unless observed. They have been inclined to deny that they are features of things in themselves and instead have regarded them as attributes of observers. Emotions have been treated in the same way and there the case was simpler. Although perceptual qualities have fairly strong claims for being attributes of objects, it seems clear that being afraid of a lion is not the same as having knowledge or true beliefs about the lion. Being frightening is clearly not a property of the lion, for whether the observer will be frightened depends largely on his state and on the circumstances. Perception, if reliable, of course also requires that the perceiver satisfy certain standard conditions. These are readily agreed upon and stated. It is much more difficult, however, if not impossible, to set standard conditions under which one might say that a person's emotions reliably informs him about their object. One can argue about what is perceived, but there is no arguing about likes and dislikes. Philosophers have therefore been content to regard emotions as noncognitive; to describe an emotion is to describe a state of a person that tells us nothing about the object occasioning that emotion. Some beliefs are true, others are false; neither of these terms can be used to apply to emotions.

On the other hand, there is a distinction between bodily sensations—for example, itches and tickles—and emotions; one ordinarily knows something about the source of the latter, but not of the former. Brentano expresses this thought by saying that emotions are intentional. In the case of an emotion but not in the case of a bodily sensation, one is always justified to expect an answer to the question ''What occasions it?'' But if emotions are noncognitive, having the emotion is not in itself sufficient to enable us to answer that question.

Hence the claim that emotions are, for the most part, accompanied by ideas, for we do know, in most cases, something about what is moving us. Because emotions are different from pure bodily states in that they have objects, they are, in Brentano's language, intentional; they must therefore be accompanied by cognitive acts of one sort or another in order for us to be able to describe their objects.

This pattern of analysis of emotions fits feelings that are not bodily—and emotions like fear, joy, anger, love, hate—rather well. (Heidegger would, of course, deny that the traditional pattern of analysis even fits these cases.) Philosophers who have offered a variety of different versions of this pattern of analysis, however, have had very little to say about a rather different range of emotional phenomena, the phenomena we usually call "moods." One suspects that this omission has to do with the greater difficulty of analyzing moods in terms of separate emotional and cognitive acts. Heidegger, on the other hand, concentrates on a discussion of moods because he is trying to replace the sharp distinction between emotional and cognitive acts so as to undermine the assumption that all knowledge is objective. To do so will enable him to show that some emotional phenomena are cognitive, although they do not yield objective knowledge.

Being pointlessly depressed or generally happy, serene or anxious, are examples of moods. They differ from the corresponding emotions of sadness or joy, of being unperturbed in the face of ———— or being afraid of ————, in that emotions have specific objects whereas moods do not. Heidegger uses the difference between fear and dread to illustrate the difference between an emotion and a mood. What one fears is always something fairly definite, an object or an event. It is characteristic of objects and events that they have a location [185]. The hungry lion that is threatening me is in a very definite place. An economic depression may be widespread, but it is always over a definite geographic area. If a world war en-

gulfs the entire globe, there may still be a peaceful refuge on
the moon. What one dreads, on the other hand

is not an entity within the world [*innerweltlich*]. . . .
Of all those entities that are ready to hand or present
on hand within the world, none function as that which
dread dreads. . . . It is characteristic of what we dread
that what threatens us is *not anywhere* [186].

. . . dread, as one way of being disposed, discloses first
of all the *world as world* [187].

One may well say, after one experiences dread, that "it was
really nothing" that one dreaded for it was indeed not any
particular object or event, or any class of objects or events.
But dread is therefore not an "objectless" emotional phenomenon. Moods, too, are intentional. It is not an emotional state
without any reference to something other than itself. What
we dread is being-in-the-world. Heidegger uses one of his new
distinctions, that between what is within the world and world
itself; he does so in order to draw the distinction between fear
and dread and more generally between emotions and moods.
World is an entity of an altogether different sort from objects
or events, or whatever else may be said to exist and to be located "within the world."

But we can also draw the distinction between emotions and
moods in the terms provided by the traditional pattern of
analysis of emotional phenomena. We can draw it without
using Heidegger's new terminology. The distinction between
emotions and moods therefore does not serve to show that the
traditional pattern is inadequate. For we might say that a
specific emotion is intimately associated with an idea of a particular event or object, and with beliefs about it, whereas a
mood is intimately associated with an indefinitely large class
of ideas and beliefs about the world. In a bad mood, we
might say, one believes many things: that men are venal and

society corrupt; that science is a sham and art an opiate to dull our pain. It is not enough to say, as some writers about Heidegger like to do, that moods differ from emotions by having more general objects. Although this is true, we must ask whether this is ontologically interesting, whether moods are of a different ontological type—require a different conceptual scheme for their analysis—from the more familiar sorts of emotions like fear, love, and hate. As we can see, the mere difference in degree of specificity of the object does not demand different conceptual schemes. The different degree of specificity in moods and emotions is thus, ontologically speaking, not an interesting difference.

The traditional pattern of analysis may well apply adequately to emotional phenomena like fear and pride as well as to the distinction between emotion and moods. Heidegger, of course, does not think so. He clearly wants to replace the pattern by a very different conception of such emotions:

It is not the case that one first establishes the existence of a future evil (*malum futurum*), which one then fears. Nor does being afraid first recognize the fact that something is impending; instead it discovers it antecedently insofar as it is frightening. . . . Circumspection sees what is frightening; it is disposed by way of being afraid. ''Fearfulness,'' that is, being afraid as a dormant possibility of our disposed being-in-the-world, has always already revealed the world as whence something like what is frightening can come toward us [141].

The first sentence rejects any analysis of fear that separates it into a belief that something evil is ahead and the emotional state proper. The second sentence in conjunction with the last denies that we are aware that there are fearful things in the world only because we have actually been frightened by them. Even if we are not afraid, and never have been, we are prepared to find things frightening: Being afraid is a ''dormant possibility.'' One knows that being frightened is one of our possibilities (in the meanings of "knowing" and "possibility" that will be discussed in the next sections of this chapter). It is therefore not true that we are frightened because we have a causal disposition to be afraid. We are susceptible to causal influences whether we know it or not. Our readiness to be afraid, however, is a kind of knowing what the world is like and what we are liable to find in it. Being prepared to be afraid is more like a vague and shadowy expectation. This expectation, the third sentence tells us, is an element of circumspection. It is an instance of what Heidegger calls "being disposed."

In this way Heidegger denies that the traditional pattern of analysis applies to fear and similar emotional states. But he does not provide even the most meager indications of an argument, perhaps because there are other cases which are more useful for rendering his views at all plausible. The cases in question are moods. They resist the traditional pattern more effectively and also illustrate more clearly what is meant by "being disposed."

In the analysis of emotions we found that philosophers agree that some belief or idea is a necessary condition for any emotional state other than mere bodily feeling. The range of possible ideas and beliefs necessary for any particular emotional state is, of course, restricted. Not every belief can make someone afraid. More important, if any particular belief makes a person afraid, acceptance of a contradictory belief will reassure him and remove his fear. If a man is afraid that he is dying of thirst, his fear is allayed by the belief that he is drinking water. His fear may be aroused again if he is told that the water is poisoned. We can calm him, once more, by proving to him that it is not. If one of two contradictory beliefs produces a certain emotion, the other will remove that emotion.

Moods are not conditional on specific beliefs and thus removable by showing these beliefs to be false. Suppose a person is in a thoroughly bad mood, about nothing in particular.

We try to cheer him up by reminding him that the sky is very blue and the sun is shining, that he is well-to-do, that he has not a care in the world, that he has a loving family and trusted friends. He may very well believe all this; in fact, he knew it all before we began talking. Quite possibly, he has no other beliefs that show the world in a bad light and that might, on balance, justify his bad mood. We might well get him to agree that few if any facts could be cited that might to any extent justify his depression. But as he is in a bad mood "about nothing in particular," we cannot change his mood by altering his beliefs. Moods are not conditioned by beliefs as, say, fear or pride are, and hence cannot be removed by replacing a belief by a contradictory belief. A given mood is compatible with any belief and the contradiction of any belief. A man may be depressed because of a certain belief, but he may also be depressed in spite of it. If we try to cheer up our friend by reciting all his good fortune to him, we may have no effect at all or we may have the opposite effect by merely deepening his depression. He may resent the blue sky or his wife's affection as a mockery of his profound sadness or a sign that she lacks genuine sympathy.

Emotions, like fear or pride, may, with some plausibility, be said to be occasioned by a certain belief under specific conditions. Lack of water will make me fear for my life, unless I believe death to be preferable to life. A beautiful wife will make a man proud unless he believes that female beauty is the work of the devil. But beliefs are not the only conditions required for some second belief to produce certain emotions. How a certain belief affects us depends largely on our moods. When we tell the man, who is profoundly sad, about all the sources of happiness in his life, he remains unmoved by them. What will cheer up people who are not depressed, what will make very happy a person who is generally in a cheerful mood, leaves him completely indifferent. Being depressed consists in part just in this: that the sorts of beliefs that cause people various emotions, pleasant and unpleasant, when they are not depressed, have absolutely no effect on a person who is. Given different moods, a person will react very differently to one and the same belief. For this reason, moods are not related to beliefs like emotions of a more specific sort, like fear or pride, because moods are themselves one of the conditions that determine how a certain belief will affect one.

This is what moods are. If we insist that the traditional pattern of analysis, with its strict distinction between cognitive and emotional phenomena, must also be applied to moods, we face several equally unattractive alternatives. Because moods will not let themselves be construed as emotional states associated with a belief, we may speak of moods as pure emotional states with no cognitive accompaniment. To do so, however, will make it difficult to separate them from bodily sensations, because, like bodily sensations, they would then not be about anything. Feeling depressed would have to be construed like feeling hot. One might then try to differentiate between moods and bodily feelings by claiming that they are intentional, whereas bodily feelings are not. But it would be difficult to decide whether that is true, if for no other reason than that the most familiar definitions of "intentional" all apply only to statements and thus are not applicable to phenomena that, by definition, cannot be analyzed into a statement plus something else as, for instance, a feeling. Besides, it would be puzzling to say that moods are about something, but that in the absence of any concomitant cognitive states we are never able to answer questions about the sources or objects of the mood. That would also be false, for we find that persons who are depressed may be, although they need not be, very voluble about the sources of their depressions. They are eager to tell us what a wretched place the world is or how all its splendors have lost their luster. They are perfectly able to explain what their mood is about.

Of course, one could also deny that moods are emotional phenomena altogether and try to construe them as a species of belief. To do so is obviously incorrect. We are left with the conclusion that the traditional pattern of analysis, when applied to moods, generates serious problems. Heidegger, of course, wants to defend a much stronger thesis, that the traditional pattern of analysis does not apply to moods at all. The foregoing discussion has indicated what sorts of arguments one would need to pursue and develop in order to take that position.

Heidegger writes:

> Moods have always already disclosed being-in-the-world as a whole; it is they, to begin with, that make it possible for us to be directed toward something [137; original italics omitted].

And again, in the passage cited earlier:

> "Fearfulness," that is, being afraid as a dormant possibility of our disposed being-in-the-world, has already revealed the world as whence something like what is frightening can come towards us [141].

Things can frighten us because we are disposed, that is, because we are in certain moods. Moods are the necessary conditions for any beliefs (or facts) to affect us with fear or any other emotion. We can have intentional objects—of an emotion, for instance—only insofar as we are antecedently in a mood and thus, in some way to be explained in more detail, already acquainted with the world as a whole. Moods are most centrally cognitive phenomena, but not in any familiar sense of "cognitive."

This polemic against the traditional pattern of analysis springs from Heidegger's refusal to take "absolute, theoretical knowledge of the 'world' " as the yardstick with which to assess all cases of knowing [138]. (The single quotes ['world'] indicate that we are speaking of "world" in the sense of the totality of objectively existing entities [65].)

If one identified what moods disclose with whatever dasein, in this mood, knows theoretically "at the same time," one would completely mistake the phenomenal characteristics of *what* moods disclose and *how* they disclose [135].

We had occasion earlier to reflect about the connection between the assumption that all knowledge is objective knowledge and the attempt to apply the traditional pattern of analysis to all emotional phenomena. Emotional predicates cannot be predicates of things in themselves, because they are subject to change as the observer changes. Different observers, moreover, react with different emotions to the same objective facts. Different reactions are explained by differences in the make-up of the observers. If one assumes that the world is what it is, whether known or observed by us or not, emotional predicates are always predicates of observers and never of the world as it is in itself, unobserved. Emotional phenomena are therefore said to be "subjective." They are always a property of persons. But it is not an external property of persons. I do not see a man's rage; I only infer that he is angry. I do not actually see the emotion he feels. Emotions are not public and external properties of persons and have therefore been regarded as "inner" properties (this is a particular application of a more general argument suggested by Heidegger [60]). But these inner states do possess a reference to something on the outside that is established by a concomitant belief. For beliefs, at least true ones, although his having them is of course a fact about a subject, do not vary with changes in the observer. They are independent of any other facts about observers and for that reason are said to be "objective."

But because he refuses to construe the sense in which we are acquainted with the world and ourselves by virtue of our moods as cases of objective knowing or as states associated with objective knowing, Heidegger also wants no part of such a dual analysis of emotional phenomena:

> Being in a mood does not primarily refer to mental states; it is not an inner state that then mysteriously gets to the outside to rub off on things and persons [137].

If we insist on the distinction between what is "inner" and what is "outer," we shall confuse our understanding of what moods are [136]. For similar reasons we shall go astray if we do not stop asking, with respect to emotional phenomena, whether they are "objective" or "subjective." This distinction has no place in this domain. Its home is elsewhere.

Accordingly, also, although moods contain a reference to something other than themselves, this reference cannot be construed as "intentional" in any familiar sense of the term. Familiar criteria for intentionality—for instance, the criteria given by Brentano—employ the concept of truth in a traditional sense. Mental acts are intentional, Brentano tells us, insofar as a true description of the act does not entail the truth of its propositional element, if it has one, or the existence of the intentional object.[6] If it is true that I am afraid of a wolf, it may still be false that there is a wolf or, even if there is one, that the wolf is threatening me. It may be a stuffed wolf. The notion of "truth" involved in this definition is one of correspondence. A statement is true if it correctly mirrors a preexistent reality. But this sense of truth is rejected as inappropriate to a discussion of moods as soon as Heidegger refuses to measure the cognitive import of moods by the standards of "absolute, theoretical knowledge of the world." He therefore also rejects Brentano's (and Husserl's) concept of intentionality. As we shall see in the next section, he is working toward a concept of knowing that is not the apprehension of preexistent facts, but can be said to transform the world that it grasps. This is the idea of "knowing" for which we saw Husserl groping in Chapter 4.

Heidegger develops Husserl's meager suggestions on this point. Heidegger understands, as Husserl did not, that such a sense of knowledge can be defended only if we surrender the concept of intentionality as the means for explicating the reference of moods and other emotional phenomena to the world or objects in it. Hence Heidegger tells us, in a passage cited earlier that "Moods . . . make it possible in the first place that we should be directed toward something" [137]. Hence, also, *S & Z* makes no reference to intentionality in spite of it being presumably a work of phenomenological philosophy. Moods are in some way a presupposition for intentional analyses. They cannot themselves be analyzed in terms of the concept of intentionality.

These last remarks need to be clarified by a detailed discussion of the sense in which moods can be said to be instances of "knowing."

II

For his new concept of knowing, Heidegger uses the term "understanding," a technical use of that word which departs from its most familiar, ordinary uses in, at least, two major ways. Ordinarily, "understanding" refers to one mental act among many. Sometimes I understand something; sometimes I do not. There are many times, for instance when I am sleeping, when one would not say that I understand or do not understand. But in Heidegger's technical vocabulary, "understanding" refers to an existential concept. It thus refers to a feature of human beings that they have always, although not necessarily always actualized [143]. This claim, that it is a permanent feature of human beings that they have understanding, comes to this: Human beings perform many different actions and find themselves in many different states. But all of these are human states or human actions. They are human, insofar as they involve that feature of human beings that Heidegger calls "understanding." These states or acts are human acts only because they presuppose that one has understanding. What does this term "understanding" mean?

It is modeled on the familiar German expression *"sich auf etwas verstehen,"* for which "knowing how to————" is the English equivalent.

> Speaking ontically, we sometimes use the expression "to understand something" in the sense of "being capable of standing at the head of an enterprise," "being equal to a task," "being able to do something" [143].

But of course Heidegger is not speaking ontically here. He is not merely telling us that when he uses the term "understand (*verstehen*)," which is used in a variety of ways in German, he is always using it in one of these ways: in the sense of "knowing how to ————." *S & Z* is an ontological inquiry. The distinction between the traditional sense of theoretical knowing (*erkennen*) and knowing how to do something is not merely a distinction between different things known—here facts, there rules of a trade or a game—but a distinction between concepts. Heidegger claims, in the first place, that knowing how to ———— differs ontologically from theoretical knowing and therefore requires a separate term to distinguish it, in philosophical discourse, from theoretical knowing. Knowing how to ———— is knowing in a different sense of that term from knowing facts or laws of nature. Second, he regards it as an important feature of dasein that it knows or understands[7] itself in this new sense. The knowledge that dasein has of itself and the world is not exclusively to be explicated as a case of theoretical knowing. Dasein also knows itself in a sense of knowing which is like knowing how to ————. Indeed Heidegger thinks that this sort of knowing of oneself and the world is "prior" to theoretical knowing. Implicit in the discussion in the next two sections are some

suggestions about what might be meant by "prior" in this
context.

I shall explain, in the present section, the respects in which
knowing how to ——— may plausibly be regarded as repre-
senting a different sense of knowing from theoretical knowing. The next section is devoted to showing in what ways this
new sense of knowing is an important ontological feature of
dasein.

For theoretical knowing, objects of knowledge exist "objectively" in the meaning of that term discussed in the
preceding chapter. We found there that any item of theoretical knowledge is compatible with two mutually incompatible
descriptions of actions. There is no logical conflict between
an item of theoretical knowledge and a description of an
action, let alone an action itself. A person who does not act
on his theoretical knowledge may be morally blameworthy,
but he has not made a logical mistake.

The independence of action from theoretical knowledge is
important here because Heidegger insists that his second
sense of "knowing" does not admit this distinction between
theory and practice. In the sense of "knowing" that he is
recommending to us, to know is to do, and vice versa.

> "Practical" conduct is not "atheoretical" in the sense
> of not possessing sight; its difference from theoretical
> conduct does not consist merely in this: that we *act* in
> the one case and observe in the other and that acting, in
> order not to remain blind, applies theoretical knowledge.
> Quite the contrary. Observing is as essentially a kind of
> concern as acting possesses *its own* sight [69; see also
> 193].

We are urged to replace the traditional distinction between
theory and practice with a distinction between theoretical
knowing and what I shall call "nontheoretical knowing,"
which has its own cognitive access to the world, "sight

(*Sicht*),'' and is, at the same time, also a kind of acting. The term ''sight'' does not literally refer to visual perception but, more generally and vaguely, to cognitive acquaintance with the world. It is undoubtedly chosen for its role in various compounds. Our knowledge of the objects of use in the world around us (*''Umwelt''*) is called *''Umsicht''*; one element of explication is called *''Vorsicht.''* Understanding, knowing how to ———, ''constitutes what we call the *sight* of dasein'' [146]. Theoretical knowledge, on the other hand, is the product of what is itself an activity, observation, and thus occurs in a context of activity.

''Practical conduct . . . does not consist merely in this . . . that acting, in order not to remain blind, applies theoretical knowledge.'' Here Heidegger rejects a possible objection to the claim that knowing how to ——— is a different sense of ''knowing'' from theoretical knowing. For someone might well claim that we do not need to introduce a new sense of ''to know'' in order to explicate knowing how to perform actions. Actions presumably obey rules. Knowing how to do something is to know these rules and to apply them correctly. Knowing rules might well be construed as having theoretical knowledge. But the sentence quoted is meant to reject that analysis of knowing how to ———. As Heidegger does not argue against this explication, we need do no more here than mention it. Before we accept Heidegger's second meaning of ''knowing'' as genuine, we of course need to be shown that our knowing about objects of use cannot be analyzed in terms of theoretical knowledge of rules plus the requisite habits that enable us to apply the rules. I am inclined to think that one can show that this analysis would not be adequate, but the argument would undoubtedly be a very long one.[8] Here I shall simply assume that such an analysis could not be defended satisfactorily.

What are the features of this second meaning of ''knowing''? We must return to the section on objects of use for an answer:

. . . the less one merely gapes at the thing that is a hammer, the more actively one uses it . . . the more undisguisedly one encounters it as what it is, an object of use. Hammering itself discovers the specific way in which a hammer is "handy." . . . However closely one merely *looks at* things that "look to be" of a certain character, one cannot discover what is ready to hand. Looking at things only "theoretically," one fails to understand what it means to be ready to hand [69].

"Knowing" may be used dispositionally, as when we say of the sleeping man that he knows French, or it may be used occurrently. In this case we speak of an actual exercise of knowledge. Exercise of theoretical knowledge may consist of making statements, providing evidence for them or asking good questions. But none of these is necessary for occurrently knowing theoretically. I may exercise my theoretical knowledge by going over a mathematical proof in my mind or by reciting the list of presidents to myself subvocally. No action is necessarily involved in the exercise of theoretical knowledge (thinking as entertaining a statement or being disposed to utter it is not an action). By contrast, to exercise nontheoretical knowledge is to act. One really knows occurrently about hammers and hammering only when one is hammering and at no other time. We do not acquire the knowledge needed for manipulating tools effectively by looking at them or observing. Observation yields theoretical knowledge. The tool, as a tool, is known only by using it. We learn to act by acting and nontheoretical knowing is a species of acting.

Since nontheoretical knowing is exercised in action, whereas theoretical knowing, if occurrent, can at best cause one to act, there is obviously a much more intimate relationship between nontheoretical knowing and "making" than there is between theoretical knowledge and the products of activity. In either case, however, "making" means producing changes in the world. But whereas theoretical knowing apprehends the world as it is, in itself, nontheoretical knowing produces what can be described only as "changes" that do not seem to lend themselves readily to a causal analysis. The discussion of tools in Chapter 2 gives obvious examples. Gear exists only in a gear context. This context consists of other gear, materials, practices and goals. What makes the difference between a hammer and a stone (or a piece of metal) to which a stick is attached consists largely in the existence of a set of practices in which the stone on a stick is used to hit other objects in prescribed ways for prescribed purposes. Attaching the stick to the stone, a purely causal operation, does not make it into a hammer, but the development of relevant skills, of nontheoretical knowledge does. Someone might tie the stick to the stone just to while away the time or just as a dirty joke. Whether the product of his activity is nothing at all, or a hammer or a phallic symbol, depends on the uses we make of it, and that depends on nontheoretical knowing. Like theoretical knowledge, nontheoretical knowledge brings about changes. Unlike theoretical knowledge, it brings about changes that cannot as readily be described in causal terms. This statement, of course, is so far one more unsubstantiated claim. It needs to be argued in order to provide a full defense of Heidegger's new vocabulary.

These are some of Heidegger's reasons for claiming that knowing nontheoretically is knowing in a different sense from theoretical knowing. In the former sense, knowing occurrently, consists of an action and is productive of results; in the second sense, knowing is independent of actions and results. This difference brings with it important other differences. In theoretical knowing, one has a belief about something. The term "belief" is, of course, ambiguous. It refers both to the psychological state of having a belief and to the belief one has. Knowing theoretically involves a psychological state and a statement or a belief, besides the object to which the true belief conforms. What I know, the statement, is distinct from the object of knowledge. If nontheoretical knowing is, occurrently, to act, the distinction between what is known and what one's knowledge is about does not apply. What I know, for instance, is how to make a clean incision for an appendectomy. What is my knowledge about, except making a clean incision for an appendectomy? In the case of occurrent nontheoretical knowing, knowledge and the known are identical. "The more vigorously we lay hold of the thing that is a hammer . . . the more directly do we encounter it" [69]. What I know is the hammer, as I grasp it when using it, but that is also what my knowledge is about.

This idea has important implications. If nontheoretical knowing does not, in its occurrent sense, admit of the distinction between what is known and the object of knowledge, we cannot very well claim that I know, in occurrent nontheoretical knowing, that a statement is true. Knowing nontheoretically cannot be explicated as having a certain psychological relation to a statement. Nontheoretical knowing is nonpropositional. This does not mean that what someone knows is some linguistic entity other than a statement (or proposition). It means on the contrary that what we know nontheoretically is how to perform an action and not any linguistic entity at all. The analysis of nontheoretical knowing cannot make reference to or mention linguistic entities. Heidegger was certainly aware of this. One aspect of discourse, as we saw earlier, is "explication." In the case of theoretical knowing, explication takes the form of interpretative statements. I explain to myself and others what I know theoretically by making statements or by means of other uses of language. In the case of nontheoretical knowing I need not talk at all to explicate what I know.

> Our original practice of explication does not consist of a theoretical statement, but in circumspectly and carefully laying down or changing the tool "without wasting any words" [157].

Heidegger's statement is more than an empirical observation that a person may know (theoretically) that a certain hammer is unsuitable for a certain job without actually uttering a statement to that effect. We are being told that knowing that a tool is not suited for a certain job, certainly an ingredient in knowing how to use that tool, does not involve any statements at all, vocal or subvocal. To know this is to put down the hammer or to reach for a different one. Hence, when we talk about particular instances of nontheoretical knowing, we are not vocalizing statements that were previously formulated, although perhaps never uttered, but we are putting into words what was previously unformulated. For that reason also one cannot infer, from his inability to talk about the exercise of his skills, that an artisan is not skilled—for possessing the skills does not involve believing that statements are true. But theoretical knowledge does involve statements; hence the man who cannot tell us about the objects of which he claims to have theoretical knowledge defeats his claims by his inability to talk.

An essential element in the analysis of theoretical knowing is the requirement that what one claims to know be true. The terms of the analysis, moreover—that what we know are true statements—determines the outline of the concept of truth employed. Statements assert something; if what they assert exists as asserted, the statement is true. What we need, therefore, in order to establish a knowledge claim is another statement concerning the relation of what we claim to know to the object of that knowledge. A knowledge claim must be supported by other statements. We use the word "evidence" to refer to the statements required to show that any given statement is true. Theoretical knowing rests on evidence. Nontheoretical knowing, on the other hand, because it does not involve statements, requires no evidence; it is, as we shall say, "nonevidential."

I know that I have theoretical knowledge of something when I know that my evidence is adequate. But if evidence is not a concept relevant to nontheoretical knowing, how do I know that I know how to do something? One might think that

I get that sort of knowledge from observation of my performances and successes. If I continually succeed, I conclude that
I am capable in my field of endeavor. But this inference from
results is an item of theoretical knowledge. I believe that a
certain statement about my capabilities is true and my past
achievements are evidence for its truth. If this were the only
way in which I could have knowledge about my nontheoretical
knowing, I would never know, while the action is still going
on and the results incomplete, that I am doing something
correctly. But I know, of course, precisely to the extent that
I am skilled in some craft, that is, possess a certain kind of
nontheoretical knowledge, when I am acting correctly so as
to achieve the desired results and when I am not. If the
enterprise threatens to miscarry at any point, I can make
corrections right then and need not wait for a failure before
discovering that I acted incorrectly. But this knowing is not
theoretical; it is itself an essential element in my skill; it is
therefore an element in nontheoretical knowing and an instance of nontheoretical knowing. What is this nontheoretical
knowledge that I know how to do something?

Consider a good craftsman at work. He not only performs
successfully, but he does so with ease and elegance. As observers, we can tell that he knows what he is doing and that
he knows this. We can tell from the confident and unhesitat-
ing manner in which he works. Nontheoretically, he knows
that he is skillful and that he can do the job well. He may
very well say at the same time, and may say so sincerely, that
he is not sure that he is competent. He may not believe theoretically that he is skillful. But once he goes to work, these
theoretical doubts, however genuine, do not affect his nontheoretical knowing, his confidence in his capabilities.

If we do not refer to a man's theoretical knowledge of
himself when we say that he knows that he is skillful, we are
saying something about the particular way in which he ex-
ecutes a piece of work. Whenever one performs a set of actions, he does so in some particular way. We describe these

ways in different terms. Actions are executed, for instance, hurriedly and distractedly, or calmly and deliberately. That they are executed in a particular way tells the observer something about the doer's present state of mind or perhaps his character and temperament. In most cases, however, it does not tell him anything about the doer's idea of his own ability. But whenever someone acts, if the action involves some skill, one may always also ask whether it was performed with assurance or with hesitation. Because the exercise of one's skill is the exercise of one's nontheoretical knowledge, exercising the skill in a particular way, with assurance or with hesitation, means also that one always has a particular sense of one's capabilities, and that sense itself is an instance of nontheoretical knowing. Knowing nontheoretically what one can do is therefore an essential ingredient in knowing how to do something. In this respect, theoretical and nontheoretical knowing differ once again. For one may possess theoretical knowledge and not know it, but one cannot know nontheoretically without also knowing that he knows nontheoretically.[9]

We have just made in an abstract way a perfectly plain point about the exercise of skills: The confidence and ease with which a skilled craftsman acts is not the result of his competence but its precondition. He is able to perform a difficult feat precisely because he approaches the work confidently. Were he to falter and hesitate, he would fail. If his hand shakes, he will not be able to complete a particularly difficult task. The belief in one's own ability is to some extent self-fulfilling. One can do what one believes one can do and only that. This point will be of considerable importance in the further development of Heidegger's concept of understanding.

The notion of acting confidently needs to be developed in some detail. This cannot be done here. But one cautionary observation is needed. When we speak of someone acting with confidence, we are not merely talking about his feeling confident. I have noted that someone may act confidently while being seriously in doubt about his ability. Conversely, because he is so utterly incompetent someone may brashly attempt a task for which he is utterly unskilled. If he possessed any of the relevant skills at all, he would be more clearly aware of the difficulties and of his own lack of capabilities. If the traditional pattern of analysis applies anywhere, it certainly applies to feelings of this sort; they seem clearly to be responses to theoretical beliefs about oneself in this case false beliefs. Acting confidently, on the other hand, is not an item of theoretical knowledge nor is it a feeling caused by theoretical knowledge or belief. It is in fact much more like being in a certain mood. When I am depressed, for instance, I do whatever I do slowly and listlessly; when joyful, with energy and grace. The nervous movements and speech of the anxious person contrast with the calm rhythm of serenity. Moods are not so much characterized by specific activities as by a certain style of action. A man's confidence that he is competent in a certain skill or his doubts about his abilities thus are specific examples of what in *S & Z* are called "moods." This use of the term is more extensive, of course, than its everyday use. But the foregoing analysis has suggested (and we shall see this in more detail in the next section) that a man's sense of his ability in the narrow sphere of skills does not differ ontologically from that more general sense of one's capacities and abilities that are ordinarily called "moods." The difference between moods, in the ordinary sense of the term, and a sense of one's competence in a craft is merely a difference in the activities in which one feels competent. For this reason, one may well extend the term "mood" to apply to one's sense of what one can do, both in the specific sphere of skills and in the more general sphere that Heidegger designates "existence."

III

What Heidegger calls "understanding" is precisely what was discussed in the preceding section as "nontheoretical knowing." Knowing how to use tools and other objects of use differs from all the other sorts of understanding that we might list in a complete inventory of human capabilities only in that they have different areas of application. The difference is ontic, not ontological. Being human, it turns out, shows important analogies to having and exercising a particular craft. Heidegger's model for his explication of what it means to be a human being is man as maker of himself and of the world, and not, what it was for so long, man as knower of ephemeral facts and eternal verities.

This choice of model is not at all surprising. We saw in Chapter 4 that Heidegger, although first and foremost interested in the question about the meaning of being, took Husserl's question about subjectivity as the point of departure for his ontological reform because the requirements for a new ontological vocabulary could not be derived from the concept of being itself, which, after all, was itself in question. Husserl's question about subjectivity, in turn, came out of the transcendental tradition that went back at least to Kant. One of the sources of his interest in this transcendental motif came to light in our previous discussion of wisdom. Heidegger diagnosed what he judged to be the failures of Kant's and Husserl's transcendental philosophies as due to the lack of a suitable vocabulary. This vocabulary is being developed here. The project, therefore, is to develop senses of "knowing" in which "knowing" is "constitutive," that is, in some way also acts, and shapes the world and the men in it.

This new sense of "knowing" is introduced in the present discussion of "understanding." If we employ it, we are able to say and make sense when we say it that self-knowledge transforms. Men are as they understand themselves. Accordingly, Heidegger insists repeatedly that it is an essential trait of dasein that it understands itself. But "understanding" must be taken in the sense of "knowing how to" or "possessing a skill." Is Heidegger telling us that in order to be a human being one needs a skill, which all possess and exercise insofar as they are human beings, whereas there are other special skills belonging to specific trades and practices? Such a claim is certainly reminiscent of Husserl's alleged discovery of transcendental constitution as an activity that any human being performs and that is distinct from all the other sorts of activities performed by some humans but not by all. One may object to what seems to be Heidegger's view on similar grounds which he objected to Husserl's: To the question "What are you doing?" we get answers like "I am building a three-mast schooner in a bottle" or "I am writing a symphony," but never "I am being a human being," for that is not a distinct activity and thus there cannot be a distinct skill concerned just with being human.

This difficulty can be resolved if we remember that we are in the middle of an ontological inquiry. Heidegger is not laying claim to discoveries of facts; he is therefore also not claiming to have discovered a special skill that one must possess and exercise in order to qualify as a member of the human race. But if that is not what he means, his claim that understanding is a necessary feature of being human seems to mean no more than that human beings possess skills. It always makes sense to ask about a person's skills, although sometimes it may turn out that a particular individual has none. Now this is undoubtedly true, but it is not interesting. Once again it looks as if Heidegger's doctrine is either false or trivial.

Heidegger makes it quite clear that he does not claim to have discovered a special skill that one must exercise to qualify as a human being:

> We are not able to perform a specific activity by virtue of understanding—taking this term as an existential concept—but are able to be in the sense of "to exist." . . . Dasein is not something present on hand that, in addition, has the gift of being able to do something; it is fundamentally being possible [*Möglichsein*]. Dasein is always what it can be and the way in which it is, its possibility [143].

But, on the other hand, he draws a distinction here that is by no means transparent. Whereas, traditionally, human beings were thought to *have* possibilities, Heidegger wants us to think that they *are* their possibilities. One may get a very vague sense of the sort of distinction that is being suggested here, but we need to put it into words if we want to understand it.

Heidegger says more than once that to be human is "to be able to be" [*ibid.*], and he says it in a tone of voice that indicates that it is a controversial assertion. But no philosopher has ever denied that men could not exist unless it were physically and logically possible that they do exist. Unless it is possible for there to be human beings, none will exist. To be human thus is to be possible. Surely there are no controversies here, at least not as long as we insist that there are roughly only two classes of possibility—logical and physical possibility. But Heidegger denies this. When he speaks of human beings as being able to be, he wants to use a concept of possibility that is different from either logical or physical possibility. Both of these concepts of possibility are, in his jargon, "categories," that is, categoreal concepts that apply to things. Categories differ from "existentials," the categoreal concepts applicable to human beings [44]. Possibility as applied to human beings, as "existential," is possibility in a different sense from logical or physical possibility. One should not take this distinction between concepts of possibility (those that are applicable only to human beings and those that are applicable to things) to imply that the concepts of logical or physical possibility cannot apply to human beings. Heidegger merely claims that these two concepts of "possibility" do not exhaust what we mean when we talk about the possibilities of human beings.

The new sense of "possible" is introduced in this passage:

> Understanding is the being of such being-able-to . . . [dasein] as understanding of this sort "knows" how things stand with it, that is, with its being-able-to-be. This "knowledge" is not the outcome of a prior act of immanent self-perception [144].[10]

"Understanding is the being of such being-able-to." Understanding, we have been told, is an essential trait of human beings. When Heidegger comes to explicating what he means by "understanding," he tells us that it consists in "being-able-to," in having possibilities in a new sense of that term. Human beings have possibilities in this sense insofar as they understand, and understand insofar as they have these sorts of possibilities. Having possibilities in this sense of the term is therefore a necessary condition for being human. It is also coextensive with understanding. It is necessary not only to have such possibilities but also to know that one has them. "Dasein . . . 'knows' how things stand with it." This suggests one difference between this sense of "possibility," which is here being introduced, and the more familiar senses of logical and physical possibility. Knowing that something is logically or physically possible for a person is not a necessary condition for his actually having possibilities in these senses. It is perfectly intelligible to speak of finding out what one can do, either by attempting a task when one is unsure whether one can complete it or by means of tests to determine one's capacities. I do not know whether I have the ability to become a pilot. I would have to take standard tests to find out. I possess all kinds of possibilities that are unknown to me, possibilities whose existence is definitely independent of my knowing about them. The possibilities in the new sense of "possible" to be introduced by Heidegger are not independent of my knowing about them.

This implies that the sense of "knowing" used in connection with the new concept of "possibility" is not that of knowing objectively, for the possibilities known are not independent of one's knowing them. Heidegger suggests this by putting "knows" and "knowledge" in quotation marks in the passage just cited and by denying, once again, that one knows oneself and one's possibilities by "immanent self-perception," that is, by self-observation, introspection, reflection or any other variant of looking at one's self [see also 115]. This suggests that we have, in fact, already encountered the new meaning of "possible" in our earlier discussion of nontheoretical knowing. I said there that in the exercise of one's skill one not only knows how to perform a certain set of manipulative acts but also knows or believes that he can or cannot perform them. An integral part of the exercise of any skill is the sense of one's capabilities. I also pointed out that this "knowledge" of one's capabilities is necessary for possessing the capabilities. For one's knowing here is nontheoretical, it is exercised in activity. To believe oneself capable is to act in a certain way, with assurance and perhaps boldness, and to do so allows one to achieve results unattainable by a more cautious and hesitant hand. (The fact that possibilities in this sense are mine only if I know they are does not mean that I may not also have theoretical knowledge of them or that they may not come to light through some standard testing procedure.) In this context it is more natural to speak of a "sense" of what one can do than of "knowledge," for we saw that the sense of one's capabilities in any particular activity is itself a mood—or something very much like a mood, differing from one only in that it has more specific objects.

The conceptual recommendation, that we use "possibility" in a new sense in which philosophers have not used it so far, is pointless, however, unless we are given some cases that demand this new sense of the term, because they remain unintelligible without it. The section on understanding does not provide any such cases; we must wait for them until Heidegger begins to discuss "being unto death" [235 ff.].

One may think, offhand, that this is a very unpromising choice of an example, first, to illustrate a sense of "possible" that is one neither of physical nor of logical possibility and, second, to show that such a sense of that concept is needed. For dying, at some time, is not only possible, but inevitable. One's dying at any particular moment, now, tomorrow or next year, is possible, but one would certainly think that this is an objective possibility. It is both logically and physically possible that I should die at any moment and this is in no way dependent on my knowledge or beliefs. Even the masters of the occult, who had thought they had discovered life everlasting, died at last. Their belief that death was not possible for them did not suffice to make them immortal.

Heidegger, of course, admits all this. Of course, my dying at any particular moment is an objective possibility. It is an extremely well-supported empirical fact that men are mortal [257]. But all this leaves open the question whether my dying is a genuine possibility for me. The fact that I am not yet at the end of my life

has the character of something, *in relation to which* dasein *takes up a stance* [*sich verhält*] [250].

Being unto death, it [viz., dasein] is dying, as a matter of facticity [*faktisch*] and that steadily . . . when we say that dasein is dying, as a matter of facticity, we say at the same time that in its being unto death, dasein has decided in this way or in that [259].

"Taking up a stance" with respect to one's death involves choices of ways to act [265]. My dying is objectively possible and I may think about that. But "taking a stance" with respect to it involves more than thinking about it [261]. It involves specific, chosen modes of conduct (*Verhaltungen*).

Except for Heidegger's use of a somewhat informal and idiosyncratic vocabulary, someone will say, the point made here is perfectly familiar and does not require the introduction of new concepts. We must take a stand with respect to our death as we must take a stand with respect to all other facts. We act in the light of facts. That one must die is one of these. We act with respect to it by making wills and taking out life insurance. Such action is related to theoretical knowledge in logical and causal ways that are perfectly familiar. One infers from a set of factual propositions that, let us say, one's family will be destitute after one dies unless specific provisions are made for them, and from that one concludes that such provisions must be made. Then one makes them.

This is a very common way of talking about dying, and Heidegger recognizes it as one of the possible stands we can take when thinking about death. One can, on the one hand, think of one's dying as an event that is certain to happen, as certain as any empirical fact, although it is quite uncertain when it will happen. In the meantime we know about dying from seeing and hearing that others die, and we think of dying as something that happens, as an impersonal event that happens to unspecified persons [252]. We think of death that way and talk about it in these terms. Such talk is not to be construed as statements that are either true or false, but as one form of articulating our unformulated, preontological understanding of dying. There are other ways of articulating this understanding, various kinds of actions—for example, in conventional ways of dealing with someone's death, conventional funeral rites, eulogies and floral tributes. Indeed, as we saw in the preceding chapter, Heidegger wants us to think even of making statements, in many cases, as a kind of action. Our talk is of one piece with our everyday actions in response to someone's death. We engage in a specific set of practices when one takes dying as an impersonal event that will, sometime, happen to us.

Heidegger regards this explication of one's preontological understanding as mistaken. As symptoms of the mistake he points to what seem to him the manifestations of conflict in everyday understanding and dealings with death, namely, the acceptance of one's dying that one then denies altogether or, less radically, refuses to grasp fully.

Evasion and concealment of death so stubbornly reigns in the everyday that the "next of kin," in the domain of being-together-with, even try to persuade the "dying man" that he will escape death and will, shortly, return to the calm everyday world about which he cares. Such "caring for" is even meant to "console" the "dying man." It wants to return him to dasein by helping him to conceal completely his most own, absolute possibility to be [253].

We deny that one dies, even at times when it is inescapably obvious. Similarly, men, upon being told that death is imminent, promptly forget what they have been told and let that fact pass completely from their minds. In other cases they accept the fact that death will come, but their understanding of it remains superficial and perfunctory.

Death is made to look as a death in the family that occurs every day with others and that at worst only assures one more plainly that "one" is after all still "alive" [254].

Death is something that happens, usually to others, and thus does not concern me now; once it happens to me, it is too late for me to be concerned about anything. Dying need not be taken as something that is involved in my own life because it is not an ingredient of life.

On the other hand, I can think of dying as something I must do myself [240] that is, for me, not an objective happening like any other—just as, for instance, my actions, for which I must take responsibility, are to that extent different

for me from the same actions performed by anyone else.
(What that difference is, however, is precisely the issue here,
namely, what it is that makes me as subject different from
other subjects and from objects.) As such, dying is not an
event that will occur at some unspecified time but is "a phenomenon belonging to life" [246]. Being alive is then being
in the process of dying or "being-unto-death." Here again
what counts primarily is not how we think about dying, but
how we conduct ourselves in relation to our dying [250].
Being unto death is not

> an isolation that flees the world, but brings us, freed
> from illusions, into the resoluteness of "action." This
> resoluteness that runs ahead [*vorlaufen*] does not spring
> from excessive "idealistic" demands that soar above ex-
> istence and its possibilities, but springs from the sober
> understanding of the fundamental possibilities that da-
> sein possesses actually. With the sober dread that brings
> us face to face with one's being-able-to-be by oneself,
> joy, arrayed in strength, goes hand in hand. In it dasein
> is freed from the "accidents" of being entertained that
> busy curiosity provides for itself from the happenings
> around the world [310; see also 264, 268, 308].

This is rather vague. Heidegger admits that. But one gets a
sense of the man who faces dying squarely as one who is in
full possession of himself, who can by virtue of this act
wholeheartedly, held back neither by unrealistic projects, by
fear or weakness, nor by excessive subservience to conventional demands and standards. Such a person is a joyful and
strong individual; he needs no diversions to protect him from
despair and anxiety; clear-eyed, he sees the world for what
it is and accepts it.

This second set of practices and attitudes is correct—Heidegger uses the term "authentic (*eigentlich*)"[11]—as the
former was incorrect.

Although everybody would admit that it is very possible

to take very different courses of action in view of one's inescapable death, it is indeed doubtful whether the distinctions suggested by Heidegger are defensible. Being in flight from death may be what Heidegger says it is and take the form of all the conventional evasions noted by him. But it is equally possible that the flight may be from what at the same time one desires, and this flight may well end in suicide, as it does in the case of the hero of Rainer Maria Rilke's *Notebooks of Malte Laurids Brigge.* Heidegger will have to explain that being in love with death, overtly one's own, or covertly by being destructive of others, is as much *uneigentlich* as evading it. Accordingly he also needs to explain the difference between this love of death, which surely is not an instance of being genuinely self-possessed, and the brave and joyful facing of death that he recommends as *eigentlich.* One may then also wonder whether the distinction can be drawn at all. Perhaps, one might say, the joyful and yet fearful anticipation of death is more accurately described as a morbid preoccupation with what one fears precisely because one loves it. A serene view of dying, on the contrary, might then consist of that very heedless ignoring of dying that Heidegger regards as an evasion.

Furthermore, in Chapter 6 I shall suggest reasons why one may be very suspicious of Heidegger's identification of an *uneigentlich* understanding of dying with sharing in communal practices and opinions. It is not obvious that one cannot be fully involved in a community and still, or precisely by virtue of that, be genuinely and joyfully in possession of oneself.

One might also wonder whether Heidegger is right when he connects being self-possessed, courageous and joyful with a correct attitude toward dying. It might be suggested instead that this genuine self-possession flows not from having made one's peace with the future as it impinges on life now, but rather from an acceptance of a past that one carries around with one, ordinarily without even knowing it.

Finally, of course, one might not even believe that being self-possessed, courageous and joyful are the marks of a life well lived, as Heidegger certainly seems to believe. One might say instead that living in this spirit is a sign of utter self-deception about one's own abjectness in the eyes of God, about the terrible punishment awaiting a sinner and the unallayed suffering that is human life here on earth. Someone might accept Heidegger's descriptions of the alternative ways of being unto death but want to reverse the labels and call "*uneigentlich*" what Heidegger calls "*eigentlich*."

To the extent that Heidegger's rather complex discussion of being unto death is in need of clarification and justification, it cannot show that a new concept of possibility is necessary. But it will show the sort of case for which Heidegger regards this new concept to be necessary and will point toward cases, less complex but also less open to objection, that will render his recommendations sufficiently plausible for us to take them seriously.

A crucial feature of the various ways in which one may respond to the idea of one's dying is expressed by saying that they are different ways of "understanding" that one must die. Genuinely self-possessed being unto death

> turns out to be a possibility of understanding one's
> *most own,* ultimate ability to be. . . . It is important to
> notice that understanding does not mean primarily staring at a meaning but understanding oneself with a view
> to what one can do [263].

Not knowing, or knowing, how to die one's own way rather than in the ways conventionally stipulated is not knowing, or knowing, how to do something. One may give different reasons for one's inability to do something. Some inabilities are congenital. A congenital idiot cannot learn to do mathematics. Other inabilities are due to circumstance. There are many things one cannot do because one has never acquired the requisite skills. But then there are also cases where there is something one cannot do because one does not want to. These cases are different from those where one can, but does not, act in certain ways because one does not want to. Refraining from an action that one dislikes is different from being unable to execute it because one dislikes it so much.

Consider a much simpler example than Heidegger's: A student is by all indications intelligent and has the opportunities to learn and does in fact learn something; however, he does very badly. His attempts at learning are listless; he is easily discouraged, inattentive and impatient with the difficulties of the tasks imposed by the teacher. As a consequence he does not learn and it is therefore true that he cannot learn. Yet the teacher insists that he could learn if he would only try. The student does not believe him and to support his view points to his consistent failure. The controversy is peculiar. The student has facts to support him; he continues to fail. But his teacher points to the style of his performance; it is uninspired, the student is somehow reluctant and rebellious. The teacher is willing to admit that the student cannot learn until he changes his attitude. But he thinks that these attitudes are changeable. What is to be changed in such a case is the student's sense that he cannot learn, as evidenced by his half-hearted attempts, disinterestedness and perhaps outright resistance to learning. His failure, the teacher suggests, is not irreversible, as it would be if it resulted from physiological deficiencies but is the result of his own attitude or stance toward learning. His saying "I can't learn" is self-fulfilling.

The student lacks a sense that he can learn. Such a sense of what one can and cannot do, we have seen, is an ingredient in any skill; a sense that one cannot do something will prevent one from exercising or even acquiring a skill. This sense of one's ability is what Heidegger calls "being disposed"; it takes the form of a mood. Having possibilities in this sense involves being in a definite mood. Moods, occurrently, consist of specific styles of acting. It is therefore a mistake to think of moods simply as inner states that come over a person and

of which he is, as it were, the victim. Nor is it true, of course,
that being in a certain mood is voluntary in the sense in which,
say, wielding a tool is (for this reason Heidegger rightly
insists both that "moods come over us" [136] and that they
are forms of turning to or away from. . . . [135]). I do not
choose to hammer in a certain style quite in the same sense in
which I choose to hammer. I cannot shake a mood at will, but
I can stop hammering at will. I cannot suddenly act with
great confidence after a long period of diffidence. Yet if someone is going to change my mood—for example, by convincing
me that I am able to learn what before I despaired of learning, he can do so only if I acquiesce in his attempts and work
along. He may begin with simple tasks that I can manage
and thus, while teaching, convince me that I can learn.[12] But
that attempt cannot succeed unless I want it to and act on that.
Moods are not voluntary in the fullest sense of the word, but
they are not involuntary either. I give more or less active support to my moods. This is quite obvious in the case of the pupil
who insists that he "can't learn." We recognize the peculiar
flavor of his statement by replying, "You mean that you
don't want to learn." His "I can't" is an expression of aversion. Hence Heidegger says

Moods do not disclose by way of looking at . . . but as
turning to or as turning away from [135].

Insofar as moods are intimately involved in possibilities, in
the new sense, and they are of my own making, in the very
tenuous sense discussed, Heidegger refers to possibility in
the sense recommended by him as something that persons
"make possible (ermöglichen)" [264]. Depending on the
case, we do hold persons responsible for their moods. We do
so, for instance, with the student whose professed inability
to learn we think merely hides his aversion. We may be willing to concede that unless someone helped him he would not
be able to overcome this aversion, but we also think that he

has to work at it himself. Not all the help in the world will change his sense of deficiency unless he wants to accept the help. In this sense we are responsible for our possibilities, which are not objective ones, and in this sense we make possible what is possible, genuinely possible for us individually.

For these reasons, Heidegger speaks of one's reaction to the fact that one must die as "taking up a stance," as "deciding" and choosing specific modes of conduct. We can see now, however, that these are somewhat special senses of "deciding" and "choosing." As our examples showed, on the other hand, there is good reason for believing that they are genuine senses of "choosing" and "deciding." One's everyday stance toward death results from failure to learn to understand dying correctly, and that is due to an unwillingness to learn. Evidence for this is the conflict manifested by everyday understanding of dying, which acknowledges the facts and then, to varying extents, goes back on this recognition by denying outright that someone is dying or by giving the most superficial interpretation of it.

If many, most immediately and most of the time, do not know about death, we cannot take this to prove that being unto death does not "in general" belong to dasein, but only that dasein, most immediately and most of the time, being in flight *from* being unto death, conceals it from itself [251].

The conceptual difficulties inherent in this claim that human beings are at fault in their inability to deal with death as they should will be discussed in the final sections of this chapter. For the present we need only note that this is what Heidegger maintains.

Everyday being unto death is an example of not being able to do something due to some resistance to the activity in question and to learning it. Should one refuse to accept Heidegger's discussion of death, there surely are cases, which one would accept, where we speak of someone not really try-

ing to learn, or not really trying to act in certain ways, of
being undecided and in conflict about something; this manifests itself in vacillations and in acting against oneself. Heidegger's discussion of dying suggests such cases. Many people
profess to want to live in ways that one might well describe
—as Heidegger describes the man who is genuinely in possession of himself—as "self-possessed, courageous and joyful," but they fail to do so; they find themselves unable to
live in that way and, what is more, unable to learn. They seem
to come no closer to the realization of their goal. Also, we do
not see them make any serious efforts to approximate it, very
much as if they did not even know where and how to begin.
In such cases one may well want to say that they do not really
want to learn to live in this way, that they are afraid of a
way of life that they, on the other hand, profess with perfect
sincerity to desire.

But one may still be unsure whether this new concept of
possibility is really necessary. The reluctant student, one may
point out, has certain objective possibilities. We may ascertain
this by various tests. He has these possibilities whether or not
he knows the results of these tests. But possibilities are actualized only under specific conditions. Powder burns and
explodes, but only if it is not wet. Human possibilities are
actualized in actions, but only if one is not afraid, for instance, to perform these actions. Our student, perhaps due
to some painful experience early in life, has become afraid of
the activities required from him if he is to learn, say, Japanese
and hence is prevented from actualizing the possibility he
does possess.

Heidegger would certainly agree that fear, in some cases,
and dread, in others, prevent us from doing what we might
do were our feelings different. Dread of facing death by oneself is what prevents one from being genuinely self-possessed.
But, one suspects, Heidegger would demur at the analogy between the conditions necessary for an explosion and those
required for being genuinely self-possessed. Powder must be

dry: This is an objective fact as is the initial possibility of exploding. But the sense of my own ability that is needed in order to learn Japanese or to be genuinely self-possessed is not in that same sense an objective condition for the actualization of possibilities that are mine whether I know that I possess them or not. What I can or cannot do here depends on my feelings, belief and sense of myself and is thus not to be construed as an objective condition for the actualization of possibilities that are mine whether or not I know that I possess them.

The new sense of possibility, assuming that it can be defended successfully, seems to be relatively restricted in applicability. It belongs in certain but not all situations that arise in connection with human beings. It does not belong anywhere else. The concept would seem to be applicable in more limited range than the concepts of logical and physical possibility. This is not Heidegger's claim, however; he asserts much more radically that

> Possibility as an existential, however, is the most fundamental and ultimate positive ontological characteristic of dasein [144].

At least as regards human beings, the new sense of possibility is the most fundamental. The preceding arguments have not shown how one would make that claim acceptable. They have not even shown unequivocally that a new sense of possibility is needed at all. But they have suggested what sorts of cases, if discussed in certain perspectives, may yield such demonstrations.

When Heidegger insists that understanding what it means to be human is an essential feature of being human, he does not claim that a particular skill is needed for being human. On the other hand, he does go beyond saying that human beings have some skills. He points to the phenomena discussed in this section, saying that the range of possibilities that human beings have—most particularly the possibility of being or not being genuinely self-possessed—is up to them and depends on their understanding of themselves as human beings. This point will come out more clearly in the following sections, in which I shall also explain Heidegger's insistence that human beings, instead of merely having possibilities, *are* their possibilities.

IV

I began this chapter by explaining Heidegger's assertion that moods, although not cases of theoretical knowing, are cognitive. The intervening discussion of "understanding" as "knowing how to" and the sense of possibility required for the explication of this sense of knowing, have made it clear that in moods I know myself, because I know what I am capable of doing. Heidegger is therefore committed to a distinction between two different senses of "self-knowledge." There is no reason to assume that he wants to deny that there is objective knowledge of oneself or wants to urge us not to speak of self-knowledge in that sense of "knowledge." Reflection is a genuine phenomenon and one that may be explicated, moreover, as a special case of knowing objectively. From this viewpoint, I know myself by and large in the same way as another person does. He has an advantage over me insofar as he can more easily observe my outward appearance, posture, facial expressions and tone of voice. But if more ready access to this sort of information about me makes it easier for him than for me to get objective knowledge of me, I have direct access to my sensations, which he knows, if at all, only by inference. With respect to objective knowledge it seems true that my ways of finding out about myself are, in principle, the same as your ways of finding out about me.[13] Heidegger fully recognizes this. Very often we try to find out about ourselves as if we were strangers to ourselves [178].

But philosophers have also wanted to say that my acquaintance with myself is more intimate than my acquaintance with anyone else. Because they construed acquaintance exclusively on the model of objective knowing, they could not claim any conceptual difference between my knowledge of myself and my knowledge of others. The difference between my acquaintance with myself and with others thus had to be construed as being factual; this led them to say that I do not possess, as a matter of fact, the same wealth of data about others as I possess about myself. Yet this factual claim is open to argument; it seems that in some respects I have more data about others than I have about myself. In other respects I have fewer data about them. Hence traditional debates about "privileged access" have been very unsatisfactory. Given that all knowing is taken to be objective, we can either deny that I am more intimately acquainted with myself than with others —and that denial seems unwarranted—or we can distinguish self-knowledge from knowledge of others on the basis of dubious factual claims. The insistence that all knowing is objective leaves us with equally unattractive alternatives.

Here Heidegger's position is promising. He can recognize that when it comes to having objective knowledge of myself, sometimes I have a better vantage point than others, and sometimes others have a better vantage point than I. But this admission does not commit him to denying that I know myself very intimately in a way in which I know no one else. I know myself, nontheoretically: I know what I am capable of. Possessing such knowledge is necessary for being able to act. In Heidegger's conceptual scheme we therefore explicate our preanalytic notion of being privy to ourselves in ways in which no one else is, not in terms of objective knowledge of ourselves that only we ourselves have, but in terms of our having knowledge of ourselves that is necessary for us to be as we are. Another person's knowledge of my capacities is not necessary in order for me to possess them. My own knowledge is necessary. This makes sense, however, only if one takes this essential self-knowledge as nontheoretical knowledge of my capacities. Such knowing is an element of my skills. Because only I possess my skills it is, indeed, true that there is knowledge of myself that only I possess.

Our sense of being more intimately present to ourselves than to anyone else also finds expression in the traditional doctrine that one's knowledge of oneself is infallible. So close are we to ourselves that we cannot be mistaken about our inner states. This claim is refuted by a large body of everyday observations. Nothing seems more common than for persons to be quite mistaken about their beliefs and feelings, goals and motives. Here again, Heidegger's doctrines promise to provide some clarification of traditional quandaries; they do so by providing a considerably more complex account of the different sorts of self-knowledge than the conceptual scheme of traditional philosophers could yield.

Let us take a moment at this point to note that knowledge of pains and other bodily sensations is not at issue here. Whether one can be mistaken about one's sensations is a very different question from the one under discussion, which concerns knowledge of all those states that are not bodily states. In Heidegger's conceptual scheme these states are known in a different sense of "knowing" from that in which one knows that he has a pain. In traditional philosophy, which did not distinguish these two senses of knowing, it was easy to confuse knowledge of bodily states with knowledge of capacities and with moods. As a consequence the preanalytic insight that we are more intimately acquainted with ourselves than with any other person could take the form of the philosophical claim that one cannot be mistaken about one's pains and other bodily sensations. But as Wittgenstein has argued persuasively, it is a conceptual mistake to claim that one has infallible knowledge of anything. This once again leaves one in a quandary about the peculiar intimacy of one's knowledge of oneself, which the Heideggerian distinction seems capable of resolving. For if we avail ourselves of his suggestions we can show the sources of the claim of privileged access to bodily sensations and show that we need not claim infallibility for our acquaintance with our bodies in order to give an account of our sense of being privy to ourselves.

But to return to the main theme of our discussion:

It is possible to distinguish theoretical knowledge of oneself, which is clearly fallible, from nontheoretical knowledge of oneself. In the case of nontheoretical knowing of oneself, the question whether knowledge of oneself is true or false involves a very different sense of "true" and "false" than does the same question about theoretical knowledge of oneself. Nontheoretical self-knowledge, for example, moods, are essentially inarticulate, as we saw earlier. Moods, occurrently, consist in specific ways of performing activities. Moods do not necessarily always take the form of definite feelings. I can be depressed without feeling depressed; being depressed consists in a certain style of acting. Nor is it necessary to being in a mood that I formulate what my sense of myself is, or in what way I am performing my activities. It is indeed even possible that I am in a certain mood but claim to be in a very different one. As it does not involve statements, the sort of knowledge of myself that I have when in a certain mood is therefore neither true nor false in the most familiar sense of "true," in which only statements may be said to be true.

Even if we broaden our notion of truth in such a way that something, not necessarily a statement, is true as long as it somehow represents what something else is like—perhaps in the sense in which we call a portrait "a true likeness"— moods could not be said to be false. They could therefore not properly be called "true" either. For the moods by which we know ourselves are at the same time conditions for our possessing definite capabilities. The sense of knowing used here is one in which knowing and making are not distinct. In our moods we do not know those properties of ourselves that we possess whether we know it or not, but rather know ourselves so that we might be as we know ourselves. I made the same point earlier by saying that moods are "self-fulfilling." For this reason self-knowledge of this sort cannot be false by reference to facts about ourselves, for as we know ourselves, in our moods, so we are. The sort of acquaintance I have with myself in moods cannot be mistaken (and thus cannot be correct) in this sense,

> Because it is in principle impossible for it [viz. dasein] to take as true (disclosed) what, after all, it wants "to have there" as true [265].

The way one knows oneself, and the world, affects what one is and what the world is.

> Dasein is always what it can be and the way in which it is its possibilities [143]. Being by nature disposed, dasein has always gotten itself already into definite possibilities; as being able to be, which it *is,* it has let possibilities pass by . . . that means: Dasein is being possible delivered unto itself [144].

There is then a clear sense in which it is impossible to be mistaken about oneself, for one is capable only of what one believes oneself capable.

But on the other hand, we saw in the preceding section that Heidegger does want to distinguish between correct and incorrect knowledge of oneself (for reasons that I will discuss in more detail in the next section). The inapplicability of the traditional notions of truth and falsity to self-knowledge does not imply that no such distinction is applicable here. In order to get some impression of the sense that Heidegger wants to give to the terms "true" and "false," we must first develop in more detail the sense in which we may say that self-knowledge transforms ourselves and the world in which we live.

Once again we need to look at some of the examples provided in *S & Z*.

Heidegger chooses the term "care for (*Fürsorge*)" to designate that particular form of care (*Sorge*) that has to do with my relations to others. In this domain, different types of conduct are open to us. Caring for

> can, as it were, relieve the other of "care" and substitute for him or *take his place* in caring . . . in such caring the other may come to be dependent and dominated. . . . there is a contrasting possibility of caring for, in such a way as not to take the place of the other but rather to prepare his place for him in existential being-able-to-be, not in order to relieve him of "care" but rather . . . to help the other to be transparent to himself *in* his care and to be *free for* it [122].

I want to illustrate the contrast—which applies, as Heidegger draws it in its full generality, to the whole range of different human relations—by referring to different ways of teaching children. On the one hand, one may teach subjects that, by general consensus, the well-educated person knows; one may teach rules governing standard practices, both social and cultural, and rules of good manners as well as of scholarly activity and artistic work; and one may also present models to be imitated by the pupils. The task of the student is to acquire knowledge and skills that are considered the mark of the accomplished adult. In this pattern, the pupil comes to be "dependent and dominated," not by any individual, but by traditions.

On the other hand, one may place central emphasis on the child's productive activity in order "to help the other to be transparent to himself *in* his care and to be *free for* it." One begins by asking what is of interest to a child of a certain age and presents subjects to him in such a way that he will want to explore them further or to retrace by himself the discoveries made by others before him. What one cannot

interest him in he need not learn. We shall want him to reg-
ulate his conduct in the light of his own wishes and a just
consideration for the wishes of others. Rules of conduct and
of good manners are to be taken into account to the extent
that they do represent the demands of a society, but they
are to be tested by the wishes and reflections of the individual.
If we introduce him to art, we shall not present him with
factual narratives and rules of, say, perspective or the com-
patibilities and incompatibilities of color, but we shall teach
him "to see" and in the light of that skill to examine the rules
that painters and artists have formulated in the past.

These very different styles of teaching determine the range
of alternative actions from which the teacher can choose. When
transmission of knowledge essential for the genuinely educated
man is at the center of teaching, the teacher may strive to be
as learned as possible and to plan his teaching schedule me-
ticulously and follow it conscientiously. Or he may be satisfied
to know the bare essentials, to be only in vague control of
class procedure. He can teach rules of conduct and artistic
practice, in a way that calls for little thought, by demanding
that rules be learned by rote: Or he may try to show the application of rules to cases and, by giving them concrete application, make them more intelligible and learning them
more useful. In this context, no genuine alternatives are open
for the man who takes the attitude that he should put on the
pupil the burden of choosing for himself, as far as possible,
what he wants to learn, how he wants to learn it and what he
wants to make of the subjects and skills that are offered him.
Teaching set subjects and rules by carefully thought-out plans
and steady procedures are not a real possibility for the man
who sees his pupils as creatively molding themselves while
they rediscover what others have discovered before them.

These two different styles of education thus determine very
different sets of alternatives and what are genuine possibilities
for each. They determine different possibilities of action for
both teacher and student; they also determine different per-

sonality types. To teach in the one vein one must be steady, methodical, proof to boredom, possess the scholarly virtues of impartiality and of respect for details as well as for the systematic interrelationships of knowledge. Such a teacher, at his best, will make contact with, and a deep impression upon, his pupils through the extent of his knowledge and the integrity of his learning. His character will be communicated indirectly through his scholarly conduct. At his worst, such a teacher will be a pedant as a scholar and a sadist as a person. The other style of teaching requires a more volatile person, one who has imagination and values it. He does not strive for knowledge as much as for a fresh view of what others know. At best he will be remembered for his passion and for the way in which he used the subject he taught to establish a bond between himself and the pupil. If he fails, he will be intellectually irresponsible and substitute disingenuous personal interest in his student for shared excitement in a subject.

The differences between these two very different kinds of teaching, teachers and students do not result from opposing opinions on the aims and methods of education. The differences are more complex and less easily identified. We could certainly get representatives of the different types to agree on a wide range of statements about teaching and learning. We might get them to agree, for instance, that a knowledge of literature and the arts is indispensable for an educated person, that we must teach students respect for learning and a sense of integrity in scholarly and artistic pursuits, and that a student must actively participate in the teaching process if his education is to be efficient and beneficial to him. The application of these maxims will differ widely, however, because in the contexts of the different educational styles the terms used in the statements accepted by all have very different meanings. Although everyone would agree that knowledge of literature and the arts is something we must teach students, representatives of the different schools attach different meanings to "knowledge." A lively and well-informed acquaintance with the classics is considered knowledge by one man. Another will dismiss it as "rote learning" and "mere information" and recommend instead that a well-trained ear for poetry, a clear eye for painterly accomplishments and a fresh and self-assured judgment are what "knowledge" means in this context. The representative of the first school would describe this as self-willed ignorance, not knowledge. There would be corresponding disagreements about the proper ways of teaching respect for learning and scholarly integrity. One school would insist, for instance, on thorough training in bibliographical materials and methods and would reject as dangerous dilettantism the other school's insistence that the student must learn to feel the genuineness of novel and self-coherent, although perhaps controversial, readings of texts. An almost artistic sense of the wholeness of a scholarly vision is recommended for which the methodical and reliable use of scholarly materials and techniques are no more than the most pedestrian tool. Exclusive insistence on that is characterized as busywork. Equally radical would be the disagreement about what constitutes interest in a subject. One side tells us that attentive listening and thoughtful reading, and questions going beyond immediate tasks, are signs of a student's interest. The other side, however, demands that an interested student be passionate, even if misguided, in his pursuit of a subject and that he feel that his own person and growth are involved in it. This view is condemned by the opposition as misusing scholarship and teaching for the very different and unrelated purpose of dubious moral education.

In this way the controversy would develop in ways that are familiar because it is constantly being argued out in different guises and between more or less clear-cut replicas of these two extremes. The difference between them, in the end, is not a difference of opinions but a difference of types of persons. The disagreements are highly emotional. One side, in each of the controversies, accuses the other of being overemotional, irresponsible, anarchical; the other comes back with accusations of overintellectualism, emotional poverty and moral sterility. What seems rigorous and productive intellectual discipline to one appears as a sign of severe repression to the other. And the latter's emotional ebullience in turn seems a destructive lack of self-control to the former. The difference, to put it very schematically, concerns different attitudes toward the expression of feeling, as manifested, for example, in different attitudes toward the extent to which the student's emotional involvement in his education should be encouraged. Accordingly there is disagreement about the extent to which a student's wishes and interest should determine what he learns, about the extent to which education should develop his feelings for and about the arts and literature, and about the importance of a free flow of feelings between teacher and student. Dividing the two views of teaching, ultimately, is a difference in people's feeling about human emotions. One type is rather afraid of emotions; they seem to be in constant need of restraint and discipline. The other type fears lack of emotion in himself as well as lack of clear signs of emotion in others. He is always asking himself what he feels and what the feelings of others are. The difference between the two versions of education thus are ultimately anchored in that sense that people have of their ability that Heidegger identifies with moods and calls "being disposed." One man feels that he cannot control emotions adequately without effort; the other fears that emotions will be depleted or hidden unless fostered and expressed.

The example illustrates how moods determine how a person conducts himself in specific spheres, how they impose on him the range of alternatives within which he can make his choices, the language in which he talks about himself and what he does, the scale of values on which he judges his own and others' actions and bestows praise and blame; how they determine what he can do and thus what he is.

Heidegger introduces the term "design (*Entwurf*)" [14] to

refer to this feature of our understanding: It determines
what we can do and thus what choices are open to us and
what sorts of persons we actually are and what we value about
ourselves and others. Human beings "design the being of
dasein with a view to its final goals (*Worumwillen*)" [145].
"Design" is clearly used in a technical sense. It does not refer to a plan drawn up on paper or developed in thought.

> Designing has nothing to do with acting on a thought-
> out plan according to which dasein arranges its being
> [*ibid.*].

In what sense must we take this new term "design"?

> The characteristic of understanding that it is design means
> also that that with a view to which it designs itself, the
> possibilities, is not itself apprehended thematically. Such
> apprehending, on the contrary, deprives the designed of
> its character of being possible [*ibid.*].

What we design are our possibilities; what is designed in this
way is not apprehended thematically, that is, is not known
theoretically. We may not know what the possibilities are to
which we have limited ourselves. In fact, once we are clearly
aware of these limitations that we impose on ourselves, we
have already altered them or are on the way to altering them.
The student who has understood that his "I can't learn" is
an expression of aversion to learning Japanese is on the way
to overcoming his aversion. The scholar who abhors the apparently undisciplined romanticism of his rival educational
theorist is at least close to surrendering his own views once he
sees that their source is in his distrust of his own emotions.
Designing is not acting on a clearly formulated plan. Impos-
ing limitations on oneself by virtue of being disposed, as il-
lustrated in our previous examples, is not a conscious process.

It is something that happens to a person. It is also, as we saw earlier, something to which one is an accomplice.

Clearly the thesis that understanding is designing is distinct from the commonplace that people have opinions and act on them. In order to distinguish the two, Heidegger insists that moods are different from beliefs or opinions, although not wholly unlike them, and that a man is not explicitly aware of the design he imposes on himself. Contained in this thesis, as well as in the preceding examples about alternative views of teaching, on the contrary, is the view that a man's explicit theoretical beliefs and opinions, as one form of explication of his inarticulate understanding of himself, are to be regarded as one more form of acting out, different only in their medium from the other activities in which he acts out this fundamental understanding of himself, acts out his sense of his capabilities and the capabilities he actually possesses. This is not to say, of course, that truth is relative to the person. It suggests, though, that different persons offer different statements with respect to reality to see whether they fit it. It is one form of explicating one's understanding of oneself, of acting out one's sense of oneself, to offer certain statements instead of others to be measured by the standard of what is real.

V

In the preceding section I used examples of the ways in which an individual conceives of himself in a very particular role, that of a teacher, in order to illustrate and explain Heidegger's account of knowing oneself. This same discussion makes clear the more general sense of ''self-knowledge'' in which Heidegger asserts that a necessary condition for being human is to know what it is to be human.

In some manner and degree of explicitness, dasein understands itself in its being. It is peculiar to such entities that their own being is disclosed to them with and by virtue of their being. *Understanding of being is itself a characteristic of the being of dasein.* Dasein is ontically distinguished by *being* ontological.

Being ontological is not developing an ontology. If we therefore reserve the term "ontology" for explicit theoretical inquiry into the meaning of entities, then we must call "preontological" the sense in which human beings are ontological [12]. Being in a world pertains essentially to dasein. Hence the understanding of being, which dasein has, is understanding both of such things as "world" and of those entities that are accessible within the world [13].

"Dasein understands itself in its being" and this understanding is here explicitly called "ontological." There is no reason whatsoever to think that the term "understanding" is used in a different sense with "ontological" from the sense in which it is used in more specific contexts. Hence the ontological features of dasein are determined by being understood and acted out in the ways in which the student's ability to learn or a teacher's conception of what it means to be a good teacher are understood and acted out and thereby determined.

"Dasein is ontological" in that the way in which one conceives of being human affects one's most particular elaborations of special roles. What I say about myself and what I do are explications or articulations, in action, of my previously less articulate understanding of myself, which includes certainly my preontological understanding of myself as a human being. As a consequence the different possible articulations of specific roles—as, for example, different types of teaching, which are instances of "caring for (*Fürsorge*)"— may be called "genuinely self-possessed (*eigentlich*)" or "not genuinely self-possessed (*uneigentlich*)"; and that is because teaching, in one way or an opposite way, or in some indistinct middle way, is attendant on the more general orientation of the individual toward being human. It elaborates his more general stance toward being a human being and thus varies with whether or not he is, in general, an *eigentlich* human being.

Heidegger does not explain how we must conceive of the connection between a man's general stance and its particular articulation in the way in which he goes about his particular business. There are several questions here. One is general and concerns the sort of vocabulary needed in order to talk about these connections. How shall we put the connection between being, in general, fallen away from and, say, very specific uses of language and the corresponding views about language? It seems fairly clear that the connection can neither be thought of as causal nor purely logico-deductive. The vocabulary we need here must also enable us to differentiate between correct and incorrect linkages of a general ontological stance and alleged specific explications of them. Once we have this vocabulary and the criteria, we need to apply them to the examples Heidegger gives in *S & Z* and ask, for instance, whether he correctly connects the sort of "caring for" that dominates the other and renders him dependent with a not genuinely self-possessed attitude toward one's dying.

To round out his account of "being disposed" and "understanding," we must now examine in what sense Heidegger could possibly insist that our understanding of ourselves may be correct but also incorrect. We saw earlier that this distinction figures prominently in his lengthy examination of being unto death and is used in the discussion of language as well as in the discussion of what it means to be an object of use. The distinction is central to *S & Z* and applies not only to understanding that is put into words but also to the inarticulate understanding called "preontological." As terms like "meaning" and "understanding" are applied to linguistic and nonlinguistic entities alike, so are "correct" and "mistaken":

Everyday dasein draws the preontological explication
of its being from the mode of being closest to it, the
mode of being that belongs to the "They" [*Das Man*].
Ontological interpretation tends, at first, to follow that
line of explication. It understands dasein in terms of the
world and discovers dasein as an entity within the world.
. . . Once we have brought to light the positive phenomenon of everyday being-in-the-world we are in a position
to see why this state of being mistakes the ontological
explication of this mode of being. *It is being-in-the-world
itself, in its everyday mode of being, that most immediately mistakes and conceals itself* [130].

Human beings tend to construe themselves on the model of
things [15, 21, 56]. This does not mean, of course, that they
overlook the ontological distinctions between "person" and
"thing" entirely but that they misstate what that distinction
is; they tend to construe the distinction between "person"
and "thing" as if it were a distinction between two classes of
things [94, 117]. But the mistake is not merely an explicit
ontological one. It does not manifest itself merely in faulty
explications of preontological understanding. It also manifests itself in various forms of behavior that are examples of
an ontological feature of human beings that Heidegger calls
"falling away from (*Verfallen*)" [175 ff.]. But behavior is a
manifestation of preontological knowledge. When we speak
of preontological knowledge, we speak of our knowing how to
behave appropriately in varied situations, thereby distinguishing different kinds of entities and recognizing their essential
features. The behavior that is called "*Verfallen*" is a case of
preontological misunderstanding. Ontological misunderstandings have their root in such preontological mistakes. These
mistakes, however, are of a peculiar sort. Preontologically,
one is not simply mistaken; instead, one acts as if one did not
know how to use the correct distinctions. It is for this reason
that Heidegger speaks of human beings (*dasein*) mistaking

and concealing their own being from themselves. Human being misleads itself [115; see also 125, 184, 189, 216 ff.].

These views need to be explicated. One can most easily understand them if one knows the problems they are designed to solve. From the very beginning it has been clear that doing ontology presupposes that human beings have preontological knowledge. This knowledge has been characterized as knowing how to behave in certain appropriate ways in different situations. Possession of preontological knowledge is manifested in standard patterns of behavior. For preontological knowledge is not theoretical; it is in some ways like making or doing. But why should we dignify these patterns of behavior with the name "knowledge"? All organisms display typical patterns of behavior and therefore might be said to draw ontological distinctions: They attack their prey and avoid those that prey on them. But it would not ordinarily occur to us to ascribe to these organisms a certain kind of "knowledge" that enables them to behave differently in different situations. Instead, we ascribe the differences of behavior to different physiological structures. Animals act in these different ways because of the way in which they are constructed. When we come to speak of human beings, there seems to be no justification for talking any differently, for explaining the typical behavior patterns by referring to preontological knowledge, whereas the same phenomenon in animals was explained by referring to physiological mechanisms. Prefacing the term "knowledge" with such qualifiers as "nonverbal," "preconceptual" and "preontological" does not make any more plausible the claim that we act in certain ways by virtue of such knowledge. We might as well say that we digest in certain ways because we have preontological knowledge of how to digest. What has been said so far about preontological knowledge does not encourage the belief that we possess such knowledge.

We might therefore, in view of these considerations, surrender the initial assumption. But along with the assumption we would surrender the very familiar description of what philosophers do, particularly in ontology. Heidegger is by no means the only philosopher who claims that his discussions of what it means to be a human being, of what it means to know and to use language, puts into words what we have known all along without having put it into words. With the initial assumption we would surrender an additional familiar philosophical claim—that philosophy examines items of common knowledge and that, therefore, the lack of methodical and exhaustive examinations of facts, in other words, the lack of experiment and observation, in no way impairs the reliability of its results. What philosophers claim to formulate is their supposed preontological knowledge. If there is no such knowledge, there is nothing for them to reflect on and nothing to be put into words. The lack of observation and experiment, under these circumstances, would be a defect. Philosophy would be, at best, an adjunct to science; at worst, a bad imitation of it.

If, in general, we want to escape conclusions of this sort and if, more specifically, we want to defend Heidegger's enterprise in *S & Z*, we must show that there is a difference between human actions that depend on preontological knowledge and those goings on in the body that do not presuppose such knowledge. We must distinguish between behavior that evinces preontological understanding and behavior that does not. To do this requires more than a merely terminological move, for example, the refusal to call digesting an example of "behavior."

A person can be said to know that something is true only if it makes sense to ask whether he has knowledge, or merely believes, or perhaps is mistaken. Analogously, the difference between digesting and knowing how to conduct oneself as human beings do is a difference between activities concerning which it makes sense to speak of making mistakes and activities concerning which it does not. The operative term is "making": Malfunctions occur in digestion as well as in other

forms of activity, and we might want to call such malfunctions "mistakes." But we could not say that the person is
making a mistake when he has indigestion. In defense of the
claim that we have preontological knowledge, we must hold
therefore that we may be preontologically mistaken. This suggests why Heidegger claims that these are preontological mistakes. We can be genuinely said to "know" preontologically
only if we can also be said to be preontologically mistaken.

Heidegger's more specific problem is this: Human beings,
he argues, by necessity know what it means to be human. But
not all past philosophers recognized that. It would seem that
not every human being possesses the knowledge of being human, which,. Heidegger claims, they possess by necessity. There
would be no problem here if he could say that philosophers
have always known preontologically what it means to be human but have simply given mistaken ontological accounts of
that preontological knowledge. But given Heidegger's conception of languages as an explication, that is, a specification
and development in detail of preontological knowledge, ontological mistakes will be reflections of preontological error, at
least in those cases in which ontological mistakes consist of
using an inappropriate vocabulary. "Meanings grow into
words." What we understand before having said it does limit
the sorts of formulations we can give it. If our formulated
ontology is radically mistaken, as Heidegger thinks most traditional ontology is, supposedly the preontological knowledge
formulated in it is not immune to criticism either. (This raises
further difficulties for Heidegger, which I will discuss in
Chapter 6.) His views about dasein and language, coupled
with his polemic against the tradition, commit him to distinguishing correct from incorrect preontological knowledge.

But it seems very difficult, if not impossible, to insist on
that distinction. By virtue of one's preontological knowledge
one conducts oneself in ways that do not violate ontological
distinctions. But I, as a human being, must respect these ontological distinctions in ways that are peculiarly human. I

must not only respect the distinction between inanimate and animate entities—between, let us say, a fire hydrant and a dog—but I must also respect this distinction in ways appropriate to a human being rather than in the ways in which a dog would draw it. Any preontological knowledge therefore presupposes and, in its exercise, involves preontological knowledge of what it means to be a human being. My knowledge of ontological distinctions is knowledge of what it means to be a human being. But how can one be mistaken about this? It would seem perfectly obvious that human beings cannot be preontologically mistaken; to be so would be to act in ways not appropriate to human beings. But if I do not act in the ways in which a human being acts, I do not fulfill the necessary conditions for being one, and hence I am something other than a human being. If I am not a human being, my not acting like one cannot be called "being mistaken about my own being." It would seem that one cannot be mistaken preontologically about the sort of entity that one is.

We might want to say, however, that an occasional mistake, an occasional failure to act in the ways essential to being a human being, is compatible with being a human being. But can we make such mistakes? To be sure, one can *act as if* he were a rock or even a monkey, but in so doing he remains a human being, one who is pretending to be what he is not. I could pretend, for instance, that I am an animal and for this reason do not know the difference between being dressed or being naked. But in order to make a bona fide mistake, I would really have to be oblivious to the distinction and to all the scruples and desires that we connect with it. We may well doubt whether that is psychologically possible. Apparently, therefore, to be preontologically mistaken, even if not logically impossible, is psychologically impossible.

In the attempt to maintain that human beings are the sorts of creatures they are by virtue of their knowing what it means to be a human being—that is, of how one conducts oneself in order to be one—Heidegger seems to be caught in a dilemma:

If he maintains that preontological knowledge is knowledge in a genuine sense, he must also maintain that some human beings may be preontologically mistaken. This contention, we have seen, is either nonsensical or false. If he denies, on the other hand, that preontological knowledge is knowledge in a genuine sense, his entire enterprise (and that of many philosophers) turns out to be chimerical. There is no point in trying to put into words what we knew, nonconceptually, all along, if there is no such nonconceptual knowledge. It seems to follow that Heidegger's undertaking in *S & Z* is impossible.

Heidegger escapes this dilemma by arguing that it is neither nonsensical nor false to say that certain human beings are preontologically mistaken. In order to maintain this argument, he must maintain that it is logically possible to be mistaken in what it means to be a human being and yet be one and that it is actually possible to be mistaken in this way. These claims may be supported as follows.

There are different ways of doing something incorrectly. A person who is completely unskilled in some performance fails because he has no control over his activity and no control, when they are involved in the performance, over his tools and materials. To the extent that a skilled person fails in some performance because he is tired, sick or absent-minded, his failure may be of the same sort. But the person who possesses a certain skill may fail on purpose. He may be acting as if he did not know how to execute the particular performance. To fail because one acts as if one did not know how to succeed is possible only for the person who does know how to succeed because he is actually exercising his skill when he fails on purpose. He can act as if he did not know how to do what he does because he really does know how to do it. It would be silly for an unskilled person to pretend that he is merely acting as if he were unskilled when he bungles his job. What is more, we can tell that he is merely pretending to be acting as if he were unskilled from the way in which he fails. He has no control over the activity as does the person who is skilled and acts as if he were not. Acting as if one did not know how to perform some activity is a very special way of failing, one that presupposes that one is able to perform correctly and is making use of this ability to be able to perform incorrectly. If I do not know how to hammer, I sometimes hit my thumb and sometimes the nail. But I do not know beforehand which it will be. I am not able to "call the shots." If, on the other hand, I act as if I did not know how to hammer, I hit my thumb on purpose. I intend to do that and I know that I will succeed under normal circumstances. But to do so requires that I hold the hammer correctly and swing it correctly. In order to act as if I did not know how to hammer I must exercise my knowledge of how to hammer.

Heidegger claims that persons who are preontologically mistaken only act as if they did not know how to use the correct ontological distinctions. This claim implies that they do know how to use these distinctions correctly and that they are exercising that knowledge. There is therefore no logical contradiction in saying that a person is preontologically mistaken about what it means to be a person, as long as his mistake is merely a case of acting as if he did not know what the correct category distinctions are. Acting as if one did not know how to use the correct distinctions is not psychologically impossible. I can certainly act as if I did not know the difference between being clothed or being naked. It is possible therefore to be preontologically mistaken as long as one is acting "as if."

There is, of course, a striking disanalogy between the instances of acting "as if," which I have discussed, and the preontological mistakes Heidegger claims to have uncovered. The person who is acting as if he did not know how to hammer knows that he knows how to hammer both nontheoretically and theoretically, and he knows in both ways that he is merely pretending. But that is not true of the person who is preontologically mistaken. He has no theoretical knowledge of correct ontological distinctions, nor that he knows these distinctions, albeit only nontheoretically. Nor does he know theoretically that he is merely acting as if he did not know what he really does know, namely, how to be a human being. As Heidegger talks about preontological error, it involves self-deception. In everyday being unto death, dasein "being in flight from being unto death, conceals it from itself" [251] and

> *It is being-in-the-world itself, in its everyday mode of being, that most immediately mistakes and conceals itself* [130].

But there is no self-deception involved in my acting as if I did not know how to hammer.

But it seems clear from the examples I have given that knowing theoretically that one is acting as if one did not know how to do something is not a necessary condition in all cases of acting as if one did not know how to do a certain thing. The student who says that he is unable to learn is behaving in just such a way, with the result that his teacher accuses him of pretending. His performance does not ring true; therefore the reply to his "I can't learn Japanese" is "You don't really want to." That means "Your actions are merely a pretense that you cannot learn; you are merely acting as if you did not know what one does when one really learns."

More generally, if all knowing were theoretical, and thus verbal knowing, it would be impossible to deceive oneself, for that would imply that one both knows and does not know something in the same sense of "to know." The notion of self-deception can be analyzed only if we recognize more than one sense of "knowing." In this case one may say that a person, because he knows one thing in one sense, refuses to know it in another. The student refuses to know theoretically that he can learn and even that he is merely pretending not to be able to learn. This requires that he knows nontheoretically how to learn and nontheoretically that he does not want to. Moods, as Heidegger says, take the form of "turning to or away

from.'' But turning away from something as much as turning
toward something involves, in some sense, a recognition of
what I turn away from. To the extent that the student turns
away from learning Japanese, he knows what that would involve and how one would do it. To the extent that I try to
escape the isolation of a genuinely self-possessed life, I know
what it would be like to live in this way. In that sense, also,
moods are cognitive. They do not yield theoretical knowledge,
of course, but they respond to some acquaintance or awareness, some sense of what it would be like to engage in certain
practices or, more generally, to live in a certain way. For a
mood, as a sense of what one can do, goes with a skill about
which one has that sense. One cannot turn either from or toward a skill unless one possesses it to some degree. But once
one possesses it one may prefer not to use it any more, let
alone perfect it; one may instead act as if one did not possess
it and may do this so effectively that one could be entirely
mistaken in one's theoretical knowledge about oneself. In
many cases to act as if one did not know how to do something
is to deceive oneself.

These considerations suggest strongly that the preontological knowledge that a human being must possess is slowly acquired as one grows up into adulthood, for it consists of various ways of acting. As one acquires these ways of acting—as
the child, for instance, discovers that people die—one may
turn away in fear from something and act afterward as if
one knew nothing of it.

It is not clear whether Heidegger would agree with this.
Nor is it clear whether it is a requirement for being human
to have preontological knowledge of being human in a particular way, that is, know how to be human in very specific ways
or merely know one particular way in which men are human,
presumably the way one has acquired as a child from one's
fellows and others. I suspect that Heidegger would choose the
former of these alternatives. I am not sure that it is not the
latter that is closer to the truth.

VI

In this way human beings determine their possibilities and do so correctly or incorrectly in view of what, by virtue of their moods, they know genuine humanity to be. What human beings are actually like, therefore, depends on them insofar as they can explicate what it means to be human in correct and incorrect ways both preontologically, in their conduct, and in their explicit ontological statements. Hence human beings cannot be said to have only logical and physical possibilities. Human possibilities are more intimately connected with them than logical and physical possibilities, for humans determine in certain ways what their possibilities are going to be. For this reason Heidegger keeps insisting that being human is "being able to be."

Insofar as human beings determine what it means to be a human being, they cannot be said to have an essence in the traditional sense of that term. They cannot be said to have certain properties regardless of how they conduct themselves or what they think they are. For this reason we are told that "the essence of dasein is its existence"; in this statement the term "existence" is to be explicated in terms of understanding. By "existence" Heidegger means that feature of dasein that its own being-able-to-be is an issue for it, that is, that it determines in its moods what is possible and what is impossible for it [179]. On the other hand, the term "essence" is used to suggest that this self-determination has definite limits. Heidegger does not deny that human beings have something like what philosophers have called an "essence." But he speaks of human beings in such a way that the traditional distinction between essence and existence no longer applies to them. The concept of essence in the traditional sense applies to things that are present on hand. That traditional concept was formed on the model of present-on-hand entities. The outcome of the preceding discussion of the new meaning assigned to "existence," namely, "understanding and designing," is that it is neither simply correct nor incorrect to speak of the essence of human beings. We can think of ourselves and treat ourselves as if we were present-on-hand entities and thus as if we had essences in the old-fashioned sense. We can think of ourselves as if we had only logical and physical possibilities and thus were in no way implicated in our possibilities. We can deny that a student aids and abets his inability to learn or that death is anything but an event that happens to us in the same sense as the sun warming a stone is an event. To the extent that we do explicate ourselves in this way, this is how we are. But it would nevertheless be preontologically and ontologically a mistake to speak about the essence of human beings, for we would be acting only as if human beings could be said to have an essence.

On the other hand, whether this choice in the attenuated sense is ours or not is not up to us. We must exist, that is, design ourselves, and this includes recognizing or concealing from ourselves that this is what we must do. In one way or another we have to be. Rather than give a new meaning to the old word "essence" for this feature of being human, Heidegger speaks of dasein as "thrown (*geworfen*)" [134]. (Except in the phrase "The essence of Dasein is its existence.") *Geworfenheit* refers to the feature of human beings that they must determine in the ways discussed in this chapter what it means to be a human being.

In our moods we turn toward or away from something. Thus we turn away from having to be, that is, from determining what it means to be a human being by acting as if we were not thrown and implicated in making human beings be what they are. We act as if we did not know preontologically what, of course, Heidegger claims, we do know. Hence the terms "true" and "false" are applicable to our preontological knowledge, our understanding of ourselves and the world, but are applicable only after having been redefined. The terms used by Heidegger in his redefinition are "uncovering (*entdeckend*)" and "covering over (*verdeckend*)" [220–221]. If we understand and design ourselves and explicate this understanding in such a way as to recognize that "we are and have to be," that "the essence of dasein is its existence," then our understanding of ourselves is true, for it uncovers and brings out into the open, in action and in talk, what we felt dimly only in our moods. If, on the other hand, we act and talk as if human beings were present on hand, and not in any sense responsible for what it means to be a human being, we turn away from what we sense ourselves to be and thus cover up our knowledge of ourselves. Such preontological knowledge may be called "false."

> Primarily "true," that is, uncovering, is dasein. Truth in the second sense means . . . being uncovered. . . . that the entities within the world are uncovered is *due* to the world being disclosed. But being disclosed is a fundamental trait of dasein. . . . Being disclosed is constituted by being disposed, understanding and discourse and pertains equiprimordially to the world, to being-in and the self. . . . [220].

Truth, defined as the state of being uncovered thus is dependent on the concepts of understanding and existence explicated in this chapter. The option of knowing ourselves truly or falsely consists of opting for (1) patterns of actions that affirm our being thrown and our having to determine what it means to be human or (2) patterns of conduct in which that determination is denied. We may say, as some commentators have, that Heidegger's "criterion" of truth is "coherence," but we must add that it is not statements or utterances that are coherent with each other. The coherence is to be looked for in our actions. The boy who claims to be unable to learn fails in fact to learn because his attempts are listless and, to the observer, unconvincing. We say that, instead of being unable to learn, he does not want to learn because we find that he does not really try. His attempts to learn are self-defeating; there is a conflict between what he does and the manner in which he does it. The incoherence that is the model for Heidegger's concept of untrue knowledge of ourselves consists of the incoherence in our actions, symptomatic of a conflict between one's striving to learn and yet being afraid to do so.

In analogous ways, human beings are said to be afraid ordinarily of the full awareness that they determine what it means to be a human being. Their self-determination thus consists of turning away from their being thrown and having to determine what it means to be human by acting in ways that are explicable by ontological theories that ascribe fixed essences, in the traditional sense, to human beings.

When fallen away from . . . dasein turns away from itself. . . . what it thus shrinks back from . . . is dasein itself [185].

6

conclusion

In the preceding chapters I
have explicated several key concepts in *S & Z* and have indicated what sorts of arguments are needed to persuade one to
accept Heidegger's recommendations. These arguments and
therefore also the recommendations have considerable plausibility. They certainly deserve to be taken seriously. Yet Heidegger abandoned the entire enterprise after publishing only
two-thirds of the first half of *S & Z*. Twenty years later he
indicates his reasons for doing so. However appealing his conceptual recommendations for talking about ourselves, they
proved inadequate to the task for which they were intended,
namely, to enable us to ask questions about the meaning of
being.[1] *S & Z* may very well help us to speak more satisfyingly about being human; it fails to enhance our ability to
speak about being. In the first section of this chapter I shall
explain this failure.

The new fundamental ontology is intended to be a system;
it is not only meant to be unified but also is said to be complete

[232, 309–310]. I shall argue in the second section that we may well feel instructed by *S & Z* without accepting Heidegger's claim for completeness, since that claim is certainly and disastrously false. A large class of phenomena, those usually called "social," would be seriously misrepresented if we applied to them the vocabulary of *S & Z*.

I

The concepts recommended in *S & Z* are not offered to us one by one; we are not free to accept some and to reject others. We are urged to accept all of them together. The shortcomings of individual traditional concepts are not enough to justify our rejecting them, for they are merely symptoms of a general and pervasive failing of the traditional conceptual schemes. Demands for a proof of the existence of the external world, for instance, must not be rejected primarily because such proofs are impossible, or perhaps not even necessary, but because they are symptoms of

> Dasein having fallen away from itself and for that reason shifting its primary understanding of being so that to be [is understood as] being present on hand [206].

Similarly, traditional conceptions of truth—for instance, the correspondence of statements to facts—are objectionable not just because there are more adequate conceptions of truth but also because the traditional conception presupposes that to be is always to be present on hand, and it is this basic ontological assumption that is open to objection and serves to invalidate traditional conceptual schemes [225]. The polemic against Descartes takes a similar form. Descartes' conceptual scheme is not objectionable because it relegates all secondary qualities to the realm of illusion but because Descartes' move

is symptomatic of a more fundamental failure, that of equating being with being present on hand [96 ff.]. The different
conceptual recommendations have a common thrust; they are
all designed to replace an ontology in which to be is to be independent of human awareness, by an ontology in which at
least some entities—human beings—depend in part for what
they are on their awareness of themselves. For human beings,
as we saw earlier, are as they know themselves.

The preceding chapter provided a more precise explication
of that conception of what it means to be human by developing the requisite sense of "knowing" in the statement "Human beings are as they know themselves." The required sense
of knowledge was that of nontheoretical knowing, one example of which is the preontological knowledge of being human
that is a necessary condition for being human. Such preontological knowledge is mistaken if it involves self-deception in
the sense discussed; otherwise it is correct. Preontological
knowledge is different from ontological knowledge insofar as
it need not be formulated. Ontological knowledge, on the other
hand, consists of explicitly formulated conceptual schemes,
their explications and defenses.

But how is our explicitly formulated ontological understanding related to our preontological understanding, which
is primarily evinced in action? In many passages, Heidegger
suggests that ontological mistakes are the consequences of preontological mistakes; we can be certain that a man who is mistaken about conceptual matters is also mistaken in his preontological understanding of himself. Thus, in the passage cited
above, it is taken as an indication that traditional philosophers were fallen away from themselves, that they tended to
overlook those features of dasein for which Heidegger has
coined the term "being-in-the-world" [206]. But to be fallen
away from is to be preontologically mistaken in that one hides
from himself what it means to be human, inasmuch as he acts
as if he did not know how to conduct himself as a human being. In similar ways, Heidegger attributes other traditional

philosophical analyses of concepts that he regards as ontologically mistaken to our being fallen away from ourselves. Ontological mistakes are consequent upon preontological mistakes.

As he begins the discussion of the concept of a self, Heidegger rejects the notion that we know ourselves primarily by way of reflection, that is, theoretically. Human beings, not being present on hand, are not known and do not know themselves primarily in the ways in which present-on-hand entities are known. But why did philosophers talk of themselves as if they were present on hand? A simple mistake? Heidegger does not think so.

> Is it not possible that this type of ''self-giveness'' [viz., reflective knowledge of oneself] of dasein is a temptation for the existential analytic, more specifically one that arises from the being of dasein? . . . Is it not possible that the characteristic of dasein that it is always mine is the source of dasein's most immediately and most frequently *being not itself*? [115–116].

Philosophers misconstrue what it means to be a person or a self and how we have access to ourselves because they are preontologically mistaken, and that means that they deceive themselves on this score. Dasein tempts itself and more often than not succumbs to this temptation to regard itself as present on hand. Ontological mistakes spring from preontological mistakes.

> Everyday dasein draws the preontological explication of its being from the mode of being closest to it. . . . it understands dasein in terms of the world and discovers dasein as an entity within the world. . . . *It is being in the world itself . . . that most immediately mistakes and conceals itself* [130].

The same conclusion must be drawn from the earlier discussion of Heidegger's views on language. We saw in Chapter 3 that language is one form of what Heidegger calls "explication," but by no means the only one. We may also explicate our nonverbal and nontheoretical understanding in actions. Language is one medium in which we explicate, that is, develop and articulate what we understand in some way before explicating it. All language is to be thought of as a case of explication regardless of whether it consists primarily of sentences making assertions or of utterances that are more clearly instances of actions [161–162]. In the case under consideration, ontological statements must therefore be considered as explications of some sort of understanding that we have already and that is also explicated in the ways in which we act. This understanding, we know, is what Heidegger calls "preontological understanding." The ontology that a philosopher provides, the explications of everyday and of more specifically philosophical concepts, puts into words the understanding of the world that he has had all along. If his conceptual explications are radically mistaken, we may infer, in this view of language, that his unformulated, preontological view of the world is mistaken in corresponding ways, for to say that one's ontology explicates one's preontological understanding is to say that incompatible ontologies cannot be sincerely defended by men with the same preontological understanding. An ontological mistake always betrays a preontological mistake.

But Heidegger does not always insist on this. He seems to be of two minds about the connection between ontological and preontological understanding. There definitely are passages that seem to imply that we cannot draw inferences from a philosopher's ontological statements to his preontological understanding of himself and of the world. Toward the end of the discussion of guilt and conscience we are told:

An existentially ontologically [existential] adequate interpretation of conscience no more guarantees that one understands its summons existentially-ontically [exis-

tentiell] than that existence is necessarily impaired directly by an ontologically inadequate understanding of conscience [295].

Existential-ontological understanding is evinced in explicit ontological discussions of concepts.[2] Such understanding of the proper concepts that are needed to speak adequately of conscience is here said to be independent of one's possibly unformulated, day-to-day harkening to the voice of conscience. This certainly suggests that Heidegger is willing to say in some cases that a man's ontological understanding may vary without corresponding variations in his preontological understanding of himself and that, consequently, we cannot always infer from his ontological mistakes that he is preontologically mistaken. We find the same suggestion in many other passages.

Existentially-ontically, individuals have definite values and have often unstated beliefs about the goals to be pursued, the ways in which they are to be pursued and at what expense. But one's existential-ontological understanding, one's ontological formulations, are independent of one's preontological understanding of oneself precisely in this respect—that one can do ontology without making any recommendations about goals or about the ways in which they are to be pursued. Heidegger insists vigorously on this independence of ontology from his own preontological understanding of the world. . . .

[If we take *S & Z*]—in spite of all expressly given warnings not to take it as an ontic characterization of man—as a philosophy of life or an ethics which appraises "human life" . . . then everything will be thrown into confusion.[3]

In the same vein he insists that his talk about "falling away from" and "idle talk" must not be taken as "moralizing criticism" [167], or as a "negative value judgment" [175] or as a statement about "the corruption of human nature" [179].

Similar disclaimers can be found throughout *S & Z*. But Heidegger is recommending that we use certain ontological concepts. He insists at the same time that he is not recommending that we live in specific ways or hold certain values rather than others. Clearly, we can change our ontological scheme and our ontological convictions without altering conduct and beliefs that evince preontological knowledge and that Heidegger calls "existential-ontic." Here, then, ontological understanding does not depend on preontological understanding.

Heidegger's vacillations are not the result of carelessness. Both his views concerning the relation of ontological to preontological knowledge are fraught with serious difficulties. If we accept the first position, that ontological mistakes are always the consequence of preontological mistakes, then a philosopher cannot be correct in his ontological recommendations unless his preontological understanding is free of mistakes. This would imply that Heidegger's claim to have an ontological understanding of the world, superior to that of his great predecessors, is justified only to the extent that his preontological understanding of the world is correct. If he recommends his new vocabulary to us, he is at the same time telling us that he is more genuinely self-possessed than, say, Kant or Spinoza. Conversely, if we want to reject Heidegger's ontological recommendations in *S & Z,* we also impugn his preontological understanding and accuse him of deceiving himself about what it means to be a human being.

But these are not the only consequences of a close connection between preontological and ontological understanding that would incline one to say that a man's ontological understanding may vary independently of his preontological understanding of himself and the world. There are corresponding difficulties when one considers the readers of *S & Z*. Heidegger is recommending a vocabulary that, he claims, flies in the face of the philosophic tradition. The tradition, moreover, represents the way men understand themselves ordinarily. They espouse the ordinary concepts because they live their lives in corresponding ways, ways that Heidegger regards as not genuinely self-possessed. If ontological mistakes spring from preontological ones, no one can possibly accept the new vocabulary unless he also manages to change his way of life, the design he makes for himself in his preontological understanding of himself. Understanding Heidegger's recommendations and adopting them requires a bona fide conversion.

But *S & Z* scorns any appeal to the reader. We are given a series of new concepts with brief explications of their new uses. No attempt is made at all to be, in Kierkegaard's terminology, "edifying," to move the reader. Only very isolated attempts are made by means of developed arguments to shake the reader's confidence in the traditional ways of thinking. Urging us to "leap into the circle" [315], Heidegger writes as if adopting the new terminology were something one did or deliberately refrained from doing. But the sort of conversion needed although voluntary, is not deliberate. This was discussed in Chapter 5 in connection with the example of the student who cannot learn because, we think, he is afraid to learn and therefore does not really try. His refusal to try, we said, may be regarded as voluntary in a very tenuous sense because one may reassure him that learning is not as frightening as he makes it out to be; but one can reassure him only if he is ready to be reassured and is willing to work along. He aids his own failure. But he cannot reverse his failure simply by "an act of will." For that reason his failure cannot be called deliberate.

If ontological failure is the result of being not genuinely self-possessed, the conversion needed to enable us to understand and perhaps adopt the terminology of *S & Z* is of the same sort, for our commitment to our present vocabulary and way of life is the same sort of commitment as that of the student to his inability to learn. If Heidegger had consistently believed that ontological knowledge is merely an elaboration of preontological knowledge, he would have had to write a very different book. The task would have been the opposite of the one tackled in *S & Z* as we know it. Here Heidegger presents a series of novel concepts that we are urged to adopt so that we can understand ourselves more adequately, as a first step toward a better understanding of being. But a book that aims at changes in our entire way of life must first strive to avoid giving the author as an authority for adopting certain turns of speech or repeating particular doctrines. For adopting new ways of talking or new opinions is not only different from transforming oneself but also an obstacle to such a transformation. Accordingly, a book that aims at changing our way of life must avoid presenting the readers with explicit theses or doctrines. Heidegger, had that been his aim, would have had to use what Kierkegaard called "indirect communication," a form of writing that, if it does not actually change its readers, at least prevents them from avoiding such change in their persons by merely changing the way in which they talk. It seems quite clear that Heidegger was not attempting to write a book of this sort. (One might note that Heidegger scolds Kierkegaard for failing to see the existential-ontological problems of the existential-ontic subjects discussed by the latter [235]. But it is not so clear that Heidegger's distinction is a happy one, or that Kierkegaard did not know a great deal more about communicating existential-ontological concepts than Heidegger.) The passages in *S & Z* that assert an intimate connection between preontological and ontological knowledge are irreconcilable with the manner in which Heidegger actually wrote *S & Z*. Throughout *S & Z* we are urged to accept a vocabulary that we are at the same time told we could not possibly accept if it were presented as Heidegger presents it. If we do not adopt it, we shall not be genuinely self-possessed. If we do adopt it, we can only use it "without adopting an original understanding and relation (*Sein*) to whatever discourse is about" [168]. What Heidegger tells his readers in *S & Z* must of necessity remain for them an instance of "idle talk." They can only *act as if* the verbal formulae in *S & Z* contained genuine understanding.

We must conclude that given Heidegger's view of language and understanding his conceptual recommendations will be accepted only by those philosophers who are predisposed to accept them. And this predisposition will exist more because of the kinds of persons they are (i.e., more because of their sense of themselves and their preontological understanding of the world) than because of their agreement with explicit arguments. One might well say that that is merely making explicit what we have known all along. Philosophers are, in some ways, extremely rational. Their main business is to construct and assess rational arguments. Yet they remain as impervious to arguments supporting alien points of views as other men and avail themselves of locutions like "nonsensical" or "not philosophical" or "not clear" to relieve themselves of the necessity of seriously meeting arguments they dislike. Criteria that are used without any argument justifying their use—of what makes sense or does not, of what is clear or is not, of what is philosophical or is not—are employed to quarantine all those thinkers whose style they dislike too much to try to grasp their substance. Heidegger, one may say, merely explains why that is so; philosophers are not narrow-minded merely out of ill will or indolence. Consistently with his own views Heidegger might still recommend his vocabulary but not hope that it would be widely accepted.

But the vocabulary discussed is a part of what Heidegger calls "fundamental ontology." Heidegger undertakes this inquiry into fundamental ontology not for its own sake but in order to make it less difficult for us to ask what being means. He thinks, apparently, when he begins to write *S & Z*, that the conceptual recommendations in it are necessary conditions for learning to ask once again the question about being. But we now see that, on the contrary, these recommendations are at best useless for most men; at worst the recommendations only harden self-deception insofar as men may be persuaded that they have learned something when they begin to talk like Heidegger, whereas to do so in fact amounts only to idle talk without the sort of conversion needed, a conversion that *S & Z* in no way helps to bring about. *S & Z* as it is available to us is at best useless; at worst, a hindrance to asking what being means. It fails in its central task with all those philosophers who cannot use the new vocabulary without self-deception.

But suppose that there are philosophical readers of *S & Z* who need no conversion because they are already genuinely self-possessed, readers for whom Heidegger's new vocabulary simply provides the medium for talking about themselves that they have needed. For them, we might think, *S & Z* would reopen the question about being. But *S & Z* would not provide them with a preontological understanding of the issue for they have presumably had one all along. It would at best make it possible for them to understand the utterance "What is the meaning of being?" by providing a more coherent explication of the key terms than that provided in traditional philosophy. It is certainly misleading to claim that such philosophers do not understand the question about the meaning of being. The claim in the beginning of *S & Z*, that the question needs to be reopened, does not apply to them. All we can say about them is that they understand being but cannot talk about it.

For the majority of us, *S & Z* offers no help in reopening the question about being. For those philosophers, few if any, who need no conversion because they are genuinely self-possessed, Heidegger's vocabulary may enable them to talk about what, before, they understood but could not articulate. But perhaps such exceptional thinkers already have the vocabulary they need and *S & Z* is therefore of no use to them either. Heidegger certainly suggests in places that the genuinely self-possessed person can make his language say what he wants it to say.

It is extremely doubtful therefore that *S & Z* makes any contribution to reawakening our understanding of the question of what being means.

The source of this failure does not lie in the particular concepts recommended, but in the fact that concepts are recommended at all. It is not that Heidegger is mistaken in recommending these particular concepts. He is mistaken in trying to illuminate what it means to ask questions about being by recommending concepts. He realized this himself. Hence we are told that the third section of the first part of *S & Z*, a section that was to have been entitled "Time and Being," and the entire second part of *S & Z*

> were withheld from publication because thinking failed to express this turn [from "being and time" to "time and being"] adequately. It was impossible for it to succeed as long as it used the language of metaphysics.[4]

The critical characteristic of the language of metaphysics that Heidegger mentions repeatedly in different works is that it is "conceptual."[5] *S & Z* fails because it recommends concepts.

One might object to this diagnosis as follows: Suppose Heidegger had adjusted his views of language and understanding in such a way that the language evincing one's preontological understanding, the ordinary language we use everyday, was to be construed as an explication of one's understanding of oneself and thus dependent on one's preontological understanding, which is to be regarded as the sort of knowing that also transforms. Suppose, further, that technical uses of language are not construed as "explication." We might then be able to say that ontological knowledge for which a special, philosophical language is used is not dependent on preontological knowledge. The difficulties just outlined would then be avoided. This adjustment would not require us to surrender the entire project of making conceptual recommendations. It would require only some changes in the most important recommendations in *S & Z*. Indeed, we have seen that there are passages in which Heidegger talks as if he were inclined to make just these adjustments; these are the passages in which he seems to regard ontological knowledge as independent of preontological knowing.

But it is not without reason that Heidegger insists most

often that preontological and ontological understanding are intimately linked, because they are both cases of knowing and understanding in the new sense of each of these terms recommended in *S & Z*. For suppose ontological knowledge were not knowledge in a new sense of that term, but in the sense familiarly used in the tradition. In that case Heideggerian ontology not only would not be circular, but could not get started because there would be no problem for it to deal with. I showed in Chapter 1 that the initial questions of *S & Z* are extremely odd and that the claim that gives rise to them (that we do not know what being means) is quite unintelligible unless we assume that Heidegger is using terms with new meanings. More specifically, it turned out in subsequent chapters that unless "knowing" is not taken in the traditional sense of "theoretical knowing" and the relation of language to reality not in the corresponding sense (developed in the first sections of the chapter on language), there is no reason to believe that the traditional account of the concept of being as the most universal, indefinable and empty concept is at all objectionable. In that case there is no reason to think that the question concerning the meaning of being needs to be reawakened. The present attempt to salvage *S & Z* by taking "knowing" as it is ordinarily understood when applied to ontology thus only succeeds in showing that the entire enterprise is utterly unnecessary. It implies that the question about the meaning of being had best be left undisturbed in the records of philosophical speculation.

For this reason Heidegger insists that his ontology is circular, that one cannot even understand the initial questions unless one has some understanding of the concepts recommended. But this implies, as we saw, that reopening the question about being requires not only that we speak a new philosophical language but also that we become new men. *S & Z* is in no way designed to produce such a change in us. It therefore remained unfinished because it could not be finished. The means adopted, conceptual analysis and recommendations, were not compatible with the goal of reopening the question about being. Heidegger's later development shows which of the incompatible alternatives he chose to retain. He surrenders conceptual language so that he might change men, particularly his compatriots.

The surrender of conceptual language in the works after *S & Z* marks a sharp break between *S & Z* and Heidegger's later works. In *S & Z* Heidegger introduced new philosophical concepts. Such an introduction is unintelligible unless we are told to what these new concepts are to be applied. Therefore we must be given examples. A term like "*zuhanden* (ready to hand)" remains a mere word unless we are told that hammers, nails and other objects of use are to be called "*zuhanden*" in order to separate them from entities to which the question "What is it for?" does not apply. In a conceptual language it is essential that we provide cases exemplifying the use of the concepts recommended. Accordingly Heidegger provides examples for the various concepts he introduces. For this reason he later describes the language in *S & Z* as "the language of metaphysics," that is, a language that allows us to talk only about entities and the being of entities but not about being as such.[6] The conceptual language of *S & Z* forbids talk about anything but entities because we must be able to show to what the concepts apply, if what we say is to be understood. In the same vein, Heidegger insists in *S & Z* that "being is always the being of entities" [9]. This is consistent with saying that "being is not something like an entity" [4] because, as I showed in Chapter 1, talk about the being of entities is talk about them that is very different from the way we talk about them ontically. Talk about being and talk about entities are two different ways of talking about entities.

In the later works Heidegger does not want to talk of being in that sense. He therefore distinguishes talk about being as such from talk about the being of entities. The latter was his topic in *S & Z*; the former is the topic of subsequent works. The latter used conceptual language; the former cannot use such language. Examples are still used for illustrative purposes, as analogies or poetic metaphors. But we no longer name entities that exemplify a given philosophical concept:

> F: *I must confess that I cannot form a conception of all that you have said. . . .*
>
> G: *One cannot form a conception of it insofar as whatever we do have a conception of has already become an object for us that stands face to face with us in a horizon.*
>
> F: *In that case we cannot really describe what has been named?*
>
> G: *No. What has been named would have to be paraded before us in the guise of an object by any description.*
>
> F: *Nevertheless it may be named and having been named thought. . . .*
>
> G: *If thinking is no longer having conceptions . . .*[7]

An entirely new kind of thinking is employed here that requires for its expression a new kind of language. It is very hard to say what sort of language that new language is. The impulse one feels, in reading the later writings, of trying to clarify the dark sayings by giving concrete illustrations must obviously be resisted. One's feeling that one does not understand is not only justified but, as we learn, indispensable:

> G: *I am not sure that I understand anything of what you are saying now.*
>
> L: *I do not understand it either, if by "understand" you mean the capacity to have a conception of what is offered us in order to subordinate it to what is familiar and thereby to safeguard it.*[8]

The relation between *S & Z* and the later works is therefore extremely complex. The clearest difference is in the languages used. The differences between these two (or more?) languages is not limited to differences in the vocabularies. As we have seen, there is also a difference in the conception of the relation of each language to what it is used to talk about, and thus a difference also in the standards for the adequate uses of that language. There is some question, as we saw in Chapter 3, about the limits to which purely formal logical standards of consistency are applicable to *S & Z*. It must be clear that, as applied to later writings like *Gelassenheit,* we do not know at all what meaning to give to the term "consistency." The term has different meanings when applied to the writings of different periods. Its meaning in the most recent writings is extremely obscure. The discussion about the consistency of individual sentences in *S & Z* with those in the middle and later works begun by Karl Löwith[9] and continued by Walter Schulz[10] is therefore misconceived. One may note the changes in Heidegger's mode of utterance, but it is extremely difficult to say in what terms the works of different periods should be compared.

II

If we do not take *S & Z* as the correct approach to a new inquiry into the meaning of being, there is still much to be learned from it. Even if some of the suggestions for talking about human beings need to be modified, much remains that is valuable and, as I have tried to show, rather plausible. In other words, we may declare *S & Z* to be a failure as a work in ontology and then take it, as many readers have done, in spite of Heidegger's vigorous objections, as a work about what it means to be a human being. In that case we must examine Heidegger's further claim that *S & Z* provides a complete vocabulary for talking about being human—complete at least in outline. I want to show that this claim is false.[11]

Heidegger does not argue at length for this claim, but it is not difficult to see why he makes it. The thrust of his polemic against his predecessors is to discredit ontologies in which to be human is a particular form of being present on hand. This is the particular form in which Heidegger wants to argue that "human beings are not things" [47]. It is clear that although objects of science are not the only instances of entities present on hand, they are certainly central instances. To treat human beings as potential objects of scientific knowledge and nothing else is to treat them as being present on hand. Clearly implied in the polemics of *S & Z* is the claim that a scientific account of human beings is not ontologically adequate. Hence the elaborate development given the claim that a man does not know himself primarily as he knows scientific truths; he does not primarily know himself theoretically. One's primary access to oneself is nontheoretical.

But of course Heidegger does not want to deny that there is a large body of scientific knowledge of human beings. They can be the objects of scientific study; they can be known theoretically. But in order to show that a scientific account can never be a complete account of human beings it is not enough to distinguish the sense of "knowing" in which one may be said to know oneself most intimately from that other sense in which one may be said to know oneself when studying the human sciences. For the distinction between the two senses of knowing, together with all the other distinctions that go with it—as, for example, the distinction between two senses of "possibility"—is compatible, as far as we know, with a neurophysiological account of the two kinds of knowledge. The Heideggerian analysis of moods, for instance, is incompatible with the traditional causal-intentional pattern of analysis of emotional phenomena used by philosophers. But we may accept Heidegger's analysis and still expect to find at some future time a biochemical theory of moods and other emotional phenomena. We may accept the concept of language offered by Heidegger and still hope that we may one day show that language, in this new sense of the term, is the product of a very complicated electronic machine. We may use Heidegger's suggestions for new concepts to show that the explications that philosophers have given in ordinary language of terms like "know," "mood," and "language" were mistaken insofar as it was tacitly assumed that "know" must always be taken in the sense in which we use it when speaking about knowing facts or scientific laws. Heidegger, we may say, has shown that these familiar words have more than one meaning. If we recognize some of the new meanings suggested by him, we can escape traditional quandaries that have long filled the textbooks. But introducing these new concepts leaves open the possibility that, eventually, both the familiar and the new concepts will be replaced by, or assimilated to the technical jargon of the natural sciences concerned specifically with the human organism. Thus far, Heidegger has not demonstrated that human beings may not in the future be shown to be objectively existing entities like the paramecia under the microscope, or remote galaxies or any other object of science.

But that is his aim. Therefore, he is not content to propose a set of new concepts to be used in some contexts in which traditional concepts have thus far been used. He makes the further claim that the traditional concepts are in some sense "derived" from the new concepts he introduces. The concepts recommended by him are "more original." More specifically, theoretical knowing is said to be a "modification" of nontheoretical knowing. We can treat ourselves as complexes of objective facts only insofar as we already know ourselves nontheoretically in moods and repertories of activities.

> In theoretical knowing dasein gains a new *ontological stance* toward the world already discovered in dasein. . . . Theoretical knowing does not first *create* a "commercium" of the subject with a world nor is it *produced* by the effects of a world on a subject. Theoretical knowing is a mode of dasein that is founded on being-in-the-world [62; italics added].

At this point, Heidegger can make two different moves. He can argue that science is an activity of the same general type as the sort of knowing, which is also acting, that he calls "understanding." In that case we would speak of science not merely as a system of true statements, but as an activity producing true statements. The truth of the statements might then still be explicated as some sort of correspondence to facts, but the criteria for truth would specify the proper way for conducting scientific research. In this scheme we tell whether scientific statements are true by the methods by which they have been obtained and confirmed. Scientific knowing, in the scheme, is a case of designing, for in the course of scientific research the scientific community itself develops the standards for correct scientific practice. It therefore determines the criteria for scientific truth.[12]

Heidegger takes the alternative route, claiming that science consists primarily of "looking at," observing entities present on hand. Presumably this claim is not a denial that a scientist performs experiments and, in so doing, performs skilled activities and uses entities ready to hand. But it does deny that the truth of scientific statements depends on anything but the facts or objects to which they are to conform. Scientific truth does not depend on officially accepted practices. Hence Heidegger does recognize a correspondence theory of truth as a perfectly genuine, although derivative, concept of truth [225]. This means, roughly, that Heidegger accepts Husserl's account of science and scientific truth but claims that it provides us with only one sense of knowing and, more generally, only one limited account of our contact with the world—a world, moreover, that can only be understood if we understand that being human is to be, in the first place, in a world in the ways discussed earlier.

The concept of scientific knowing is thus to be derived from the concept of understanding oneself and the world. The former concept is related to the latter as a deficiency in "caring for," and having to do with the world. By abstaining from all production, handling, and so on, "caring for" adopts the

> only mode of being-in now available to it, namely, being only present at. . . . *On the basis* of this mode of being with respect to the world, which lets us encounter whatever we encounter within the world purely as *what it looks like* [εἶδος] . . . it is possible to look deliberately at what is encountered in this way [61].

Fully developed being-in is understanding, that is, knowing that is also doing, and is thus true or false in the ways described earlier. The derivative sense of being-in as merely looking-at, which yields truths therefore merely by correspondence, is attained by refraining from all producing, handling and other activity to the extent that they would affect the result of research. Heidegger is committed to deriving the traditional concepts used to describe scientific knowledge from the new concepts proposed by him in *S & Z,* because he subscribes to the Husserlian view that scientific knowledge is objective in the strong sense of being completely independent of all human knowers and thus also of their scientific practices.

There are only occasional references to this derivation in *S & Z* [e.g., 59 ff., 224 ff., 363]. Heidegger does not try to support by argument his claim that the concepts needed to describe science are derived from those recommended by him for describing human beings. Nor is he very explicit about the meaning of "derivation." But because it is a fundamental thesis of *S & Z* that to be human is to understand what that means, he is committed to saying that any human pattern of conduct is a modification of complete understanding of being human in the sense of that term discussed earlier. This understanding of oneself involves recognition or concealment of those features of dasein that the terms "understanding" and "being thrown" refer to: that in some way it is incumbent on human beings to shape the world in which they find themselves. "Understanding oneself as dasein" means that one either recognizes or conceals from oneself that the world does not exist objectively in just that way in which this is claimed by science on Husserl's view of science, that Heidegger adopts. It seems then that Heidegger must present as the product of human beings, who conceal from themselves what it means to be a human being, the scientific enterprise and the concepts that science demands for an account of itself. The tendency is therefore for Heidegger to develop the concepts that, he thinks, science calls for as instances of being fallen away from.

Thus the traditional concept of truth as some sort of correspondence of a statement to a fact seems to be derived by Heidegger from his proposed concept of truth, by presenting it as a consequence of men being fallen away from themselves. In his new vocabulary, "true" applies primarily to human beings and is intimately connected with dasein explicating its understanding of itself so as to hide it or reveal it (see the last part of Chapter 5). Fallen away from itself, dasein hides from itself also the genuine sense of truth and thus speaks of truth as a present-on-hand relationship between present-on-hand entities, statements and facts [219 ff.; particularly, 224]. Concepts familiar to philosophers are derived from those proposed by Heidegger, insofar as dasein fallen away from itself acts as if it did not understand the correct concepts. Analogous derivations are given in the discussion of "being fallen away from" [175–176], of fear as "dread that is fallen away from itself to the world" [189], as well as in the lengthy discussion of temporality that culminates in the section in which Aristotelian definitions of time, as well as the preontological understanding of time as clock time that it formulates, are presented as instances of being fallen away from [420 ff.].

The implicit suggestion that scientific pursuits are always symptomatic of preontological mistakes is extremely puzzling. Perhaps this is not what Heidegger means by "derivation."

But we need not discuss this in more detail here. It is clear that, as far as Heidegger is concerned, to regard dasein as ontologically different in important respects from the way in which it is presented in *S & Z* will never be correct. In order to bolster his claim he must insist that no new scientific knowledge can ever invalidate the ontological claims of *S & Z* because concepts applicable to science and supported by the results of science presuppose Heideggerian concepts, in the manner indicated or in some other way. Only beings who are as Heidegger describes dasein could gain and have scientific knowledge. For the same reason Heidegger claims completeness for his scheme. Possible challenges to his fundamental ontology, for instance, from the sciences, are ruled out once and for all because science and its concepts are derived from dasein's understanding of itself. This is true for all concepts applicable to entities of a different type than dasein, and thus, even if *S & Z* should turn out to be incomplete in that it has ignored a mode of being, it is at least complete in principle in that procedures are available for showing that this other mode of being is dependent on and derived from dasein and its concepts. The conceptual structure that is provided enables us to understand any element in human life. This is what Heidegger means by the completeness of *S & Z* [see 232 ff.].

It is not difficult but extremely important to show that Heidegger's account of being human is not complete. We must not only reject his claims in the opening passages of *S & Z* that he is opening up the question about being; we must also reject the lesser claim that his account of what it means to be human is complete.

If all ontological concepts not applicable to dasein are dependent on dasein's understanding of itself or on some distortion or modification of that understanding, then all concepts a philosopher might want to use are in specific ways tied to individual persons. For dasein, as Heidegger insists repeatedly, is "always mine (*je meines*)" [41]. Its own being is an issue for it, and that means, as Heidegger explains gradually, dasein has the option of being or not being genuinely self-possessed. It is in some sense up to me whether or not I am a genuine individual. Whether I am depends on my understanding of myself, specifically, on my understanding of my being unto death [297 ff.]. When using the concepts Heidegger recommends, we always use concepts applicable to specific individuals. In order to make clear what, say, "understanding" means, we must speak, as we did in the preceding chapters, about the conduct of individuals and about the sense they have about their own individual capabilities to master the world. If we talk about language, we talk about it as a form of, or as analogous to, action, and actions are always someone's actions. Dasein is capable of being fallen away from. If we want to explicate that, we must speak of someone's attempts to hide from himself that he must die and is, indeed, dying now. This involves his acting as if he did not know how to do something that he knows how to do. Genuinely self-possessed understanding of time is always someone's understanding of the future that he designs for himself and that it is his task to design for himself [323 ff.]. Whether this concept and understanding of temporality is modified by way of falling away from or in some other way, what is being modified is always someone's preontological understanding, a certain way of conducting oneself. An explication of genuinely self-possessed understanding of time, as well as of not genuinely self-possessed understanding of time, thus must always make reference to some individual, real or imaginary. Insofar as Heidegger's concepts are either concepts directly applicable to genuinely self-possessed dasein or modifications of such concepts, the complete analyses of these concepts must always contain a place for the names of individuals. We need not name any particular individual in our analysis of the concept. But when we actually use it, the analysis requires that we always apply it to a particular individual who is named or otherwise identifiable.

But there are a series of phenomena that Heidegger mentions and in part discusses in the course of his analyses, that do not meet that requirement. They are the sort of phenomena we call "social." They are intimately connected with the existence and activity of persons but not of any particular person. We need not refer to individuals in the analysis of these concepts or name individuals when we use them.

In the discussion of gear, Heidegger insists that there is no such thing as one item of gear. In order for gear to exist there must be a gear context. But what is the ontological type of gear contexts? Entities occurring in gear contexts are ready to hand. Gear contexts themselves, however, are not used, misused or abused; they are not in the place where they belong or out of place; they do not have the characteristic features of entities ready to hand. Therefore they must be of a different ontological type. It is clear that they are not merely present on hand. They must therefore be of the same ontological type as dasein, and that seems to be what Heidegger wants us to think [64, 75]. But clearly we cannot accept this.

Contained in a gear context are not only different things like tools, materials, workshops, means of transportation and products but also artisans and their skills. There are, besides, the standard practices in which artisans are skilled, which they need to learn before they gain recognition as artisans and by reference to whose standards their performances are judged. Involved in any gear context are standard techniques, practices, customs. Archaeologists, for instance, can date prehistoric Japanese pottery by its shape, size and ornamentation; the pottery in different regions of Japan today still displays unmistakable features. In a given place pottery will be made in a particular way and in no other way. The standard way of making pottery differs in different regions. These standard practices that belong to a given gear context could not belong to the same ontological type as dasein because standard practices are not always someone's. Dasein, Heidegger tells us, is always individuated (*je meines*). But that is not true of standard practices. Most characteristically, they are still standard practices when not practiced by anyone, as when one deplores the loss of certain established skills in a community because all the practitioners of a given craft are badly trained and incompetent.

This point can be strengthened and clarified by reflecting about the relation of practices to skills. A skill is always the skill of a person and is therefore of the ontological type of dasein. If one wants to determine whether someone possesses a skill he claims to possess, we have to assess his activities and products by the established standards. This judgment must be made by someone, but the validity of the judgment does not depend on the identity of the individual who does the judging as long as he is a qualified judge. Although judgments of course are always made by a person, the standards by which someone's actions are judged are not. Such standards are one element in what we call "practices."

Practices are, of course, related to skills. Existing practices are transformed and new practices introduced only by virtue of the skilled actions of individuals. But not all the actions of a craftsman are instances of a practice. A skilled craftsman may handle a given tool in a novel way. But if no one tries to do the same, the novel technique will remain his alone and not become a practice. It becomes a practice, on the other hand, precisely insofar as it becomes dissociated from his individual person and skill and becomes something everyone practices. Whether a new practice is adopted depends in part and to varying degrees in different situations on specific individuals. Where a new technique is developed, its adoption depends on the prestige and age of the craftsman developing it or on the prestige or age of others who now also use it. But this is true while the new technique still is not a full-fledged practice, but is in the process of becoming one. To the extent that the new technique has been adopted, it depends less and less on any particular individual's actions. If I follow what is now a standard technique, I cannot claim to contribute to its adoption or even to its preservation. Christmas cards will be sent even if I refuse to do so. To the extent that a particular activity is a genuine social practice, it is independent of individuals. It is partly dependent on individuals only insofar as it is a practice that is less than full-fledged and less than full-fledged either because it is beginning or ceasing to be so.

To the degree that the concepts of *S & Z* are always applicable to specific individuals, they cannot be used to give an adequate account of social practices. To the degree that such practices are elements in gear contexts, Heidegger is unable to give an adequate account of a gear context. This shows that, contrary to his claim, *S & Z* does not provide a complete conceptual scheme in principle.

But does Heidegger not provide just such an account of practices when he speaks of "They (*Das Man*)"? It would certainly seem so:

> In using public means of transportation, in using the communications media (newspapers), every one is like every other one. This being with one another dissolves one's own dasein into the mode of being of "the others," so that. . . . They establish their real tyranny. We enjoy and amuse ourselves, as they enjoy; we read, see and judge about literature and art as they see and judge [126–127].

And Heidegger describes the standard practices surrounding someone's death—funeral services, funerals and care of graves —as instances of the falling away from dasein into "They" [238–239]. Heidegger does refer to common practices but always as instances of the concept of They, that is, of dasein falling away from itself.

It seems very implausible that a craftsman making pottery in a traditional way or that a man, say Heidegger, riding the streetcar is thereby manifesting that he is preontologically mistaken. But being firmly committed to the thesis that all his concepts are either directly applicable to genuinely self-possessed dasein or are derivable from such concepts and that dasein is always mine, Heidegger cannot give an account of practices that are not in this way intimately tied to individuals. His attempt to identify practices with "They" ignores an important distinction. There is a clear-cut distinction between common practices in any area and the uses that any person makes of them. Given any action, requiring some skill, there are two distinct questions to be asked about it. First, does the action exemplify a social practice? If a man builds a model of the Empire State Building from subway tokens, his actions do not exemplify a common practice. If he makes copper and enamel earrings, his actions do exemplify such a common practice. In the latter case we ask our second question: Is his work purely imitative, humdrum and undistinguished or, on the contrary, does he make brilliant and original use of established techniques, employ familiar motifs in startling and interesting new ways and thus show new possibilities for other makers of copper and enamel earrings? No such questions are applicable to the man who builds the model of the Empire State Building. When Heidegger talks about the They and brings in common practices, he draws this second distinction. They always practice common skills and techniques in an uninspired and timidly conventional way. The genuinely self-possessed person, on the other hand, puts standard practices to his own uses and thus gives them new vitality. That is a good distinction but one that presupposes the earlier distinction between actions that do and those that do not exemplify standard social practices. But that distinction Heidegger has not drawn when he talks about the They. We have seen that he cannot draw it.

One might still try and defend *S & Z* against the charge of being seriously incomplete by pointing to Heidegger's discussion of being-with (*Mitsein*) and by arguing that here Heidegger definitely does recognize the existence of practices and, more generally, of social phenomena. We encounter others, we are told by Heidegger, in our everyday dealings with objects of use. The tools and what we produce with them are "tailor-made" to fit myself and others; their scale is a human scale and, more specifically, the scale of the people with whom I live. Where the average height differs significantly from ours, as, for example, in the Orient, the scale of automobiles, houses and streets is very different from ours. The scale of the environment, insofar as it is man-made, is determined not by any particular person's height but by the average height [117 ff.].

Heidegger speaks of social phenomena like average height. But what he says does not provide the vocabulary for a proper ontological account of such phenomena. The discussion of *Mitsein* fails to give an ontological account of genuinely social phenomena like human scale or average height. For *Mitsein* is always referable to individuals. Average height, on the other hand, is not any one person's height. To be sure there are individuals who are of average height. But whether they exist or not has no influence at all on what the average height happens to be. Only the existence of individuals who are not of average height influences that figure in any way. Although Heidegger refers to a phenomenon as human scale, he has no concepts to speak of it because he can speak only of those phenomena that are referable to individuals. Human scale and average height are not such phenomena; they do not refer to specifiable and nameable human individuals.

Similar problems arise elsewhere in *S & Z*. Dasein, we are told, determines by virtue of understanding and designing what it means to be human. But do I determine what it means for any human being to be human? If I determine it only for myself, I do not determine what it means to be human but only what it means to be myself. If I determine it also for others, it is false to say that they too determine what it means to be human, unless we determine this together. But how that will be done we shall not learn from a study of *S & Z*.

The failure of *S & Z* to provide a vocabulary appropriate

to social phenomena is particularly serious in the context of Heidegger's discussion of language. He wants to argue that any given language is a medium in which we formulate and articulate our preontological understanding. If we choose a different language, that is, a different medium, the same preontological understanding would find a very different articulation. No sharp distinction is to be drawn, therefore, between talking about a language and using it to talk about the world. Insofar as two languages differ, so will the worlds that we use them to talk about.

Neither Heidegger's text nor any explications of it have at all specified what is meant by "language" in this discussion. Are German and English different languages, or are Kant's and Heidegger's German philosophical vocabulary? Whatever Heidegger's intention on this point may have been, he also draws a distinction between genuinely and not genuinely self-possessed uses of any given language. The latter he calls "idle talk." What the world appears as to me depends on the language I speak, but it also depends on the sort of use I make of that language, for the use I make of it depends on my preontological understanding of myself; and depending on whether I am or am not genuinely self-possessed, I use language either to shield myself against understanding that I am dying or, on the contrary, to explicate that fact to myself. If I use language to deceive myself, I shall use it to suggest that I am not an individual confronting his death but a person like any other to whom death will happen at some unspecified time. The language I speak, then, is designed to reenforce my anonymity as "some person," and thus my language will be anonymous. I shall talk like the next fellow, using clichés, jargon and a generous number of the latest fad words. The genuinely self-possessed person, on the other hand, will use language to express himself as an individual and thus will use language in ways novel and peculiarly expressive of what he has to say [167 ff.]. But it is just as possible to use language vigorously and expressively without violating any of the rules of language as it is to use language in hackneyed ways. The difference between hackneyed and expressive uses of language does not coincide with the difference between correct and incorrect uses. Whenever someone speaks a language badly, we can say neither that he is making very expressive use of it nor that he is using conventional and hackneyed speech. There are two separate distinctions here where Heidegger draws only one.

We may try to defend him by pointing to his remark that words are ready to hand [161]. Words are comparable to tools in their ontological characteristics. Language thus is of the same ontological type as gear contexts. But that merely confirms what was said earlier. For the same difficulties that Heidegger encounters in connection with gear contexts he encounters in the discussion of language. He can speak of the different uses that persons make of language and of standard practices. But he can no more give an account of language as a rule-governed activity than he can of the different rule-governed activities that we call "social practices." One may say that it is merely a modification of dasein whether or not I use language in a genuinely self-possessed way, but the language I use is independent of me in the ways in which a social practice is. This is quite obvious if we think of English or German as instances of "language." It is also true, although perhaps less obviously so, in the case of a philosophical vocabulary. It is introduced by one man and thus is his, but to that extent it is a particular use of a language and not a language. It becomes a language only insofar as its rules are regarded as valid apart from the speech or writing of any particular person. Of language, in that sense, there is no account in *S & Z*, just as there is no account of social practices.[13]

Heidegger's blindness to the difference between social phenomena and the attributes and acts of individuals had disastrous consequences in the years following the publication of *S & Z*. His political conduct in 1933 has been both widely attacked and defended. The details of his position are still being debated, but the outlines are clear. Available documents indicate clearly that Heidegger was in sympathy with, and gave active support to, the new Nazi regime.[14] Little is known, of course, about his personal motives—for instance, his motives in taking over the *Rektorat* of Freiburg University at this crucial time. But his personal motives are Heidegger's concern, not ours. What does concern us is the connection between *S & Z* and his eager adoption of the slogans of the Third Reich.

It is often alleged that the insistence on being "resolute" in *S & Z* leads directly to Heidegger's political stand. The authentic human being is resolute. He chooses, it is said, but no criteria are provided for distinguishing correct from incorrect choice. A choice is justified by having been made. Thus choosing to join the National Socialist party would justify itself as would any other choice.[15] But this explanation is a gross misreading of *S & Z*. It is by no means true that any choice is regarded as genuinely self-possessed. Heidegger's term *"entschlossen* (resolute)*"* is a technical term. To be resolute is to be open to being, is to be "in the truth"; hence only those choices that are genuinely self-possessed, in which we do not act as if we did not know the correct category distinctions, are to be regarded as resolute choices [196–197]. There is, then, a criterion for action implied in Heidegger's ontological vocabulary. Actions cannot be acceptable as long as they involve self-deception about the true nature of being human. It is by no means true that Heidegger would applaud any choice as long as it has been made vigorously.

It is true, however, that the only characteristic of actions that Heidegger recommends is that they are chosen by a person who does not act in this way in order to deceive himself about what it means to be human. For Heidegger, to be human means that one may deceive oneself into thinking that there are impersonal truths that determine what actions are to be done or that there is a divine judge who discriminates good from bad for us. But all such appeals to objective standards are being rejected. The good choice is the one that is made in full awareness of this lack of objective and impersonal guidance of our actions. Fallen away from himself, man conducts himself according to socially imposed tasks and fulfills them in order to fulfill generally accepted standards [268]. There is no such impersonal guidance and justification for genuinely self-possessed choices. Properly understood, conscience is not the voice of God or of the introjected authority of parents [275] but the voice of myself [276]. In harkening to this voice and accepting that I am "my own, thrown ground" [284] I become truly myself [322]. Whatever the technical details, the stress of Heidegger as a moralist is on moral self-reliance and a bold acceptance of one's own choices to the extent that one can assure oneself that they are not self-delusive or self-destructive or evasions of painful truths about oneself.

One may well doubt whether this is an adequate discussion of morals. Because Heidegger—not quite consistently, as we have seen—denies being a moralist at all, we may leave this question aside. But the tenor of his remarks about conduct surely would lead us to expect that his political sympathies would incline him toward an anarchism like that of Henry David Thoreau, who proclaims, "That government is best which governs least." Where all authority is suspect and feared as a temptation for the individual to give over his responsibility for choosing genuine self-possession, one is not surprised to read that

> Resoluteness constitutes the *fidelity* of existence to its own self. As resoluteness which is ready for *dread*, fidelity is at the same time respect for the only authority that existing freely can have [391].

Yet four years after *S & Z* appeared, we find Heidegger taking up what seems to be a diametrically opposed position.

Instead of supporting the widest possible scope for the movement and choices of the individual, he supports the restrictive
Hitler regime. Instead of vigorously defending traditional
freedoms, he has this to say in his inaugural address as *Rektor*
of Freiburg University:

> The highly touted "academic freedom" is being ban-
> ished from the German university; being merely negative,
> this freedom was spurious. It meant indifference, arbi-
> trariness of goals and inclinations, actions without re-
> straint.[16]

The argument is astonishing. Heidegger ignores altogether
the difference between the personal attitudes necessary to give
full expression to the possibilities inherent in certain institutions and those institutions themselves. Even if we wanted
to say that being fully free involves personal attitudes and
the sort of conduct, more specifically, that Heidegger labels
"being genuinely in possession of oneself," certain institu-
tional arrangements are certainly necessary if we are to be
considered free. One can perfectly well be genuinely self-
possessed in a concentration camp, but one cannot be free
there. Unless academic freedom is in some sense guaranteed,
all the integrity in the world will not be enough to permit a
scholar to follow his interests. If certain pursuits will land
him in jail, his choice is between not pursuing his interests in
jail or not pursuing them at home. To choose the one may be
more admirable and genuinely self-possessed than the other,
but neither can be regarded as an exercise of freedom.

Heidegger's argument is not surprising, however, in the
light of the difficulties we examined before. We found that
he is unable to distinguish between the practices constitutive
of a gear context and the uses individuals make of them or
between the standard linguistic practices of a community as
formulated in dictionaries and grammar books and the uses
that an individual makes of them. Now we find that he fails
to distinguish between the political practices of a people as

expressed in their legislation and constitutional guarantees and the use individuals make of those practices. Unfortunately, one no longer needs to argue that this distinction is indispensable to any complete account of what it means to be a human being. The absence of this distinction characterizes Heidegger's entire inaugural address. The stress is on the "resoluteness" of the members of Freiburg University as well as of the German people as a whole. Nothing reveals more strikingly Heidegger's blindness to the peculiar features of social phenomena than his attempt to speak of an entire nation as if it were one individual. His hope clearly was that the coming to power of the National Socialist regime represented a sort of collective conversion similar to the one he thought any individual would need in order to turn from being fallen away from himself to being genuinely self-possessed. Anarchism, as a political position to be espoused by genuinely self-possessed individuals, is crudely collectivized into the anarchism of a whole people, which now recognizes no authority except its own "choices." It took Heidegger some time to see, apparently, that such a collective anarchism is most aptly called "totalitarianism." This not only shows lack of political judgment; it also exhibits a closely related philosophical failure—the failure to provide the vocabulary in which to express the distinction between individuals and their lives and the community to which they belong.

The conclusion is inescapable that the conceptual vocabulary of S & Z is incomplete. This does not force us to reject all of S & Z. But it does force us to reject Heidegger's claim that the distinctions that he introduces in his new vocabulary may never be restated in the vocabularies of more fully developed sciences. This claim, we saw, rested in part on the insistence that dasein is always something possessed by a person. We may well want to retain that view but reject the further claim that all the concepts needed for talking about the world are to be taken as forms of human preontological understanding of oneself or as modifications of that under-standing. The preceding arguments suggest strongly that Heidegger's claims about the "modification" and "deriva-tion" of concepts are to be rejected. (This might incline us, but would not force us, to reject the Husserlian account of science and scientific knowledge, which Heidegger had re-tained, thus claiming that there are either no entities, or very few, that are known theoretically or are properly said to be present on hand. Instead we would construe science and sci-entific knowing as versions of understanding. This could be done satisfactorily, of course, only if we were able to do what the Heideggerian vocabulary now does not permit: to distin-guish between talk about individuals and their understanding of themselves and talk about social phenomena and our under-standing of them.)

The suggestion that Heidegger's claims about "modifica-tion" and "derivation" of concepts are to be rejected is further supported by the fact that this part of Heidegger's scheme is more scantily developed than most others and is the one that we can relinquish with least damage to the system of concepts presented in $S \& Z$. The account of being human would remain essentially intact although we would have to recognize its incompleteness. $S \& Z$ does not provide the foundations for a philosophy of science or for social and political philosophy. It does not even provide the outline for a complete philosophy of language.

It is also clear, of course, that aside from its failure to lead to a reopening of the question about the meaning of being, $S \& Z$ fails not only because it does not forestall any possible future replacement of its vocabulary by one developed by neurophysiologists or biochemists but also precisely because it tries to rule out such a replacement. Many points that are unclear in the discussion of gear and gear contexts, of lan-guage and language use and, generally, of the individual's contacts with a community spring from Heidegger's claim to completeness, which forces him to neglect specifically social

254 Martin Heidegger on Being Human

phenomena and to confuse them with the peculiar uses individuals make of them.

This failure is more serious than has been indicated so far. *S & Z* attempted, in a phrase Heidegger was to use much later, to "restore the dignity of man," [17] presumably by insulating him, once and for all, from all attempts to present him as the object of scientific knowledge and no more. Insofar as this attempt and the doctrines of *S & Z* that came of it led without inconsistency to fascism, that attempt failed tragically. But *S & Z* also attempted, as I showed in Chapter 4, to restate in an adequate form the transcendental motif that Heidegger had found in Kant, Hegel and Husserl. The task was to provide a vocabulary in which one could make sense of the traditional claim that the world is "constituted" by human beings. But the upshot of the preceding arguments is that Heidegger did not succeed in this either. For what was needed was an account not only of those phenomena that might be said to be constituted by some specific individual, but also of those phenomena that are the creations of a community. Phenomena like social practices, whether in the domain of skills, language or the legal order are not constituted by individuals but by a collective. The vocabulary of *S & Z* does not illuminate constitution in that domain.

notes and index

notes

CHAPTER 1 Ontology

1. Martin Heidegger, *Sein und Zeit* (Halle, Germany: 1927; 11th ed. Tübingen: 1967). References to the book appear in brackets in the text. English translation: *Being and Time,* John Macquarrie and Edward Robinson (trs.), (New York: 1962). I have used my own translations but owe many valuable suggestions to Macquarrie and Robinson for elegant and ingenious solutions to problems of translation. Being undertaken for different purposes from theirs, my translations are occasionally freer. I have indicated in footnotes where my translations diverge in important ways from those of Macquarrie and Robinson.
2. The German word here is "*Vorurteile,*" which has all the pejorative connotations of the English word "prejudices." This term is, therefore, preferable to the word "presuppositions" used in the translation of Macquarrie and Robinson.
3. Otto Pöggeler, *Der Denkweg Martin Heideggers* (Pfullingen, Germany: 1963), p. 49; and Albert Chappelle, *L'Ontologie phénoménologique de Heidegger* (Namur, Belgium: 1962), p. 10.
4. Martin Heidegger, "Grundprobleme der Phänomenologie" (unpublished lectures, Marburg, Germany: 1927), p. 39. See also Heidegger's *Kant und das Problem der Metaphysik* (Frankfurt, Germany: 1951; first printing, 1929), p. 210. (This book will be referred to as *Kant.*)
5. Heidegger, *Kant, op. cit.,* p. 204.
6. *Ibid.,* p. 205.
7. *Ibid.*
8. *Ibid.,* p. 204.
9. See, for example, Walter Biemel's work (which in other respects is

often instructive) *Le Concept de monde chez Heidegger* (Paris: 1950), p. 18. Also see Heidegger, *Being and Time*, Macquarrie and Robinson (trs.), *op. cit.*, p. 31, trs. *n* 3. A notable exception is Frederick A. Olafson, *Principles and Persons, An Ethical Interpretation of Existentialism* (Baltimore: 1967), pp. 79–94. Olafson not only devotes some space to an attempt to clarify the notion of ontology in Heidegger (and Sartre) but his conclusions are very close to mine, that what English speaking philosophers call ''conceptual analysis'' of the revisionary variety is very close to what Heidegger calls ''ontology.''

10. Martin Heidegger, *Unterwegs zur Sprache* (Pfullingen, Germany: 1959), p. 91.

11. The German terms ''*vorhanden*'' and ''*zuhanden*'' are translated as ''present at hand'' and ''ready at hand'' respectively by Macquarrie and Robinson.

12. Heidegger, *Kant, op. cit.*, p. 210.

13. William J. Richardson, *Heidegger, Through Phenomenology to Thought* (The Hague: 1963), pp. 38, 42.

14. *Ibid.*, pp. 33, 34.

15. Also see Heidegger, *Sein und Zeit, op. cit.*, pp. 140, 150 ff., 232.

16. Martin Heidegger, *Platon's Lehre von der Wahrheit, mit einem Brief über den ''Humanismus''* (Bern: 1954), pp. 109 ff. and *passim*. This work will be referred to as *Humanismusbrief*.

17. For example, Heidegger, *Unterwegs zur Sprache, op. cit.*, pp. 85 ff.

CHAPTER 2 Things

1. Edmund Husserl, *Ideen zu einer reinen Phänomenologie und phänomenologischen Philosophie*, Vol. II. *Husserliana*, Vol. IV. Marly Biemel (ed.) (The Hague: 1952), p. 45.

2. *Ibid.*, p. 31.

3. *Ibid.*, pp. 29 ff.

4. I translate ''*Zeug*'' as ''gear.'' Macquarrie and Robinson prefer the word ''equipment.''

5. I translate Heidegger's ''*Zeugganzes*'' as ''gear context.'' Macquarrie and Robinson prefer ''totality of equipment.''

6. I have suggested some of the relevant arguments in my paper ''Heidegger's Analysis of 'Tool,' '' *The Monist*, XLIX (1965), 70–86.

7. Heidegger uses the word ''*Sorge*'' and the corresponding verb ''*besorgen*'' which I render as ''care'' and ''caring for.'' Macquarrie and Robinson use ''concern'' and ''being concerned for.''

CHAPTER 3 Language

1. Martin Heidegger, *Die Kategorien und Bedeutungslehre des Duns Scotus* (Tübingen, Germany: 1915).

2. Edmund Husserl, *Logische Untersuchungen*, 2nd ed., 2 vols. (Halle, Germany: 1913). This work will be referred to as *LU* I (first volume and *LU* II (second volume).

3. This was also Husserl's understanding of Heidegger's book on Scotus. See Edmund Husserl, *Formale und Transcendentale Logik* (Halle, Germany: 1929), p. 43. This work will be referred to as *FTL*.

4. Heidegger, *Scotus, op. cit.*, p. 91.

5. Husserl, *FTL, op. cit.*, pp. 44, 66. The details of this distinction are by no means clear.

6. Chauncey Downes, "On Husserl's Approach to Necessary Truth," *The Monist*, XLIX (1965), 87–106.

7. Dagfinn Føllesdal, "Husserl and Frege," *Avhandlinger utgift av det Norske Videnskap—Akademi i Oslo*, II, Hist.—Filos. Klasse. 1958, 2.

8. Cf. Ludwig Wittgenstein, *Tractatus Logico-Philosophicus* (London: 1922), 3.323–3.325: "In the language of everyday it very often happens that the same word signifies in two different ways. . . . In order to avoid these errors, we must employ a symbolism . . . of *logical* grammar—of logical syntax."

9. See, for example, Husserl, *FTL, op. cit.*, pp. 87–88.

10. *Ibid.* See also Hans Ulrich Hoche, *Nichtempirische Erkenntnis, Analytische und Synthetische Urteile a priori bei Husserl und bei Kant, Monographien zur Philosophischen Forschung*, No. 35 (Meisenheim am Glan, Germany: 1964), p. 155, *n* 264.

11. Heidegger, *Scotus, op. cit.*, p. 143.

12. *Ibid.*, p. 108.

13. *Ibid.*, pp. 90 ff.

14. *Ibid.*, p. 120.

15. *Ibid.*, p. 161.

16. *Ibid.*, p. 163.

17. *Ibid.*, pp. 149–150.

18. *Ibid.*, p. 161.

19. Cf. Pascal's *Pensées* (New York: 1958), #50: "The meaning changes with the words that express it. Meanings receive their dignity from words instead of giving it to them. . . ."

20. Translated in Marjorie Greene, *Heidegger* (New York: 1957), p. 24.

21. Cf. Ludwig Wittgenstein, *Philosophical Investigations* (New York:

1953), par. 23: "Review the multiplicity of language games in the following examples, and in others. . . . It is interesting to compare the multiplicity of kinds of word and sentence with what logicians have said about the structure of language." I shall point to other parallels between Wittgenstein's later views on language and those of Heidegger in his middle period. For more striking but also more controversial parallels between the early Wittgenstein and the later Heidegger, see Ingvar Horgby, "The Double Awareness in Heidegger and Wittgenstein," *Inquiry,* II (1959), 235–264.

22. Husserl regarded *S & Z* as definitely psychologistic. See Alwin Diemer, *Edmund Husserl, Versuch einer systematischen Darstellung seiner Phänomenologie* (Meisenham am Glan, Germany: 1965), p. 30. It would be a very complex task to show that this judgment is not false but inappropriate. The pro- and antipsychologism controversy presupposes not only a set of doctrines about words and their relations to what they mean, as represented by Husserl's theses, but also involves definite conceptions about the relations of bodies and their actions—for example, speaking—to minds and their states—for example, thoughts or intentions. Of crucial importance, furthermore, is a definite view of the sense in which formal logic is formal and in which statements in logic differ from statements about facts. In order to escape the alternatives set up by Husserl and his predecessors, Heidegger must relativize the distinctions between word and meaning, mind and body, and logical and empirical knowledge.

23. Wittgenstein, *Philosophical Investigations, op. cit.,* par. 560: "The meaning of a word is what is explained by the explanation of meaning."

24. Macquarrie and Robinson translate "*Auslegung*" as "interpretation." I prefer "explication" because it contains the same concrete images as "*auslegen,*" namely, of taking a great many things thrown together helter-skelter in a bundle and laying them out separately so that they can be seen more clearly for what they are. This would be an example of what Heidegger means by "*auslegen.*"

25. Wittgenstein, *Philosophical Investigations, op. cit.,* par. 177, speaks in comparable ways of looking at something "through the medium of a concept."

26. *Ibid.,* par. 78: "Compare *knowing and saying*: How many feet high Mont Blanc is—; how the word 'game' is used—; how a clarinet sounds—. If you are surprised that one can know something and not be able to say it, you are perhaps thinking of a case like the first. Certainly not of one like the third." What about the second case?

27. Wittgenstein, *Philosophical Investigations, op. cit.,* par. 31: "We may say: only someone who already knows how to do something with it may significantly ask a name."

28. *Ibid.*, par. 19. Different languages make us see the world in different ways; they involve us in different practices, goals, products and skills. These are part of what Heidegger calls "world." Wittgenstein calls them a "form of life" when he says that "to imagine a language means to imagine a form of life."
29. *Ibid.*, par. 84: ". . . the application of a word is not everywhere bounded by rules."
30. *Ibid.*, par. 81: ". . . in philosophy we often *compare* the use of words with games and calculi which have fixed rules, but cannot say that someone who is using language *must* be playing such a game."
31. *Ibid.*, par. 11: "Think of the tools in a tool box. . . . the function of words is as diverse as the functions of these objects."

CHAPTER 4 Phenomenology

1. I have argued this point in more detail in my paper "Phenomenology and Analysis," *Philosophy and Phenomenological Research*, XXIII (1962), 421–428.
2. Edmund Husserl, *Ideen zu einer reinen Phänomenologie und phänomenologischen Philosophie*, in Walter Biemel (ed.), *Husserliana* (The Hague: 1950), Vol. III. This work will be referred to as *Id.* I.
3. See my paper "Husserl's Transcendental-Phenomenological Reduction," *Philosophy and Phenomenological Research*, XX (1959), 238–245. Also see Rudolf Boehm, "Basic Reflection on Husserl's Phenomenological Reduction," *International Philosophical Quarterly*, V (1965), 183–202.
4. Edmund Husserl, "Philosophie als Strenge Wissenschaft," *Logos*, I (1910), 289–314. This article will be referred to as "Strenge."
5. Edmund Husserl, "Phenomenology," *Encyclopedia Britannica*, 14th ed. Different versions of this article have now been reprinted in Walter Biemel (ed.), *Husserliana* (The Hague: 1962), Vol. IX. The article will be referred to as *Encyc.*
6. Edmund Husserl, *Die Idee der Phänomenologie*," in Walter Biemel (ed.), *Husserliana* (The Hague: 1950), Vol. II. This work will be referred to as *Idee.*
7. Husserl's writings on ethics have been available thus far only in the summary by Alois Roth. See Alois Roth, *Edmund Husserl's ethische Untersuchungen* (The Hague: 1960).
8. Edmund Husserl, "Amsterdamer Vorträge," in Walter Biemel (ed.), *Husserliana* (The Hague: 1962), Vol. IX, p. 344.
9. *Ibid.*, p. 333.
10. *Ibid.*, p. 320.
11. See, for example, the opening paragraph, *ibid.*, p. 302.
12. *Ibid.*, p. 345. "The will to be ultimately responsible" gives a hint

of the great struggle that Husserl fought in order to reach even
this very partial understanding of what was troubling him.

13. Walter Biemel (ed.), *Husserliana* (The Hague: 1954), Vol. VI, p.
    508.

14. See also Walter Biemel, ''Husserl's Encyclopedia Britannica Artikel
    und Heidegger's Anmerkungen dazu,'' *Tijdschrift voor Philosophie*,
    XII (1950), 246–280.

15. This account is oversimplified. It ascribes, in the interest of clearer
    exposition of Heidegger's views, clearcut doctrines to Husserl where,
    in fact, we find him struggling uncertainly with the problem of dif-
    ferentiating the pure from the empirical ego. The problem is simple:
    In the so-called natural attitude, objects exist independently of be-
    ing known. Their existence and their essence is, according to Husserl,
    not relative to anyone's subjectivity. But in phenomenology we dis-
    cover that objective existence *is* relative to subjectivity. How are
    we to reconcile this contradiction between the natural and phe-
    nomenological standpoint?

    We may wish to regard the views of the natural attitude as mis-
    taken and claim that the world is dependent, in the requisite sense
    of that term, on the empirical self. This view amounts to psy-
    chologism and Husserl had earlier argued vigorously against this
    position. The experienced world cannot be dependent on the em-
    pirical self. Accordingly we need a distinction between the empirical
    and the transcendental self.

    Husserl tries to draw this distinction in a variety of ways. Some-
    times it seems that the difference is that between the full self,
    which includes my body, and my mind considered in isolation from
    my body [See Id I, 130–136]. At other times it seems that the dif-
    ference between empirical and transcendental subject is one in the
    attitude of the inquirer, it depends on whether he has performed
    the transcendental epoche. The first formulation of the distinction
    is not adequate for the mind, considered in isolation from the body,
    still is the empirical mind. Similarly the mind (or subject) con-
    sidered from different points of view is one and the same empirical
    mind. Thus the problem of the distinction between empirical and
    transcendental subject remains and recurs in passage after passage.

    Husserl's perplexity in the face of this problem is exemplified by
    passages like this one: ''My transcendental ego is evidently 'dif-
    ferent' from my natural ego insofar as it is the ego of the tran-
    scendental experience of myself and yet it is nothing less than a
    second ego, that is separate, in any ordinary sense. There are not
    two egos, external to each other . . . [Encyc. 342].'' It was Husserl
    himself who put the word ''different'' in quotation marks to indi-

cate that the meaning of that term, however crucial, is quite unclear. The passage merely states the perplexity of how to differentiate the empirical from the transcendental ego and yet to maintain that they are one and the same. Husserl never manages to solve that difficulty.

There are corresponding difficulties in the notion of ''constitution.'' If the two egos are distinct, so are their activities and we can, if we want, call those of the transcendental ego ''constitution.'' But if the two egos are identical, are not their acts also identical? If they are identical we must identify constitution with ordinary mental acts. But that identification leads back into psychologism.

16. Philosophers in rather different traditions would agree with Heidegger on this point. See Wilfred Sellars, *Science, Perception and Reality* (New York: 1963), p. 6. The all-important question is how different philosophers work out that claim, for example, what explication is given of the term ''conceiving.'' Sellars uses statements in science and scientific theories as paradigms of his explication; Heidegger, as we have seen, rejects this paradigm. Corresponding differences show up in the explications of other key terms.

17. See, for example, Biemel, ''Husserl's Encyclopedia,'' p. 276.

18. The term ''objectivism'' must be used with care. Husserl calls Heidegger an objectivist, according to Alwin Diemer. See Alwin Diemer, *Edmund Husserl, Versuch einer systematischen Darstellung seiner Phänomenologie* (Meisenheim am Glan, Germany: 1965), p. 30. By ''objectivist'' Husserl presumably means that Heidegger makes no mention in *S & Z* of constitution by a transcendental subject. Husserl mistakenly takes Heidegger to reaffirm what Husserlian phenomenology had been at pains to deny: that the world is what it is, independent of any subject. I use the term ''objectivism'' in a related but more restricted sense to refer to a specific view about human knowledge, namely, that knowledge is by definition objective.

19. Martin Heidegger, ''Grundprobleme der Phänomenologie'' (unpublished lectures, Marburg, Germany: 1927), p. 31. ''And for this reason we may also call this science of being, inasmuch as it is a critical science, the transcendental science.''

20. For an illuminating account of Heidegger's development in the years between the Scotus book and *S & Z*, see Otto Pöggeler, *Der Denkweg Martin Heideggers* (Pfullingen, Germany: 1963).

21. This shift has been clearly outlined in Laszlo Versenyi, *Heidegger, Being and Truth* (New Haven, Conn.: 1965).

CHAPTER 5   Understanding

1. This term renders Heidegger's ''*Befindlichkeit*,'' a neologism with several roots. A doctor will ask a patient about his ''*Befinden*'' to

find out how he feels. One says that things *"sich befinden"* somewhere when one speaks about their location. The corresponding ad-
verb to this second meaning of *"befinden"* is *"befindlich."* *"Befindlichkeit"* also carries overtones of *"Empfindlichkeit,"* sensibility
or sensitivity, and of *"sich finden,"* to find oneself. All welded together into one word refer to the capacity for an emotional awareness of one's situation. "Being disposed" renders part of this web
of ideas by reminding us, on the one hand, of "being indisposed,"
not feeling well, and of "being of a sunny disposition," inclined to
be in a good mood—and, on the other hand, of "being disposed,"
as being placed in a certain orderly arrangement. The translation is
awkward but, I think, a shade less misleading than William J. Richardson's "disposition," a word that will remind philosophers forci-
bly of "potentiality." Because Heidegger is trying to reform traditional concepts of consciousness and therefore very carefully avoids
familiar terms like *"Bewusstsein,"* Macquarrie and Robinson's
use of "state of mind" to translate *"Befindlichkeit"* is seriously
misleading and should be changed in later editions of their translation.

2. From the very outset of his analyses, Heidegger indicates that he
uses the term *"Erkennen"* to designate that meaning of "knowing" that traditional philosophy had discussed in the context of the
"Erkenntnis-problem" and that refers to knowledge of objects existing independently of human knowing [61]. Elsewhere, Heidegger
himself uses the adjective "theoretical" for this kind of knowing.
I therefore translate *"Erkennen"* as "theoretical knowing" or
"theoretical knowledge." These terms refer to the meaning of
knowing preferred by Husserl, in which "Knowledge is objective"
is true by virtue of the meanings of terms.

3. Franz Brentano, *Von der Klassifikation der psychischen Phänomene*
(Leipzig, Germany: 1911).

4. Immanuel Kant, *Critique of Judgment*, Introduction, par. III.

5. David Hume, *Treatise of Human Nature*, Book II, Part I, Sec. I.

6. Brentano, *op. cit.*, p. 122.

7. Because "understanding" stands for the new concept of knowing,
I frequently use "knowing" as synonymous with "understanding,"
in the sense in which that term is used in *S & Z*. Both terms are
contrasted with "theoretical knowing" or "objective knowing."

8. I have made a few suggestions about the necessary arguments in
my paper "Two Senses of Knowing," *The Review of Metaphysics*,
XVIII (1965), 657–677.

9. It has recently become a matter of controversy whether one can

know that p without knowing that one knows that—nor, of course, is that the first time that this controversy has been raised. See Jaako Hintikka, *Knowledge and Belief* (Ithaca: 1962) and Charles Pailthorp, "Hintikka and Knowing That One Knows," *Journal of Philosophy*, LXIV (1967), 487–499. I am inclined to side with Pailthorp.

10. For Heidegger's *"Seinkönnen"* I use "being-able-to-be," and Macquarrie and Robinson write "potentiality-for-being."

11. The German terms *"eigentlich"* and *"uneigentlich"* are customarily translated as "authentic" and "inauthentic," presumably because *"eigentlich"* ordinarily means "genuine" or, adverbially, "really." But Heidegger uses these terms in a technical sense, playing on the meaning of *"eigen,"* which means "own." To be *eigentlich* is to be an individual in the fullest sense of that term; it is to be in possession of oneself. To be *uneigentlich* is to be "fallen away" from oneself (*Verfallen*) or, in a familiar expression, to be alienated from oneself. To be in full possession of oneself is, of course, also to be most genuinely a human being. Hence to translate *"eigentlich"* as authentic, although not wrong, is a bit misleading; more clumsy, but more accurate, is "genuinely self-possessed."

Furthermore, it is inappropriate to translate *"eigentlich"* as "authentic," because Heidegger makes a distinction between conduct that is *"eigentlich"* and conduct that is *"echt* (genuine)," and similarly between *"uneigentlich"* and *"unecht* (not genuine)" conduct [146]. See Martin Heidegger, "Grundprobleme der Phänomenologie" (unpublished lectures, Marburg, Germany: 1927), p. 289. Everyday understanding of myself in terms of what I do— "We are what we are occupied with"—is not to be genuinely self-possessed (*uneigentlich*) but may for all that be quite *echt* while "extravagant rummaging around in one's psyche may be to the highest degree not genuine (*unecht*) and pathological." Heidegger never comes any closer to giving a more specific explication of the difference between behavior that is *uneigentlich* and behavior that is *unecht*.

12. Illuminating examples of such attempts are to be found in Bruno Bettelheim, *Love Is Not Enough* (New York: 1950).

13. Gilbert Ryle, *The Concept of Mind* (London: 1949), p. 156.

14. I shall use "design" for *"entwerfen"* so as to avoid possible misunderstanding. "Project," used by Macquarrie and Robinson, means planning or designing but also "casting something onto something" as in "projecting a picture on a screen." This latter meaning is not part of the meaning of *"entwerfen"* but misleads Macquarrie

and Robinson to translate *"das woraufhin es entwirft"* [145] as "that upon which it projects," whereas the translation should have been "that with a view to which it projects."

CHAPTER 6 Conclusion

1. *Humanismusbrief*, p. 72.
2. Heidegger distinguishes a person's understanding of existence that takes the form of being able to talk about it from an understanding that is evinced in conduct. The first sort of understanding produces an ontology and is called *"existential"*; the latter is manifested in correct dealings with everyday facts and events in existence. Heidegger calls it *"existentiell"* understanding. Macquarrie and Robinson took the German word *"existentiell"* into English to mark that distinction. I prefer to speak of existential understanding that deals with ontology or with the ontic, respectively, and therefore translate *"existential"* as "existential-ontological" and *"existentiell"* as "existential-ontic."
3. Martin Heidegger, *Kant und das Problem der Metaphysik* (Frankfurt, Germany: 1951), p. 213. See also *Humanismusbrief*, pp. 59, 78.
4. *Humanismusbrief*, p. 72.
5. *Humanismusbrief*, p. 92; Martin Heidegger, *Unterwegs zur Sprache* (Pfullingen, Germany: 1959), pp. 112 ff.; Martin Heidegger, *Vom Wesen der Wahrheit*, p. 72.
6. *Humanismusbrief*, p. 65.
7. Martin Heidegger, *Gelassenheit* (Pfullingen, Germany: 1959), p. 43. Now available in English as *Discourse on Thinking*, John M. Anderson and E. Hans Freund (trs.) (New York: 1966).
8. Heidegger, *Gelassenheit, op. cit.*, p. 40.
9. Karl Löwith, *Heidegger, Denker in dürftiger Zeit* (Göttingen, Germany: 1960; first edition, Frankfurt, Germany: 1953).
10. Walter Schulz, "Über den philosophiegeschichtlichen Ort Martin Heideggers," *Philosophische Rundschau*, I (1953–1954), 65–93, 211–231.
11. At the end of the first half of *S & Z*, Heidegger asks whether the analyses provided so far have encompassed the entire subject of *S & Z* [*in die Vorhabe gebracht*, 232]. He answers in the negative and then proceeds to make up this deficiency. As the ontological vocabulary of *S & Z* explicates preontological understanding, the question about the completeness of the vocabulary leads to the question of how it is possible for dasein to understand itself as a whole. The question about the completeness of *S & Z* leads into the question of dasein's capacity for being whole (*Ganzseinkönnen*) [233–234].

That question is answered later [309, 373 ff.]. Having thus shown what it means for dasein to be complete and to understand itself as such, he has also indicated that, at least in outline, the vocabulary we are asked to use in talking about human beings is complete because it allows us to express dasein's complete preontological understanding of itself. It allows us to put that complete understanding of dasein into words, and that is all that is needed for the vocabulary to be complete.

12. A view of this kind is defended in Thomas Kuhn, *The Structure of Scientific Revolutions* (Chicago: 1962).

13. In my discussion of language in Chapter 3, I pointed to analogies between *S & Z* and Ludwig Wittgenstein's *Philosophical Investigations*. Wittgenstein's use of the notion of a game in his discussion of language suggests that he was more aware of the peculiar social nature of language.

14. Guido Schneeberger, *Nachlese zu Heidegger, Dokumente zu seinem Leben und Denken* (Bern: 1962). Some of the documents are now available in English translation in Dagobert D. Runes (ed.), *Martin Heidegger, German Existentialism* (New York: 1965).

15. See, for instance, Karl Löwith, ''Les Implications politiques de la philosophie de l'existence chez Heidegger,'' *Les Temps modernes*, II (1946), 346 ff.

16. Martin Heidegger, *Die Selbstbehauptung der Deutschen Universität* (Breslau, Germany: 1933), p. 15.

17. *Humanismusbrief*, p. 75. The entire passage [67 ff.] expresses quite clearly Heidegger's determination to oppose all attempts to assimilate philosophical explications with scientific accounts of what it means to be human.

index

A Priori: 58, 107, 141
Auslegung: 258n.; *see also* Explication
Authentic: 184; *see also* Genuinely self-possessed

Bedeutsamkeit: 84, 87
Befindlichkeit: 261–262n., *see also* Being disposed
Being:
  question about, 4ff., 10, 228–229, 231
  requires different vocabulary than entities, 9, 232
  in ontology, 13
  preconceptual understanding of, 14, 204
  preontological understanding of, 18–19, 147
  exhibited in phenomenology, 146–147
  no starting point provided by question about, 176
Being disposed: 159, 162, 187, 201
Being-in-the-world: 157, 204
  deceives itself, 206
  foundation of theoretical knowing, 236

and understanding, 238
Being thrown: 216–217
Being-together-with: 183
Being-unto-death: 181ff.
  genuinely self-possessed, 185–186
  case of understanding, 189
Being with: 245ff.
Brentano, Franz: 150–151, 153–154, 164

Care: 197
Care for: 197ff., 237–238
Categories: 17, 178
Conscience: 223–224
Constitution: 119, 130–131
  transcendental, 133–134
  not a distinct activity, 137–138

Dasein:
  exists, 15
  meaning and denotation of, 15
  is being-in-the-world, 27
  is being able to be, 27
  is being with, 27
  "essence" consists of its existence, 27, 138, 215–216
  never a "real fact in the world," 134ff.

Moods (*continued*)
  independent of specific beliefs,
    159–160, 203
  conditions for other types of
    emotional states, 160
  not analyzable in traditional
    terms, 161
  disclose being-in-the-world, 162
  not instances of theoretical
    knowing, 162ff,
  cases of non-theoretical know-
    ing of action, 175, 180, 187,
    201

Object of use: *see* Gear
Objective:
  two senses of, 52
  relation to the subjective, 118ff.
  reexamination, 132
  what is present on hand, 133
  not applicable to emotional
    phenomena, 163–164
Ontic: *see* Ontology
Ontology:
  deals with being, 13
  fundamental, 16, 133, 228
  differs from ontic discourse,
    16ff., 29
  provides vocabulary for for-
    mulating preontological un-
    derstanding, 18
  provides new criteria for con-
    cepts, 21
  gives reasons for accepting new
    criteria, 22
  and positive science, 23
  reasons for lack of criteria,
    25–26
  circularity, 25, 27
  differs from other philosophi-
    cal discourse, 26
  conceptual, 29–30

and phenomenology, 104, 143
as fundamental concept, 133
formulates preontological understanding, 204, 208

Persons:
  different from things, 21, 32
  their difference from things
    often misconstrued, 206
  mistake by philosophers about,
    222
Phenomenological psychology:
  116
Phenomenology:
  disagreement between Heideg-
    ger and Husserl, 104
  theory of theories, 106
  and the sciences, 107ff.
  descriptive, 108ff., 140
  intuits essences, 109, 139
  reflects about consciousness,
    110
  early and middle views of Hus-
    serl, 112ff.
  disruptive motifs in Husserl's,
    113–114, 123ff.
  eidetic and egological, 117
  and science, 128
  not a science, 131
  discussion by Heidegger of,
    143ff.
Phenomenon: 145ff.
Philosophical vocabulary:
  if applicable to entities not to
    being, 9
  need for refurbishing, 11–12
  proposals in S&Z, 13, 150
  not coining new words, 19
  shortcomings of the traditional,
    20, 41
  new criteria involved in new
    system, 21

Philosophical vocabulary (*continued*)
definite view of language presupposed in new system, 71
theoretical and practical consequences of a different, 93–94
Possibility:
as category and as existential, 178
not independent of one's knowing, 179–180
Heidegger's sense of, 187ff.
fundamental characteristic of dasein, 191, 215
designed, 202–203
Present on hand:
restricted use of German word, 19
entities, 39, 45ff., 49, 235
in itself, 50ff.

Rationality: 98–99
Ready to hand:
a neologism, 19
entities, 45ff., 49, 150, 232
knowing what is, 47, 169
in itself, 50ff.
Rede: see Discourse
Resolute: 249ff.
Richardson, William: 29

Science:
discusses present on hand entities, 235ff.
Heidegger accepts Husserl's account of, 237
Seiendes: 9
Sein: see Being
Sein und Zeit:
difficulties in understanding, 4ff.

proposes a new philosophical vocabulary, 13, 30, 150
widespread misunderstandings, 26ff.
our explication of, 28, 95ff.
gives cursory development to many of its claims, 45
the central problem of, 133–134, 148
fails to reawaken the question about being, 219, 229–230
Heidegger claims completeness for, 219–220, 240
why it remained unfinished, 231–232
Heidegger's later works, 232ff.
Seinkönnen: 263n.
Self knowledge:
not always reflective, 141–142, 222
two senses of, 192ff.
and privileged access, 193–194
infallibility, 194
and truth, 196–197
Sicht: see Sight
Sight: 168
Sinn: 84, 87
Social institutions: 251ff
Social phenomena: 246ff
Social practices: 243ff
Sorge: 256n.; *see also* Care
Sprache: see Language
Statements: 80–81; 100–101
Subject:
Husserl's transcendental, 111ff.
Husserl's problem about, 118ff.
pure, 129
two senses of, 137
Heidegger's new concept of, 138
not known by reflection, 141–142

16⁹⁵

19.95